Byron
Interviews and Recollections

BYRON

Interviews and Recollections

Edited by

Norman Page

Professor of English
University of Alberta

Humanities Press
Atlantic Highlands, New Jersey

Selection and editorial matter © Norman Page 1985

First published 1985 in the United States of America by
HUMANITIES PRESS INC.
Atlantic Highlands
N.J. 07716

ISBN 0–391–03216–X

Printed in Hong Kong

Library of Congress Cataloging in Publication Data
Main entry under title:
Byron: interviews and recollections.
Includes index.
1. Byron, George Gordon Byron, Baron, 1788–1824 –
Biography – Addresses, essays, lectures.   2. Poets,
English – 19th century – Biography – Addresses, essays,
lectures.   I. Page, Norman.
PR4381.B79   1985   821'.7 [B]   84-19209
ISBN 0–391–03216–X

To Sydney and Rita Singh

Contents

List of Plates   ix

Introduction   xi

A Byron Chronology   xix

INTERVIEWS AND RECOLLECTIONS
Schooldays in Aberdeen   *Anonymous*   1
'Little Deevil Geordie Byron'   *R. E. Prothero*   3
Harrow   *Thomas Moore*   4
Cambridge   *Anonymous*   5
'I Shall Go Mad'   *James T. Hodgson*   7
Byron Takes his Seat in the House of Lords   *R. C. Dallas*   8
An Adventure in Greece   *J. C. Hobhouse*   11
In England Again (1811–14)   *J. C. Hobhouse*   12
First Impressions   I (1809)   *John Galt*   14
First Impressions   II (1811)   *Samuel Rogers*   18
First Impressions III (1813)   *Leigh Hunt*   20
First Impressions IV (1821)   *Thomas Medwin*   23
First Impressions   V (1822)   *E. J. Trelawny*   24
First Impressions VI (1823)   *Lady Blessington*   28
Byron's Snobbery   *John Galt*   30
The Effects of Fame   *R. C. Dallas*   31
'Soothed by Success'   *John Galt*   34
'As Playful as a Kitten'   *Sir Walter Scott*   35
Later Recollections   *Sir Walter Scott*   38
Life in London   *R. H. Gronow*   40
Byron's Marriage and Departure from England   *J. C. Hobhouse*   43
Travelling with Byron in Europe   *J. W. Polidori*   47
Italian Travel   *J. C. Hobhouse*   50
Meetings with Byron (1818–21)   *P. B. Shelley*   51
'A Lost Man'   *Mary Shelley*   55
A Visit from Thomas Moore   *Thomas Moore*   57
Moore Recalls his Visit   *Thomas Moore*   58

'A Thoroughly Spoilt Man'   *E. J. Trelawny*   62
'A Most Eccentric Character'   *Anonymous*   71
Teresa Guiccioli   *Thomas Medwin*   74
'The Handsomest of Men'   *Teresa Guiccioli*   76
Life at Pisa I   *Edward E. Williams*   84
Life at Pisa II   *Leigh Hunt*   90
The Cremation of Williams and Shelley   *E. J. Trelawny*   94
A Clergyman Visits Lord Byron   *Anonymous*   98
Byron's Conversation I: On Books and Authors   105
   Shakespeare and Pope – Dr Johnson – Johnson and
   Pope – Voltaire – Madame de Staël – Sir Walter Scott –
   Wordsworth – Southey and Landor – Thomas Moore –
   Leigh Hunt – Shelley – Shelley and Other
   Contemporaries
Byron's Conversation II: On Other Topics   113
   Ambition and Authorship – Love, Friendship and
   Marriage – Religion – Death – Miracles – Cant and
   Gossip – His Lameness – Lord and Lady Holland –
   Ravenna – Air Travel – A Storm at Sea
With Byron to Greece I   *J. H. Browne*   125
With Byron to Greece II   *E. J. Trelawny*   137
In Greece   *Julius Millingen*   139
Last Days I   *Count Gamba*   150
Last Days II   *William Fletcher*   155
Last Days III   *Julius Millingen*   160
'More Beautiful in Death than in Life'   *E. J. Trelawny*   167
Preparations for the Last Journey   *Edward Blaquière*   169
'A Great Sensation'   *Mary Shelley*   171
Byron's Funeral Procession   *Thomas Moore*   173
Last Recollections (1824)   *J. C. Hobhouse*   175

Index   180

List of Plates

1. Byron at Harrow (1801), pencil sketch, signed T. W.
2. Byron and Robert Rushton (1808), by George Sanders (Newstead Abbey Collection, Nottingham City Library)
3. Portrait of Byron (1813), by Richard Westall (National Portrait Gallery)
4. Byron in Albanian dress (1814), by Thomas Phillips (National Portrait Gallery)
5. Byron aged 26 (1814), by Thomas Phillips (Newstead Abbey Collection, Nottingham City Library)
6. Byron at Pisa (1822), engraving by C. Turner based on painting by W. C. West (Newstead Abbey Collection, Nottingham City Library)
7. 'A Noble Poet Scratching up his Ideas', cartoon (1823) (British Museum)
8. 'The Burning of Shelley's Body' (1889), by L. E. Fournier (Walker Art Gallery, Liverpool)

Introduction

The cult of literary personality begins in England with Byron, and begins specifically in the second decade of the nineteenth century. With the publication of the first two cantos of *Childe Harold* in 1812, Byron had, famously, become famous overnight; but it was in the heady postwar atmosphere of 1816 that scandal – not only the separation from his wife, but rumours of an incestuous relationship with his half-sister – and the grand gesture of self-exile set the seal on that fame. Byron's separation and his departure from England took place within months of the Battle of Waterloo; and that battle was not yet a year old when he rode over the battlefield (4 May 1816) at almost exactly the same time that work was resumed on *Childe Harold*. It is natural to link Byron's name with Napoleon's as Romantic archetypes. When Byron later took the name Noel and signed himself 'Noel Byron', he was gratified at sharing his new initials with Napoleon Bonaparte. (For his dismay and disgust on hearing of the latter's defeat, see pp. 42–3 below.) P. G. Trueblood's wide-ranging survey of European Byronism, *Byron's Political and Cultural Influence in Nineteenth-Century Europe* (New Jersey, 1981), has as its epigraph an observation by Northrop Frye: 'European nineteenth-century culture is as unthinkable without Byron as its history would be without Napoleon.'

The time-scale of Byron's fame during his lifetime is not long: only a dozen years elapsed between the rise to fame in 1812 and the perhaps unnecessary but in mythic terms inevitable death at Missolonghi in 1824. But it was an extraordinary phenomenon, volcanic in its effects, and the far-flung tidal waves and sunset glows were not quick to diminish. Byron was certainly not the best poet of his generation, but as a candidate for contemporary fame he possessed an unbeatable combination of qualities. Snobbery, sexual attraction, an appetite for scandal (the offences, actual or alleged, ranging from incest to using a skull as a drinking-cup), and the appeal of exoticism were all ingredients in the Byron craze (the word 'craze' itself seems to have appeared in this sense in 1813). Byron himself once remarked in connection with the success of one of his poems that 'I may place a great deal of it to being a lord';[1] his film-star good looks are obvious from numerous portraits (as his tendency to run to fat is not) as well as from verbal descriptions; from being conventionally dissipated in the brothels and gambling-hells of London and Brighton he moved on to more perverse pleasures, for which the most famous lameness since Oedipus seemed to be a strangely apposite outward token (he had 'the feet and legs of a sylvan satyr' declared, implausibly, the egregious Trelawny after inspecting his corpse); and the guidebook element in his work made a strong appeal to a generation whose mobility had been limited by a long war. He also spoke out against the decadence and corruption of royalty and politicians and was an angry young man a century and a half before that phrase became a cliché. With his knack of making enemies by ridiculing fellow authors, allied to his photogenic qualities, he would have been a brilliant success as a television personality.

But above all he had prodigious abilities. To read some of Byron's biographers is to receive the impression that, like Wilde, he put his genius into his life and his talent into his work. Certainly, he was a witty and delightful companion with numerous and diverse friendships (though he could also be moody and quarrelsome), and his letters are as good as anything he ever wrote. (His autobiography is, of all lost books, perhaps the one many of us would most wish to read.) But, for all his aristocratic scorn for the tribe of authors, he was also a hard-working writer whose output, even given his remarkable facility, is staggering.

Byron's death produced a reaction that it is hard to parallel in the history of literature. Within a few weeks, Sir Cosmo Gordon had published a volume, *Life and Genius of Lord Byron*, that opens with the words, 'Lord Byron is no more!', and it is difficult to think of any other writer whose passing might have been hailed in quite that plangent and portentous tone. More privately, the fourteen-year-old Alfred Tennyson carved on a rock the words 'Byron is dead'; later in life he described the reception of the news as 'a day when the whole world seemed to be darkened for me'.[2] In America a sermon on Byron's life and works was preached to the text 'The memory of the wicked shall rot', and the twelve-year-old daughter of the evangelical preacher (herself to win astonishing fame a generation later as the author of *Uncle Tom's Cabin*) lay down on the grass and prayed that she might take upon herself a portion of the dead poet's sufferings. Another of Byron's instant biographers (and they were legion) referred to him as 'one upon whose most trifling action the eyes of all Europe have been fixed for ten years with an anxious and minute curiosity, of which the annals of literature afford no previous example'.[3]

Such hero-worship inevitably provokes, both in the short run and in the long run, opposition and reaction; and the detractors were at work even during Byron's lifetime. The first substantial biography is that by John Watkins, whose *Memoirs of the Life and Writings of Lord Byron*, published anonymously in 1822, accused him of being the founder of a 'school of immorality and profaneness' and a 'new academy of blasphemy'.[4] After Byron's death, as the air became noisy with the scratching of pens, the chorus of grief and adulation was not unanimous. As the *British Critic* observed tartly in April 1831, 'We do not know whether the public is one half so sick as we are of the apparently interminable inquest which has been sitting upon the case of this noble "Martyr of Genius" (as Mr Moore is pleased to style him) from the day of his decease unto the present hour.' The interesting thing, however, is that a journal as heavily theological as the *British Critic*, with a readership mainly among the clergy, should have been publishing an article on Byron at all (and subsequently reprinting it as a small volume); and the editor, no doubt conscious of this, felt constrained to state his reasons explicitly – reasons that constitute an oblique if unintended tribute to Byron's fame and influence:

> The works of Lord Byron are so much in the hands of almost every class of society, that it is highly important to point out his true principles and character. While his writings tend to render vice more attractive, by clothing it with gaiety and grace, it is well that the young should see it exhibited in himself, under its true features of wretchedness and deformity.

As it turned out, with friends such as Edward Trelawny, Leigh Hunt and Samuel Rogers ready to publish reminiscences shot through with envy and prejudice, not to mention downright fabrication, Byron hardly needed enemies.

The Victorian reaction against Byron was hardly surprising: an age that prized earnestness and high seriousness was unlikely to find in Byron an eligible sage, prophet, or moral guide. Matthew Arnold, visiting Byron's former stamping-ground in Switzerland, could only find him irrelevant to the needs of the new hour:

> What helps it now, that Byron bore,
> With haughty scorn which mocked the smart,
> Through Europe to the Aetolian shore
> The pageant of his bleeding heart?
> That thousands counted every groan,
> And Europe made his woe her own?
>   ('Stanzas from the Grande Chartreuse')

A few years later, George Eliot's Maggie Tulliver turned away from Byron's poems, perceiving that their effect was 'to dull her sensibility to her actual daily life'; and John Stuart Mill recorded his disappointment in the famous fifth chapter of his *Autobiography*:

> In the worst period of my depression, I had read through the whole of Byron (then new to me), to try whether a poet, whose peculiar department was supposed to be that of the intenser feelings, could

rouse any feeling in me. As might be expected, I got no good from this reading, but the reverse. The poet's state of mind was too like my own. His was the lament of a man who had worn out all pleasures, and who seemed to think that life, to all who possess the good things of it, must necessarily be the vapid, uninteresting thing which I found it. His Harold and Manfred had the same burden on them which I had; and I was not in a frame of mind to desire any comfort from the vehement sensual passion of his Giaours, or the sullenness of his Laras.

It was for later generations to rehabilitate Byron, not as a moral guide but as a highly intelligent, linguistically resourceful writer who showed a mastery alike of the long poem, the lyric and the familiar letter, and as the only verse satirist since Pope to compare with that master.

The present volume assembles the testimony of many witnesses, famous and obscure, impartial and partisan, who knew Byron for long or short periods. The extracts have been selected from a very large corpus of material: as the useful bibliography in Samuel C. Chew's *Byron in England* (1924) makes clear, there survives an enormous quantity of writing about Byron, most of it from the years immediately following his death (including the reminiscences of some who never set eyes on him); and, though the flood abated as time passed and memoirists died, it continued for over half a century. Much of it is ephemeral and unworthy of disinterment: books such as *The Private Life of Lord Byron*, for instance, which promised an 'Exposé of Fashionable Frailties, Follies, and Debaucheries' at about the time that Victoria came to the throne, like the more soberly titled *Enquiry into the Moral Character of Lord Byron* (1826) by one J. W. Simmons of Philadelphia, can be allowed to rest undisturbed by the anthologist. But a surprising amount is of interest, and some of it is by friends of Byron – Scott, Shelley, Mary Shelley and others – who are of importance in their own right.

Memoirs and reminiscences are not history or biography, though they may make an important contribution to history and biography; and several caveats need to be entered – in Byron's case, more rather than less forcefully than usual. Some of the recollections are, fairly obviously, coloured by their authors' enthusiasm and admiration, or their eagerness to tell a colourful story, and display a proneness to exaggeration that is one of the occupational hazards of the hagiographer as well as the pornographer. As one of his earliest biographers, George Clinton, writes in relation to some of the accounts of Byron's youth, 'Many strange stories are told of him at this period, the greater part of which are the fruitful inventions of his friends and acquaintances, founded perhaps upon some slender fact, which has been so much exaggerated and altered that it bears no longer any resemblance to the truth.'[5] (Clinton assures us that, while Byron undoubtedly *owned* a drinking-cup made from a human skull, he 'never used it to drink out of'. Another book of the same year, *Anecdotes of Byron*, informed its delighted or horrified readers that the skull was often filled with claret and passed around the circle of his drinking-companions.) We can spot this tendency in yet another publication of the same busy year, where the superlatives betray the writer's tendency to depict his subject as a little (or more than a little) larger than life:

> Lord Byron ran into excesses, particularly in two things, riding and swimming. Immoderately addicted to the latter, he might have been denominated as amphibious; for he has been known to sport on the water five hours, without once coming to land: his exercise on horseback was very violent, always proceeding at a hard gallop and taking the most desperate leaps, swimming his horse through rivers, and spurring him up precipices where few were able or willing to follow him, even on foot.[6]

In another passage of the same work, we can see the Byron legend coming into existence before our eyes (the author is recounting Byron's visit to Juliet's tomb in Verona):

> Lord Byron hung over it a few minutes in mournful silence, and I thought I perceived a tear glistening in his eye; whether as a tribute to the sainted memory of the fair Juliet, or the no less sainted one of our immortal bard, I shall not pretend to determine. Whatever were his feelings, he kept them to himself; for he suddenly rushed out of the ruined building, as if overcome by internal emotion, hurried away through the streets, leaving us to follow him at our leisure, and shut himself up till the next day, without uttering a syllable to any person whomsoever.[7]

If this is not how Romantic poets actually behave, it is certainly how they ought to behave. John Galt's account of another incident makes a somewhat similar point with less straining for effect:

> It was in the course of the passage to the island of Zea, where he was put on shore, that one of the most emphatic incidents of his life occurred; an incident which throws a remarkable gleam into the springs and intricacies of his character – more, perhaps, than anything which has yet been mentioned.
> One day, as he was walking the quarter-deck, he lifted an ataghan (it might be one of the midshipmen's weapons), and unsheathing it, said, contemplating the blade, 'I should like to know how a person feels after committing murder.'[8]

However, Byron had the habit of repeatedly disconcerting those around him by a rapid fluctuation between acting out the role of a Byronic hero and scoffing at the Romantic archetype in his other capacity as wit, satirist and cultivated, aristocratic man of the world. Many informants were perplexed by the complexity and contradictions of his personality and behaviour: expecting to meet Childe Harold in the flesh, they encountered a Byron who undermined his own myths.

In the other direction, many accounts are, as already suggested, characterised by the envy or malice of their authors; and in reading (for instance) Trelawny or Hunt, allowance must be made for their very evident bias. In both the instances cited there are different versions, written at different times and showing signs of different degrees of prejudice, of the same events; and I have given samples of these variations of detail, emphasis and tone. In the same way, where two accounts from the same hand exist, one written immediately after the event and the other at a distance in time (for instance, Thomas Moore first describing a visit to Byron in his journal, and then recalling it in his biography), I have sometimes given both, since the comparison can be instructive.

Another kind of allowance has to be made for the discrepancy between the claims of memoirists and the limitations of memory. The evidence suggests that Byron was a brilliant conversationalist, vigorous, irreverent, unpredictable in the turns taken by his wit, and also capable of being utterly serious. We need not be surprised that those recalling his conversation, sometimes after many years, are incapable of reproducing it verbatim; instead of recognising their limitations, however, they follow the absurd convention of feigning total recall and give the reader lengthy 'conversations' in which, all too often, Byron's language has obviously been emasculated and standardised. It seems likely that his spoken style was much closer to his wonderfully fertile and energetic epistolary style than is suggested by, for instance, Lady Blessington. As that lady was shrewd enough to acknowledge, repeatedly, Byron was in conversation very often a performer, talking for (and to great) effect:

I was this day again struck by the flippancy of his manner of talking of persons for whom I know he expresses, nay, for whom I believe he feels a regard. Something of this must have shown itself in my manner, for he laughingly observed that he was afraid he should lose my good opinion by his frankness; but that when the fit was on him he could not help saying what he thought, though he often repented it when too late. . . .

He talks for effect, likes to excite astonishment, and certainly destroys in the minds of his auditors all confidence in his stability of character. . . .

Byron takes a peculiar pleasure in opposing himself to popular opinion on all points; he wishes to be thought as dissenting from the multitude, and this affectation is the secret source of many of the incongruities he expresses.[9]

Much of that effect has inevitably been lost with the transposition of his spontaneous speech into the formality of written style; but enough remains for us to be aware of its quality and range, even though we may be able to hear no more than faint echoes of it.

The arrangement of the following extracts is not relentlessly chronological, since it has sometimes seemed preferable to juxtapose accounts of different dates (for example, the bouquet of 'first impressions'). In any case, to have preserved a strictly chronological sequence would have involved breaking up some of the longer extracts into fragments, thereby sacrificing the sense of the writer's personality and attitude that a longer piece provides. Broadly speaking, however, the underlying narrative of Byron's life from school and university to final illness, death and burial has been observed. Like all who study Byron's life, I have relied heavily on the three volumes of Leslie A. Marchand's *Byron: A Biography* (New York, 1957), referred to throughout as 'Marchand', and the eleven volumes of the same scholar's edition of Byron's letters and journals (1973–81; with index, 1982). Ernest J. Lovell Jr's substantial anthology *His Very Self and Voice: Collected Conversations of Lord Byron* (New York, 1954) has also been useful. The place of publication of books cited is London unless otherwise stated.

NOTES

1. R. C. Dallas, *Recollections of the Life of Lord Byron* (1825) p. 244
2. *Alfred Lord Tennyson: A Memoir by his Son* (1897) I, 4.
3. George Clinton, *Memoirs of the Life and Writings of Lord Byron* (1825) p. 715.
4. Samuel Chew describes Watkins's book as 'violently hostile to Byron' – *Byron in England* (1924) p.112. Shelley wrote to Leigh Hunt on 24 June 1822 that Byron was 'in a state of supernatural fever about some lying memoirs published of him' – *The Letters of Percy Bysshe Shelley*, ed. F. L. Jones (Oxford, 1964) II, 441.
5. Clinton, *Memoirs of Byron*, p.113.
6. *The Life, Writings, Opinions and Times of . . . Lord Byron . . . by an English Gentleman in the Greek Military Service, and Comrade of his Lordship* (1825) III, 65. See p. 74 below.
7. Ibid., I, 398.
8. John Galt, *The Life of Lord Byron* (n.d.) p. 171.
9. *Lady Blessington's Conversations of Lord Byron*, ed. E. J. Lovell Jr (Princeton, NJ, 1969) pp.10, 33, 204.

A Byron Chronology

1788   (22 Jan) George Gordon Byron born at 16 Holles Street, Cavendish Square, London, son of Captain John Byron and his second wife Catherine, who separate in 1790 after five years of marriage.

1789   Byron's mother moves to Aberdeen.

1791   (2 Aug) Byron's father dies in France.

1794–8   Byron attends Aberdeen Grammar School.

1798   (21 May) On the death of his great-uncle, the fifth Lord Byron, George Gordon Byron becomes the sixth Baron Byron of Rochdale. (Aug) He is taken by his mother to the ancestral seat, Newstead Abbey, Nottinghamshire.

1799   After a period spent with a private tutor in Nottingham, Byron is taken to London and (Sep) enters Dr Glennie's School in Dulwich.

1801   (Apr) Byron enters Harrow School, remaining there with interruptions until 1805.

1805   (24 Oct) Byron enters Trinity College, Cambridge.

1806   (Nov) *Fugitive Pieces* privately printed.

1807   (Jan) *Poems on Various Occasions* privately printed. (June) *Hours of Idleness* published. (Christmas) Byron leaves Cambridge without a degree.

1808   Byron lives in London and Brighton, and at Newstead. (Mar) He publishes *Poems Original and Translated*.

1809   (13 Mar) Byron takes his seat in the House of Lords. *English Bards and Scotch Reviewers* published the same month. (20 June) He sets off for Falmouth, accompanied by Hobhouse. (2 July) They embark for Lisbon, arriving there five days later. The Grand Tour takes them through Portugal and Spain to Gibraltar, whence (16 Aug) they sail for Malta, arriving the 31st. (19 Sep) They set off for Greece and Albania, landing at Patras on the 26th. (31 Oct) Byron begins *Childe Harold*. (Christmas Day) They arrive in Athens.

1810   The tour continues via Smyrna and Ephesus to Constantinople, where they arrive on 13 May. (28 Mar) Byron finishes the second canto of *Childe Harold*; (3 May) he swims the Hellespont. (17 July) Hobhouse bids Byron farewell and returns to England. Byron spends the rest of the year and part of the next in Greece.

1811   Byron returns to England via Malta, landing at Sheerness on 14 July. (1 Aug) Death of Byron's mother. (3 Aug) Death of Byron's friend Charles Matthews. (Oct) Byron hears of the death of John Edleston. (4 Nov) Byron dines with Samuel Rogers and meets Thomas Moore.

1812   (27 Feb) Byron delivers his maiden speech in the House of Lords. (10 Mar) Publication of the first two cantos of *Childe Harold*, bringing instant fame to Byron. Byron has affairs with Lady Caroline Lamb and Lady Oxford; (Oct) he proposes to Annabella Milbanke, whom he has seen for the first time in March, but is rejected.

1813   (20 May) Byron visits Leigh Hunt in jail. (5 June) *The Giaour* published. (20 June) Byron meets Madame de Staël. (Aug) He conducts a liaison with his half-sister Augusta. (2 Dec) *The Bride of Abydos* published.

1814   (1 Feb) *The Corsair* published; 1000 copies are sold on the day of publication. (6 Aug) *Lara* published. (Sep) Byron again proposes to Miss Milbanke, and is accepted.

1815   (2 Jan) Byron marries Annabella Milbanke. They honeymoon in Yorkshire. (29 Mar) The Byrons settle at 13, Piccadilly Terrace, London. (7 Apr) Byron meets Scott. *Hebrew Melodies* is published the same month. (Nov) Bailiffs enter the Byrons' London home. (10 Dec) Birth of Byron's daughter Ada.

1816   (15 Jan) Lady Byron leaves London with Ada to visit her parents and never returns to live with Byron, who (2 Feb) receives a letter from his father-in-law suggesting an amicable separation. (7 Feb) *Siege of Corinth* published. (Mar or Apr) Byron meets Claire Clairmont. (21 Apr) He signs a deed of separation, and (23 Apr) leaves London for Dover, setting sail for Ostend on 25 Apr. Travelling via Bruges, Ghent and Antwerp, he reaches Brussels, where (early in May) he begins Canto III of *Childe Harold*. (4 May) He visits the battle-field at Waterloo. (6 May) He leaves Brussels and goes via Louvain, Cologne, Bonn, Coblenz, Mannheim and Basle to Geneva. (27 May) Byron meets Shelley at Sécheron, near Geneva. (10 June) Byron moves into the Villa Diodati near the Lake of Geneva. (5 Oct) He sets off for Italy with Hobhouse, arriving in Milan on the 12th and meeting Stendhal in that city; then he goes via Verona, Vicenza and Padua to Venice, arriving there on 10 November. (18 Nov) Canto III of *Childe Harold* published. (5 Dec) *The Prisoner of Chillon and Other Poems* published.

1817   (12 Jan) Allegra, child of Byron and Claire Clairmont, born in England. (17 Apr) Byron travels via Bologna and Florence to Rome, arriving on the 29th; by 28 May he is back in Venice. (4 June) He leases the Villa Foscarini at La Mira. (16 June) *Manfred* published. (13 Nov) Byron returns to Venice. (Dec) Sale of Newstead Abbey.

1818   (22 Jan) Byron meets the Countess Guiccioli. (28 Feb) *Beppo* published. (28 Apr) Canto IV of *Childe Harold* published. (2 May) Allegra arrives in Venice. (3 July) Byron begins *Don Juan*.

1819   (June) Byron goes to Ravenna to visit the Guicciolis, and in August follows them to Bologna. (15 July) Cantos I and II of *Don Juan* published. (Sep) Teresa and Byron at La Mira. (11 Oct) Byron gives Moore his memoirs, Moore having arrived at La Mira on the 7th. In November Teresa returns with her husband to Ravenna. Byron arrives in Ravenna on Christmas Eve.

1820   (July) Byron meets Count Pietro Gamba. (14 July) Teresa's separation decree arrives.

1821   (1 Mar) Allegra is sent to a convent school. (July) Teresa's father and brother are banished, and she goes to join them in Florence. (Oct) Byron leaves Ravenna to rejoin Teresa in Pisa. (Nov) Byron meets Edward Williams and Thomas Medwin.

1822   (15 Jan) Byron meets Edward Trelawny. (20 Apr) Death of Allegra. (July) Leigh Hunt and his family arrive in Pisa. (8 July) Shelley and Williams are drowned in the Bay of Spezia. (Oct) Byron arrives in Genoa. (15 Oct) *A Vision of Judgment* published.

1823   (1 Apr) Byron meets Lady Blessington. (13 July) He embarks on the *Hercules* for Greece, but owing to delays the ship does not set off until the 16th. (3 Aug) Byron lands at Argostoli, Cephalonia. (30 Dec) Byron sets sail for Missolonghi.

1824   (4 Jan) Byron arrives in Missolonghi. (15 Feb) He suffers a violent fit but gradually recovers. (19 Apr) Weakened by blood-letting, Byron dies of fever. (14 May) News of Byron's death reaches England. (17 May) Destruction of Byron's memoirs. Byron's body reaches England at the beginning of July. (12 July) The funeral procession leaves London, and (16 July) burial takes place at Hucknall Torkard, Nottinghamshire.

Schooldays in Aberdeen*

ANONYMOUS

It is the custom of the grammar school at Aberdeen, that the boys of all the five classes to which it is composed, should be assembled for prayers in the public school at eight o'clock in the morning; after prayers a censor calls over the names of all, and those who are absent are punished.

The first time that Lord Byron had come to school after his accession to his title, the rector had caused his name to be inserted in the censor's book *Georgius Dominus de Byron* instead of *Georgius Byron Gordon* as formerly. The boys, unaccustomed to this aristocratic sound, set up a loud and involuntary shout, which had such an effect on his sensitive mind, that he burst into tears, and would have fled from the school had he not been restrained by the master. . . .

A school-fellow of Byron's had a very small Shetland pony, which his father had brought him, and one day they went to the banks of Don to bathe: but having only one pony, they were obliged to follow the good old practice called in Scotland 'ride and tie'. When they came to the bridge, over that dark, romantic stream, Byron bethought him of the prophecy which he has incorrectly quoted (from memory, it is true) in *Don Juan*:[1]

> Brig o' Balgownie! wight is thy wa',
> Wi' a wife's ae son an' a mare's ae foal,
> Down shalt thou fa'.

He immediately stopped his companion, who was then riding, and asked him if he remembered the prophecy, saying, that as they were both only sons, and as the pony *might* be 'a mare's ae foal', he would rather ride over first, because he had only a mother to lament him should the prophecy be fulfilled by the falling of the bridge, whereas the other had both a father and a mother to grieve for him. . . .

---

*Anecdotes of Lord Byron, from Authentic Sources: with Remarks Illustrative of his Connection with the Principal Literary Characters of the Present Day (London: Knight and Lacey, 1825) pp.1–3, 5–6.

1

While at the grammar school, in all the boyish sports and amusements he would be the first, if possible. Notwithstanding the weakness of his constitution and the mal-conformation of one of his feet, no boy could outstrip him in the race, or in swimming. His desire for supremacy in the school games led him into many combats. In these he shewed himself no mean proficient at 'England's darling science' – he came always off with honour, almost always victorious. Upon one occasion, a boy pursued by another took refuge in his mother's house; the latter, who had been much abused by the former, proceeded to take vengeance on him, even on the landing-place of the drawing-room stairs, when young Byron came out at the noise, and insisted that the refugee should not be struck in his house, or else he must fight for him. The pursuer, 'nothing loath', accepted the challenge, and they fought for nearly an hour, when both were compelled to give in from absolute exhaustion. . . .

An answer which Lord Byron made to a fellow-scholar, who questioned him as to the cause of the honorary addition of '*Dominus de Byron*' to his name, served at that time, when he was only ten years of age, to point out that he would be a man who would think, speak, and act for himself; who, whatever might be his sayings or his doings, his vices or his virtues, would not condescend to take them at second hand. This happened on the very day after he had been menaced with being flogged round the school, for a fault which he had not committed; and, when the question was put to him, he replied: 'It is not *my doing*. Fortune was to whip me yesterday for what another did, and she has this day made me a Lord for what another has ceased to do. I need not thank her in either case; for I have asked nothing at her hands.'

NOTES

Anecdotes of Lord Byron, published anonymously, was compiled by Alexander Kilgour. Byron was at Aberdeen Grammar School between the ages of six and ten (1794–8).

Teresa Guiccioli (see p. 83) recounts the incident that took place on 'the banks of Don', but places it 'on the river Dee' – *My Recollections of Lord Byron, and Those of Eye-witnesses of his Life* (New York, 1869) pp. 176–7. She adds two other anecdotes of this period as well as some rather fulsome commentary:

The anecdotes told of him at this time all prove his fine nature, and show the goodness and greatness of soul which characterised him up to his last day.

All the qualities which are to shine in the man will be found already marked in the child. On one occasion he was taken to see a piece at the Edinburgh theatre, in which one of the actors pretends that the moon is the sun. The child, notwithstanding his timidity, was shocked by this insult to his understanding, rose from his seat, and cried out, 'I assure you, my dear sir, that it is the moon.' Here, again, we can trace that love of truth which in after life made him so courageous in its proclamation at any cost. . . .

On another occasion he saw a poor woman coming out of a bookseller's shop, distressed and mortified at not having enough to buy herself the Bible she wanted. The child ran after her, brought her back, made her a present of the desired book, and, in doing so, obeyed that same craving of the heart to do good which placed him all his life at the service of others.

1. *Don Juan*, X.xviii.

'Little Deevil Geordie Byron'*

R. E. PROTHERO

The few personal reminiscences [of Byron's childhood] that have been gleaned in later years scarcely deserve the same credence as those that belong to an earlier date. Some, however, are sufficiently characteristic to be chronicled. Here, for example, is a story which illustrates the love of practical joking that marked the 'young English nickom', the 'little deevil Geordie Byron'. His mother had taken him to visit Lady Abercromby of Birkenbog: the two ladies were talking in the parlour window; the boy escaped to the room above. Suddenly a piercing scream was heard, and an object, clad in the boy's coat and hat, shot headlong past the window where the ladies sat. Byron had dressed a pillow in his clothes and, with a shriek, launched it from the room above, in the hope of persuading his mother that he had accidentally fallen. It is, perhaps, as a sequel to this story that the following is told: Lady Abercromby advised his mother to punish him for some offence. He received his chastisement; but, that ended, walked up to Lady Abercromby and struck her in the face, saying, 'That's for meddling. But for you I should not have been beaten.' Another reminiscence is that of Mr Stephen, mealmaker at Inchmarnock, near Ballaterich, who remembered him as 'an ill-deedie laddie; he was aye pittin' bits o' sticks and orra things in my mill-wheel, and brook it in twa-three places'.

*'The Childhood and School Days of Byron', *Nineteenth Century*, XLIII (1898) 72–3.

Other recollections, gathered by the Rev. J. Michie, of the Manse, Dinnet, relate to Ballaterich, on Deeside, where the boy was first sent to recover from illness, and where he afterwards spent portions of his summer holidays.

My informant [writes Mr Michie] was Mrs Calder, the widow of the farmer of Greystone, in the immediate vicinity of Ballaterich, and the daughter of the carpenter referred to. She was born in 1791, died years ago at the advanced age of 86, and remembered Byron and his ways very distinctly. Even at that early age (eleven or twelve) the wilful, intractable disposition which in riper years too much distinguished the character of the noble bard had begun to display itself. I give the following in the words of my informant: 'He was a very takin' laddie, but no easily managed. He was fond of coming up to see my father's shop, and particularly fond o' the turning-lathe; but he wadna haud his hands frae ony o' the tools, and he spoiled them completely before he would let them go. My father couldna lay hands on him, and he wad tak nae telling; so at last he set some o' us to watch when we would see him coming up the brae frae Ballaterich, and when he got word that he was coming he would lock the door of the shop, and gang awa' out about. There was nae ither way o' deean wi' him.'

Harrow*

THOMAS MOORE

Arrived at Harrow about half-past six [on 3 July 1827]: no one but Drury[1] himself (who received me most hospitably) and his family at dinner. Dr Butler[2] joined us in the evening. A good deal of desultory talk about Byron; his quarrel with Butler; could not bear his succeeding Dr Drury; organised a rebellion against him on his arrival; wrote up in all parts of the school, 'To your tents, O Israel!'[3] dragged the desk of the master into the middle of the school, and burnt it.[4] Lived in Dr Butler's house; pulled down the blinds of his study or drawing-room (?); when charged with it by Dr B and asked his reason, said 'They darkened the room.' Afterwards, however, when Butler threatened him, cried and blubbered like a child. Always at the head of every

---

*The Journal of Thomas Moore, 1818–1841, ed. Peter Quennell (London: Batsford, 1964) pp. 153–4. The Journal was originally published in 1853–6.

mischief. His lameness, they both agreed, was from an accident, being let fall when at nurse; might have been removed if he had not been obstinate at school, and resisted all the precautions and remedies adopted. Was very idle; learnt nothing. His mother a coarse, vulgar woman.

NOTES

On Moore, see p. 58. He visited Harrow in the course of collecting material for his biography of Byron.

After being removed from Aberdeen Grammar School, Byron was placed with a private tutor and then sent to Dr Glennie's School in Dulwich. He entered Harrow School in April 1801 and remained there until 1805.

1. Moore's meeting was with Henry Drury, son of Dr Joseph Drury, who had been Byron's headmaster at Harrow. Henry Drury had been Byron's tutor. At his first interview with Byron, Dr Drury found that 'a wild mountain colt had been submitted to my management. But there was mind in his eye. . . . His manner and temper soon convinced me, that he might be led by a silken string to a point, rather than by a cable; – on that principle I acted' (quoted by Marchand, p. 64).

2. Dr George Butler succeeded Drury in 1805 after the latter had spent twenty years in the headship. Francis Hodgson reports that Byron used to speak of Drury as 'the *dear* Drury, in contradistinction to his successor, whom he maliciously designated the *cheap* Butler, but whom he afterwards learned to estimate at his proper value' — *Memoir of the Rev. Francis Hodgson, BD* (London: Macmillan, 1878) I, 36.

3. 1 Kings 12:16.

4. A different version of this episode is given in *Anecdotes of Lord Byron*, p.6:

The boys at Harrow had mutinied, and, in their wisdom, had resolved to set fire to the scene of all their ills and troubles – the school-room. Byron, however, was against the motion, and by pointing out to the young rebels the names of their fathers on the walls, he prevented the intended conflagration. This early specimen of his power over the passions of his school-fellows, his Lordship piqued himself not a little upon.

Cambridge*

ANONYMOUS

From Harrow Lord Byron was removed, and entered of Trinity College, Cambridge. Here, however, he did not mend his manners, nor

Anecdotes of Lord Byron, pp. 6–7.

hold the sages of antiquity in higher esteem than when under the command of old Drury at Harrow. He was above studying the Poetics, and held the rules of the Stagyrite[1] in as little esteem as, in after life, he did the 'invariable principles' of the Rev. Mr Bowles.[2] Reading after the fashion of the studious men of Cam, was to him a bore; and he held a senior wrangler in the greatest contempt. Persons of real genius are seldom candidates for college prizes, and Byron left 'the silver cup' for those plodding characters, who, perhaps, deserve them, as the guerdon of the unceasing labour necessary to overcome the, all but invincible, natural dullness of their intellects. Byron, instead of reading what pleased tutors, read what pleased himself, and wrote what could not fail to displease those political weathercocks. He did not admire their system of education, and *they*, as is the case with most scholars, could admire no other. He took to quizzing them, and no one likes to be laughed at. Doctors frowned, and Fellows fumed, and Byron, at the age of nineteen, left the university without a degree. . . .

Whilst at Cambridge, he kept a young bear in his room for some time, and it is reported, that he told the master, he intended that his bear should sit for a fellowship. But however much the Fellows of Trinity may claim acquaintance with the '*Ursa Major*',[3] they were by no means desirous of associating with his Lordship's *élève*.

NOTES

Byron went up to Trinity College, Cambridge, on 24 October 1805 (three days after the Battle of Trafalgar), and left Cambridge for good at the end of 1807. His rooms were in the south-east corner of Trinity Great Court, and his bear was kept in a turret at the top of the stairs.

1. Aristotle (so called because he was born in Stageira), whose *Poetics* was a text prescribed for study.

2. William Lisle Bowles (1762–1850), whose *Fourteen Sonnets* (1789) enjoyed a considerable vogue, and whose edition of Pope (1806) sparked off a controversy in which Byron joined in 1821.

3. The Great Bear constellation (the rather laboured allusion is to the mathematical and astronomical studies at the College). Byron wrote to Elizabeth Bridget Pigot on 26 October 1807, 'I have got a new friend, the finest in the world, a *tame bear*, when I brought him here, they asked me what I meant to do with him, and my reply was, "*he should sit for a Fellowship*" ' – '*In my hot youth': Byron's Letters and Journals*, I, ed. Leslie A. Marchand (1973) pp. 135–6. Medwin (see p. 24) reports Byron as saying, 'I had a great hatred of College rules, and contempt for academical honours. How many of their wranglers have distinguished themselves in the world?' – *Conversations of Lord Byron*, ed. Ernest J. Lovell Jr (Princeton, NJ, 1966) p. 67.

'I Shall Go Mad'*

JAMES T. HODGSON

That Byron was his own worst enemy has often been noticed by his biographers. His extraordinary love of a bad reputation, of exhibiting himself in the most unfavourable aspect, amounted almost to insanity, and was in nothing more conspicuous than in his determination to represent his religious opinions as far more sceptical than they really were. Many of his friends, and in particular Hodgson and Scrope Berdmore Davies,[1] a fellow of King's at this time [1808–9] and mutual friend of Byron and Hodgson, used constantly to make fun of this idiosyncrasy. Byron, when absorbed in thought and indulging in reckless speculations, used often, as he expressed it, to suffer from 'a confusion of ideas', and would sometimes exclaim in his most melodramatic manner, 'I shall go mad.' Scrope Davies, a true friend, and a charming vivacious companion, who had a quaint dry manner of speaking and an irresistible stammer, used quietly to remark in answer, 'Much more like silliness than madness.'

*Memoir of the Rev. Francis Hodgson, BD (London: Macmillan, 1878) I, 103–4.

NOTES

Francis Hodgson (1781–1852) was educated at Eton and King's College, Cambridge, and became an assistant tutor at King's in October 1807. Byron met him at about that time. In the same year Hodgson published a translation of Juvenal that was attacked in the Edinburgh Review. They remained friends until Byron left England for good, though, as Marchand comments, 'this friendship was one of Byron's strangest. Hodgson's moral earnestness and sometimes humourless conventionality were at complete odds with Byron's sceptical proclivities' (p. 141). Hodgson took orders in 1812, but his attempts to convert Byron met with no success: 'As to your immortality,' Byron wrote to him on 7 September 1811, 'if people are to live, why die? And our carcases, which are to rise again, are they worth raising? I hope, if mine is, that I shall have a better pair of legs than I have moved on these two-and-twenty years, or I shall be sadly behind in the squeeze into Paradise.' Hodgson's urging that he should 'examine the whole of Paley's Evidences' fell on stony ground.

1. Scrope Berdmore Davies, dandy and gambler, was a close associate of Byron during his London years and visited him at Newstead. Davies became a Fellow of King's College, Cambridge, and Byron visited him at Cambridge in 1811. When Byron left England in 1816, Davies accompanied him as far as Dover. He visited Byron at the Villa Diodati in August of that year. According to *Anecdotes of Lord Byron*, p. 6, 'This gentleman and Byron once lost all their money at "Chicken hazard", in one of the hells of St James's, and next morning Davies sent for Byron's pistols to shoot himself with. Byron sent a note refusing to give them, on the ground that they would be forfeited as a deodand. This comic excuse had the desired effect.' See T. A. J. Burnett, *The Rise and Fall of a Regency Dandy: The Life and Times of Scrope Berdmore Davies* (1981).

Byron Takes his Seat in the House of Lords*

R. C. DALLAS

I saw Lord Byron daily. It was about this time that Lord Falkland[1] was killed in a duel, which suggested some lines as the Satire was going through the press. Nature had endowed Lord Byron with very benevolent feelings, which I have had opportunities of discerning, and I have seen them at times render his fine countenance most beautiful. His features seemed formed in a peculiar manner for emanating the high conceptions of genius, and the working of the passions. I have often, and with no little admiration, witnessed these effects. I have seen them in the glow of poetical inspiration, and under the influence of strong emotion; on the one hand amounting to virulence, and on the other replete with all the expression and grace of the mild and amiable affections. When under the influence of resentment and anger, it was painful to observe the powerful sway of those passions over his features: when he was impressed with kindness, which was the natural state of his heart, it was a high treat to contemplate his countenance. I saw him the morning after Lord Falkland's death. He had just come from seeing the lifeless body of the man with whom he had a very short time before spent a social day; he now and then said, as if it were to himself, but aloud, 'Poor Falkland!' He looked more than he spoke – 'But his wife, it is she who is to be pitied.' I saw his mind teeming with benevolent

Recollections of the Life of Lord Byron, 1808–14 (London: Knight, 1824) pp. 48–55.

intentions – and they were not abortive. If ever an action was pure, that which he then meditated was so; and the spirit that conceived, the man that performed it, was at that time making his way through briers and brambles to that clear but narrow path which leads to heaven. Those, who have taken pains to guide him from it, must answer for it!

The remembrance of the impression produced on Lord Byron by Lord Falkland's death, at the period I am retracing, has excited this slight, but sincere and just, effusion; and I am sensible that the indulgence of it needs no apology.

The Satire was published about the middle of March, previous to which he took his seat in the House of Lords, on the 13th of the same month. On that day, passing down St James's Street, but with no intention of calling, I saw his chariot at his door, and went in. His countenance, paler than usual, showed that his mind was agitated, and that he was thinking of the nobleman to whom he had once looked for a hand and countenance in his introduction to the House. He said to me – 'I am glad you happened to come in; I am going to take my seat, perhaps you will go with me.' I expressed my readiness to attend him; while, at the same time, I concealed the shock I felt on thinking that this young man, who, by birth, fortune, and talent, stood high in life, should have lived so unconnected and neglected by persons of his own rank, that there was not a single member of the senate to which he belonged, to whom he could or would apply to introduce him in a manner becoming his birth. I saw that he felt the situation, and I fully partook his indignation. . . .

After some talk about the Satire, the last sheets of which were in the press, I accompanied Lord Byron to the House. He was received in one of the antechambers by some of the officers in attendance, with whom he settled respecting the fees he had to pay. One of them went to apprise the Lord Chancellor of his being there, and soon returned for him. There were very few persons in the House. Lord Eldon[2] was going through some ordinary business. When Lord Byron entered, I thought he looked still paler than before; and he certainly wore a countenance in which mortification was mingled with, but subdued by, indignation. He passed the woolsack without looking round, and advanced to the table where the proper officer was attending to administer the oaths. When he had gone through them, the Chancellor quitted his seat, and went towards him with a smile, putting out his hand warmly to welcome him; and, though I did not catch his words, I saw that he paid him some compliment. This was all thrown away upon Lord Byron, who made a stiff bow, and put the tips of his fingers into a hand, the amiable offer of which demanded the whole of his. I was sorry to see this, for Lord Eldon's character is great for virtue, as well as talent; and, even in a political point of view, it would have given me inexpressible pleasure to have seen him uniting heartily with him. The

Chancellor did not press a welcome so received, but resumed his seat; while Lord Byron carelessly seated himself for a few minutes on one of the empty benches to the left of the throne, usually occupied by the Lords in opposition. When, on his joining me, I expressed what I had felt, he said: 'If I had shaken hands heartily, he would have set me down for one of his party – but I will have nothing to do with any of them, on either side; I have taken my seat, and now I will go abroad.' We returned to St James's Street, but he did not recover his spirits. The going abroad was a plan on which his thoughts had turned for some time; I did not, however, consider it as determined, or so near at hand as it proved. In a few days he left town for Newstead Abbey, after seeing the last proof of the Satire, and writing a short preface to the Poem.

NOTES

Robert Charles Dallas (1754–1824) met Byron in January 1808. 'Dallas, more than thirty years his senior, became devoted to Byron, aided him, sometimes officiously, in putting his poems through the press, and was a frequent caller for several months' (Marchand, p. 143). Byron took his seat in the House of Lords on 13 March 1809; his satire *English Bards and Scotch Reviewers* was published later in the same month.

1. Charles John Cary, ninth Lord Falkland (1768–1809), was wounded in a duel with Sir Arthur Powell at Chalk Farm on 28 February 1809 and died at the latter's home in Devonshire Place two days later. On 8 February, Byron, plagued by debts, had announced his intention of sailing with Falkland 'for Sicily'. After Falkland's death he stood godfather to his posthumous child and gave his widow £500. Byron described himself (letter of 6 March) as having been 'under great depression of spirits from poor Falkland's death'. There is a reference to Falkland in *English Bards and Scotch Reviewers*, lines 685–6:

> The mangled victim of a drunken brawl,
> To live like CLODIUS, and like FALKLAND fall.

Byron's interesting note on the allusion to Falkland is quoted in Lord Byron, *The Complete Poetical Works*, ed. Jerome J. McGann, I (Oxford: Clarendon Press, 1980) p. 412.

2. John Scott Eldon (1751–1838), lawyer and politician, was Lord Chancellor almost continuously from 1801 to 1827 and was a notable reactionary and opponent of reform.

An Adventure in Greece*

J. C. HOBHOUSE

The pass through the hills lasted half an hour; and after travelling an hour more over a slippery plain, we arrived at the village just as the evening set in very dark, and the rain began to pour down in torrents. My friend [i.e. Byron], with the baggage and servants, was behind, and had not been in sight for some time.

After stumbling through several narrow lanes, we came, at last, to the miserable hovel prepared for our reception. . . .

We were very uneasy that the party did not arrive; but the Secretary assured me, that the guides knew every part of the country, as did also his own servant, who was with them, and that they had certainly taken shelter in a village at an hour's distance. Not being satisfied with this conjecture, I ordered fires to be lighted on the hill above the village, and some muskets to be discharged; this was at eleven o'clock, and the storm had not abated. I lay down in my great coat; but all sleeping was out of the question, as any pauses in the tempest, were filled up by the barking of the dogs, and the shouting of the shepherds in the neighbouring mountains.

A little after midnight a man, panting and pale, and drenched with rain, rushed into the room, and, between crying and roaring, with a profusion of action, communicated something to the Secretary, of which I understood only – that they had all fallen down. I learnt, however, that no accident had happened, except the falling of the luggage horses, and losing their way, and that they were now waiting for fresh horses and guides. Ten were immediately sent to them, together with several men with pine torches; but it was not till two o'clock in the morning that we heard they were approaching, and my friend, with the Priest and the servants, did not enter our hut before three.

I now learnt from him, that they had lost their way from the commencement of the storm, when not above three miles from the village; and that after wandering up and down in total ignorance of their position, had, at last, stopped near some Turkish tomb-stones and

---

*A Journey through Albania, and Other Provinces of Turkey in Europe and Asia, to Constantinople, During the Years 1809 and 1810 (London: John Murray, 1813) I, 79–80.

a torrent, which they saw by the flashes of lightning. They had been
thus exposed for nine hours; and the guides, so far from assisting them,
only augmented the confusion, by running away, after being
threatened with death by George the dragoman, who, in an agony of
rage and fear, and without giving any warning, fired off both his pistols,
and drew from the English servant [Fletcher] an involuntary scream of
horror; for he fancied they were beset by robbers.

NOTE

John Cam Hobhouse (1786–1869), later Lord Broughton, politician and
memoirist, became Byron's executor. Near the beginning of his *Recollections* he
writes, 'At Cambridge I formed an acquaintance with Lord Byron, and, having
taken my degree, I travelled with him across Portugal and Spain to Gibraltar
and Malta, and thence to Albania, Greece, and Constantinople.' Byron and
Hobhouse set off on the Grand Tour on 2 July 1809, sailing from Falmouth to
Lisbon and travelling thence via Seville, Cadiz and the other places mentioned
by Hobhouse. They arrived in Greece on 26 September 1809 and Byron began
Childe Harold on 31 October. For John Galt's account of Byron in Gibraltar and
Sardinia, see below.

Hobhouse's *Contemporary Account of the Separation of Lord and Lady Byron; also of
the Destruction of Lord Byron's Memoirs* was privately printed in 1870.

In England Again
(1811–14)*

J. C. HOBHOUSE

[16 July 1811.] I heard today from Byron, by a letter written at Malta,
appointing a meeting at Sittingbourne, to which place I went the next
day, where I met my friend after an absence of one year. We spent the
next two days in visiting Canterbury and the neighbourhood, and I left
Canterbury on the 19th, after having parted with my dear friend.

[1811.] During the month of November I prepared, in frequent consultation with Byron, my work on our travels in Albania, the proofs of
which I got by the end of the year.

Recollections of a Long Life (London: John Murray, 1909–11) I, 35, 36, 38, 45,
86, 98–9, 100, 105–6, 125.

[19 Feb 1812.] Lord Byron made his maiden speech today on the Nottingham Riot Bill.

[21 Apr.] Stayed up all night at the House of Lords. Debate on the Catholic question. Heard Byron, who kept the House in a roar of laughter . . . .

[14 Aug.] Went to Garroway's Coffee House to the sale of Newstead Abbey by auction by a Mr Fairbrother, where, having just secured myself with Byron, I bid twelve times, and left off at 113,000 guineas for the large lot, which was bought in at 113,500 guineas, B having fixed £120,000 as the price. The second was bought in at 13,100 guineas. Never having done the like before, I was, before the thing began, in a complete fever, but was told by Hanson, B's solicitor, that I came off most admirably. I had just then only one pound one shilling and sixpence in the world.

[18 Feb 1814.] Its success [*The Corsair*] has been astonishing, 13,000 copies sold in a month. The abuse showered upon Byron for the 'Weep, Daughter of a Royal Line', helped it along.[1]

[21 Mar.] This evening I went to a very small early party at Lady Lansdowne's, where there were not above 150 people present. . . . Lord Byron, whom I love more and more every day, not so much from his fame as his fondness – I think not equivocal, for me – introduced me, at her desire, to Lady Melbourne . . . .

[23 Mar.] Call on Lady Portsmouth with Byron, and on Lady Westmoreland, but did not go, as intended, to Murray's, in whose reading-room there is daily an assembly of *Quarterly* and other wits, into which, as an author or a gentleman, or more as a friend of Lord Byron's, whose works are Murray's income, I enter.

[28 Mar.] He says himself that his poems are of that sort, which will, like everything of the kind in these days, pass away, and give place to the ancient reading, but that he esteems himself fortunate in getting all that can now be got by such a passing reputation, for which there are so many competitors.

[12 Apr.] Byron goes not to Paris. He is a difficult person to live with . . . .

[19 May.] Went with Byron and Tom Moore to the Orchestra to see Kean[2] in *Othello*. For two acts and a half the play was tame, but from the sentence, 'Not a jot', he displayed his extraordinary powers, and, as

Byron said, threw a sort of Levant fury of expression into his actions and face, to which we Orientalists had been accustomed, and which we could appreciate. His stabbing himself was a masterpiece.

NOTES

After visiting Constantinople with Byron, Hobhouse had parted from him on 17 July 1810 and had made his way back to England.

1. John Murray, Byron's publisher, wrote to him early in February 1814 to tell him that 10,000 copies of *The Corsair* had been sold on the day of publication – 'a thing perfectly unprecedented'. Within the next few weeks Murray 'printed seven editions and sold twenty-five thousand copies' (Marchand, p. 433). On 22 February 1812, at a banquet held at Carlton House, the Prince Regent had 'abused all his Whig friends in violent language. His little daughter, Princess Charlotte, who was present, wept at her father's treachery to those who had befriended him and to the party in which she and her mother had put all their hope. She was ordered out of the room with the Duchess of York' (Marchand, pp. 318–19). Early in March, Byron sent a poem, 'Sympathetic Address to a Young Lady', to the *Morning Chronicle*, to be published anonymously. It appeared on 7 March 1812. When its authorship became known, the attack on the Regent ('A Sire's disgrace, a realm's decay') aroused an outcry.

2. Edmund Kean (1789–1833), Shakespearean actor. Byron, accompanied by Thomas Moore, had seen Kean on 7 May, and Byron and Hobhouse had seen him as Richard III on 19 February.

First Impressions I (1809)*

JOHN GALT

It was at Gibraltar that I first fell in with Lord Byron. I had arrived there in the packet from England, in indifferent health, on my way to Sicily. I had then no intention of travelling. I only went a trip, intending to return home after spending a few weeks in Malta, Sicily, and Sardinia; having, before my departure, entered into the Society of Lincoln's Inn, with the design of studying the law.

At this time, my friend, the late Colonel Wright, of the artillery, was

The Life of Lord Byron (London: Sisley's, n.d.) pp. 62–7. Originally published in 1830.

secretary to the Governor; and during the short stay of the packet at the Rock, he invited me to the hospitalities of his house, and among other civilities gave me admission to the garrison library.

The day, I well remember, was exceedingly sultry. The air was sickly; and if the wind was not a sirocco, it was a withering levanter[1] – oppressive to the functions of life, and to an invalid denying all exercise. Instead of rambling over the fortifications, I was, in consequence, constrained to spend the hottest part of the day in the library; and, while sitting there, a young man came in and seated himself opposite to me at the table where I was reading. Something in his appearance attracted my attention. His dress indicated a Londoner of some fashion, partly by its neatness and simplicity, with just so much of a peculiarity of style as served to show, that although he belonged to the order of metropolitan beaux, he was not altogether a common one.

I thought his face not unknown to me; I began to conjecture where I could have seen him; and, after an unobserved scrutiny, to speculate both as to his character and vocation. His physiognomy was prepossessing and intelligent, but ever and anon his brows lowered and gathered; a habit, as I then thought, with a degree of affectation in it, probably first assumed for picturesque effect and energetic expression; but which I afterwards discovered was undoubtedly the occasional scowl of some unpleasant reminiscence: it was certainly disagreeable – forbidding – but still the general cast of his features was impressed with elegance and character.

At dinner, a large party assembled at Colonel Wright's; among others the Countess of Westmorland, with Tom Sheridan and his beautiful wife; and it happened that Sheridan, in relating the local news of the morning, mentioned that Lord Byron and Mr Hobhouse had come in from Spain, and were to proceed up the Mediterranean in the packet. He was not acquainted with either.

Hobhouse had, a short time before I left London, published certain translations and poems rather respectable in their way, and I had seen the work, so that his name was not altogether strange to me. Byron's was familiar – the *Edinburgh Review* had made it so, and still more the satire of *English Bards and Scotch Reviewers*, but I was not conscious of having seen the persons of either.

On the following evening I embarked early, and soon after the two travellers came on board; in one of whom I recognised the visitor to the library, and he proved to be Lord Byron. In the little bustle and process of embarking their luggage, his Lordship affected, as it seemed to me, more aristocracy than befitted his years, or the occasion; and I then thought of his singular scowl, and suspected him of pride and irascibility. The impression that evening was not agreeable, but it was interesting; and that forehead mark, the frown, was calculated to awaken curiosity, and beget conjectures.

Hobhouse, with more of the commoner, made himself one of the passengers at once; but Byron held himself aloof, and sat on the rail, leaning on the mizzen shrouds, inhaling, as it were, poetical sympathy, from the gloomy Rock, then dark and stern in the twilight. There was in all about him that evening much waywardness; he spoke petulantly to Fletcher, his valet; and was evidently ill at ease with himself, and fretful towards others. I thought he would turn out an unsatisfactory shipmate; yet there was something redeeming in the tones of his voice, when, some time after he had indulged his sullen meditation, he again addressed Fletcher; so that, instead of finding him ill-natured, I was soon convinced he was only capricious.

Our passage to Sardinia was tardy, owing to calms; but, in other respects, pleasant. About the third day Byron relented from his rapt mood, as if he felt it was out of place, and became playful, and disposed to contribute his fair proportion to the general endeavour to wile away the tediousness of the dull voyage. Among other expedients for that purpose, we had recourse to shooting at bottles. Byron, I think, supplied the pistols, and was the best shot, but not very pre-eminently so. In the calms, the jolly-boat was several times lowered; and, on one of those occasions, his Lordship, with the captain, caught a turtle – I rather think two – we likewise hooked a shark, part of which was dressed for breakfast, and tasted, without relish; your shark is but a cannibal dainty.

As we approached the gulf, or bay, of Cagliari, in Sardinia, a strong north wind came from the shore, and we had a whole disagreeable day of tacking, but next morning, it was Sunday, we found ourselves at anchor near the mole, where we landed. Byron, with the captain, rode out some distance into the country, while I walked with Mr Hobhouse about the town: we left our cards for the consul, and Mr Hill, the ambassador, who invited us to dinner. In the evening we landed again, to avail ourselves of the invitation; and, on this occasion, Byron and his Pylades[2] dressed themselves as aides-de-camp – a circumstance which, at the time, did not tend to improve my estimation of the solidity of the character of either. But such is the force of habit: it appeared a less exceptionable affectation in the young peer than in the commoner.

Had we parted at Cagliari, it is probable that I should have retained a much more favourable recollection of Mr Hobhouse than of Lord Byron; for he was a cheerful companion, full of odd and droll stories, which he told extremely well; he was also good-humoured and intelligent – altogether an advantageous specimen of a well-educated English gentleman. Moreover, I was at the time afflicted with a nervous dejection, which the occasional exhilaration produced by his anecdotes and college tales often materially dissipated, though, for the most part, they were more after the manner and matter of Swift than of Addison.

Byron was, during the passage, in delicate health, and upon an abstemious regimen. He rarely tasted wine, nor more than half a glass, mingled with water, when he did. He ate little; no animal food, but only bread and vegetables. He reminded me of the ghoul that picked rice with a needle; for it was manifest, that he had not acquired his knowledge of the world by always dining so sparely. If my remembrance is not treacherous, he only spent one evening in the cabin with us – the evening before we came to anchor at Cagliari; for, when the lights were placed, he made himself a man forbid, took his station on the railing between the pegs on which the sheets are belayed and the shrouds, and there, for hours, sat in silence, enamoured, it may be, of the moon. All these peculiarities, with his caprices, and something inexplicable in the cast of his metaphysics, while they served to awaken interest, contributed little to conciliate esteem. He was often strangely rapt – it may have been from his genius; and, had its grandeur and darkness been then divulged, susceptible of explanation; but, at the time, it threw, as it were, around him the sackcloth of penitence. Sitting amid the shrouds and rattlins, in the tranquillity of the moonlight, churming[3] an inarticulate melody, he seemed almost apparitional, suggesting dim reminiscences of him who shot the albatross.[4] He was as a mystery in a winding-sheet, crowned with a halo.

NOTES

John Galt (1779–1839), Scottish novelist. Byron was in Gibraltar from 4 to 16 August 1809; his meeting with Galt apparently took place on the 15th. They were fellow passengers to Malta and met again in Athens on 21 February 1810, continuing to meet from time to time until Byron's departure from that city on 5 March. A few weeks later they saw each other in Smyrna. During the winter of 1811–12 Galt saw Byron 'frequently' (by his own account) in London. Their last meeting was on 5 December 1813.

    1. Strong easterly wind in the Mediterranean.

    2. In Greek legend, the close friend of Orestes; hence, a faithful companion.

    3. Dialect term for making 'a confused, intermingled noise or hum' (*English Dialect Dictionary*).

    4. Coleridge's Ancient Mariner.

First Impressions II (1811)*

SAMUEL ROGERS

Neither Moore nor myself had ever seen Byron when it was settled that he should dine at my house to meet Moore; nor was he known by sight to Campbell, who, happening to call upon me that morning, consented to join the party. I thought it best that I alone should be in the drawing-room when Byron entered it; and Moore and Campbell accordingly withdrew. Soon after his arrival, they returned; and I introduced them to him severally, naming them as Adam named the beasts. When we sat down to dinner, I asked Byron if he would take soup? 'No; he never took soup.' – Would he take some fish? 'No; he never took fish.' – Presently I asked if he would eat some mutton? 'No; he never ate mutton.' – I then asked if he would take a glass of wine? 'No; he never tasted wine.' – It was now necessary to inquire what he *did* eat and drink; and the answer was, 'Nothing but hard biscuits and soda-water.' Unfortunately, neither hard biscuits nor soda-water were at hand; and he dined upon potatoes bruised down on his plate and drenched with vinegar. – My guests stayed till very late, discussing the merits of Walter Scott and Joanna Baillie[1]. – Some days after, meeting Hobhouse, I said to him, 'How long will Lord Byron persevere in his present diet?' He replied, 'Just as long as you continue to notice it.' – I did not then know, what I now know to be a fact – that Byron, after leaving my house, had gone to a Club in St James's Street, and eaten a hearty meat-supper.

Byron sent me *Childe Harold* in the printed sheets before it was published; and I read it to my sister. 'This,' I said, 'in spite of all its beauty, will never please the public: they will dislike the querulous repining tone that pervades it, and the dissolute character of the hero.' But I quickly found that I was mistaken. The genius which the poem exhibited, the youth, the rank of the author, his romantic wanderings in Greece – these combined to make the world stark mad about *Childe Harold* and Byron. I knew two old maids in Buckinghamshire who used to cry over the passage about Harold's 'laughing dames' that 'long had fed his youthful appetite', etc.[2]

Recollections of the Table Talk of Samuel Rogers, ed. M. Bishop (Lawrence, Kan.: University of Kansas Press, 1953) pp. 188–91.

After Byron had become the *rage*, I was frequently amused at the manœuvres of certain noble ladies to get acquainted with him by means of me: for instance, I would receive a note from Lady —— requesting the pleasure of my company on a particular evening, with a postscript, 'Pray, could you not contrive to bring Lord Byron with you?' – Once, at a great party given by Lady Jersey, Mrs Sheridan ran up to me and said, 'Do, as a favour, try if you can place Lord Byron beside me at supper.'

Byron had prodigious facility of composition. He was fond of suppers; and used often to sup at my house and eat heartily (for he had then given up the hard biscuit and soda-water diet): after going home, he would throw off sixty or eighty verses, which he would send to press next morning.

He one evening took me to the green-room of Drury Lane Theatre, where I was much entertained. When the play began, I went round to the front of the house, and desired the box-keeper to show me into Lord Byron's box. I had been there about a minute, thinking myself quite alone, when suddenly Byron and Miss Boyce[3] (the actress) emerged from a dark corner.

In those days at least, Byron had no readiness of reply in conversation. If you happened to let fall any observation which offended him, he would say nothing at the time; but the offence would lie rankling in his mind; and perhaps a fortnight after, he would suddenly come out with some very cutting remarks upon you, giving them as his deliberate opinions, the results of his experience of your character.

Several women were in love with Byron, but none so violently as Lady Caroline Lamb.[4] She absolutely besieged him. He showed me the first letter he received from her; in which she assured him that, if he was in any want of money, 'all her jewels were at his service'. They frequently had quarrels; and more than once, on coming home, I have found Lady C. walking in the garden, and waiting for me, to beg that I would reconcile them. – When she met Byron at a party, she would always, if possible, return home from it in *his* carriage, and accompanied by *him*: I recollect particularly their returning to town together from Holland House. – But such was the insanity of her passion for Byron, that sometimes, when not invited to a party where he was to be, she would wait for him in the street till it was over! One night, after a great party at Devonshire House, to which Lady Caroline had not been invited, I saw her – yes, saw her – talking to Byron, with half of her body thrust into the carriage which he had just entered.

NOTES

Samuel Rogers (1763–1855), poet, banker and malicious gossip. His *Pleasures of Memory* (1792) and *Italy* (1822–8) enjoyed a considerable success, and

Rogers was offered (but declined) the Laureateship on Wordsworth's death in 1850. He visited Byron in Pisa in April 1822. For Byron's lampoon on Rogers, see Marchand, pp. 724–5. The meeting described took place on 4 November 1811. For Moore's first impressions of Byron, see p. 77. The third member of the party was Thomas Campbell (1777–1844), Scottish poet.

1. Joanna Baillie (1762–1851), Scottish poetess and dramatist, and a friend of Sir Walter Scott.

2. *Childe Harold*, I. xi.

3. Byron had an affair with the actress Susan Boyce in the winter of 1815–16; for details see Marchand, pp. 548–50.

4. Lady Caroline Lamb (1785–1828), daughter of the Earl of Bessborough, had in 1805 married William Lamb, later Lord Melbourne. Byron met her at Holland House in 1812, she became infatuated with him, and their affair was public knowledge. Eventually he repulsed her. See also p. 33 below. Her novel *Glenarvon* (1816) contains a portrait of Byron.

First Impressions III (1813)*

LEIGH HUNT

The first time I saw Lord Byron, he was rehearsing the part of Leander, under the auspices of Mr Jackson,[1] the prize-fighter. It was in the river Thames, before he went to Greece. I had been bathing, and was standing on the floating machine adjusting my clothes, when I noticed a respectable-looking manly person, who was eyeing something at a distance. This was Mr Jackson waiting for his pupil. The latter was swimming with somebody for a wager. I forget what his tutor said of him; but he spoke in terms of praise. I saw nothing in Lord Byron at that time, but a young man, who, like myself, had written a bad volume of poems; and though I had a sympathy with him on this account, and more respect for his rank than I was willing to suppose, my sympathy was not an agreeable one; so, contenting myself with seeing his Lordship's head bob up and down in the water, like a buoy, I came away.

Lord Byron was afterwards pleased to regret that I had not stayed. He told me, that the sight of my volume[2] at Harrow had been one of his incentives to write verses, and that he had had the same passion for friendship that I had displayed in it. To my astonishment, he quoted

Lord Byron and Some of his Contemporaries (Philadelphia, 1828) pp. 9–11.

some of the lines, and would not hear me speak ill of them. This was when I was in prison, where I first became personally acquainted with his Lordship. His harbinger was Moore. Moore told me, that, besides liking my politics, he liked *The Feast of the Poets*,[3] and would be glad to make my acquaintance. I said I felt myself highly flattered, and should be proud to entertain his Lordship as well as a poor patriot could. He was accordingly invited to dinner. His friend only stipulated, that there should be 'plenty of fish and vegetables for the noble bard', his Lordship at that time being Brahminical in his eating. He came, and we passed a very pleasant afternoon, talking of books, and school, and the Rev Mr Bowles;[4] of the pastoral innocence of whose conversation some anecdotes were related, that would have much edified the spirit of Pope, had it been in the room.

I saw nothing at first but single-hearted and agreeable qualities in Lord Byron. My wife, with the quicker eyes of a woman, was inclined to doubt them. Visiting me one day, when I had a friend with me, he seemed uneasy, and asked without ceremony when he should find me alone. My friend, who was a man of taste and spirit, and the last in the world to intrude his acquaintance, was not bound to go away because another person had come in; and besides, he naturally felt anxious to look at so interesting a visitor: which was paying the latter a compliment. But his Lordship's will was disturbed, and he vented his spleen accordingly. I took it at the time for a piece of simplicity, blinded perhaps by the flattery insinuated towards myself; but my wife was right. Lord Byron's nature, from the first, contained that mixture of disagreeable with pleasanter qualities, which I had afterwards but too much occasion to recognise. He subsequently called on me in the prison several times, and used to bring books for my *Story of Rimini*,[5] which I was then writing. He would not let the footman bring them in. He would enter with a couple of quartos under his arm; and give you to understand, that he was prouder of being a friend and a man of letters, than a lord. It was thus that by flattering one's vanity, he persuaded us of his own freedom from it; for he could see very well, that I had more value for lords than I supposed. . . .

[After leaving prison] I was then living at Paddington. I had a study looking over the field towards Westbourne Green; . . . I received visits in it from two persons of a remarkable discrepancy of character – Lord Byron and Mr Wordsworth. Of Mr Wordsworth I will speak hereafter. Lord Byron, I thought, took a pleasure in my room, as contrasted with the splendour of his great house. He had too much reason to do so. His domestic troubles were just about to become public. His appearance at that time was the finest I ever saw it, a great deal finer than it was afterwards, when he was abroad. He was fatter than before his marriage, but only just enough so to complete the manliness of his person; and the turn of his head and countenance had a spirit and elevation in it, which though not unmixed with disquiet, gave him altogether a nobler look, than I ever knew him to have, before or since. His dress, which was black, with white trousers, and which he wore buttoned close over the body, completed the succinctness and gentlemanliness of his appearance.

NOTES

James Henry Leigh Hunt (1784–1859), poet and essayist, was imprisoned in 1813 for libelling the Prince Regent in the *Examiner*, of which he was editor. His first meeting with Byron was in May of that year, when Byron and Tom Moore dined with him in prison. Later Shelley, apparently at Byron's suggestion, invited Hunt to join them in Pisa to establish a new journal, the *Liberal*. Hunt arrived in July 1822 with his disgruntled wife and unruly children, and relations soon became strained. The first number of the *Liberal* appeared on 15 October 1822 and contained Byron's *Vision of Judgment*; only three more issues of the periodical were published. Byron helped Hunt financially but the continued requests for more money wore out his patience and his generosity (Dickens thirty years later portrayed Hunt as Skimpole, the calculatingly irresponsible artist–sponger in *Bleak House*). Hunt's *Lord Byron and Some of his Contemporaries* gives a very unfavourable portrait of Byron: S. C. Chew described it as 'so distorted as to be scandalous', and a contemporary reviewer wrote that 'it is by much too bad . . . that [Byron's] bones must be scraped up from their bed of repose to be at once grinned and howled over by creatures who, even in the least hyena-like of their moods, can touch nothing that mankind would wish to respect without polluting it' – *Quarterly Review*, XXXVII (1828) 423–4. Hunt's *Autobiography* (1850; rev. edn, 1860) admits that his earlier judgement was unfair, pleads youth as his excuse, and tones down the acerbity of the comments on Byron in many places: for instance, the phrase 'a nobler look, than I ever knew him to have, before or since' near the end of the above extract was revised to read 'a very noble look . . .'. On Hunt, see biographies by Edmund Blunden (1930) and (in French) Louis Landré (1935–6); also William H. Marshall, *Byron, Shelley, Hunt, and 'The Liberal'* (Philadelphia, 1960).

   1. John Jackson (also known as 'GJ'), pugilist and former champion, taught Byron boxing.

   2. Hunt's *Juvenilia* (1801).

   3. Published in 1814.

   4. See p. 6.

   5. Hunt's *The Story of Rimini* was published by John Murray in 1816, having been recommended to him by Byron.

First Impressions IV (1821)*

THOMAS MEDWIN

During the few minutes that Lord Byron was finishing his letter, I took an opportunity of narrowly observing him, and drawing his portrait in my mind. Thorwaldsen's bust[1] is too thin-necked and young for Lord Byron. None of the engravings gave me the least idea of him. I saw a man about five feet eight, apparently forty years of age: as was said of Milton, he barely escaped being short and thick. His face was fine, and the lower part symmetrically moulded; for the lips and chin had that curved and definite outline which distinguishes Grecian beauty. His forehead was high, and his temples broad; and he had a paleness in his complexion, almost to wanness. His hair thin and fine, had almost become grey, and waved in natural and graceful curls over his head, that was assimilating itself fast to the 'bald first Cæsar's'. He allowed it to grow longer behind than it is accustomed to be worn, and at that time had mustachios, which were not sufficiently dark to be becoming. In criticising his features it might, perhaps, be said that his eyes were placed too near his nose, and that one was rather smaller than the other; they were of a greyish brown, but of a peculiar clearness, and when animated possessed a fire which seemed to look through and penetrate the thoughts of others, while they marked the inspirations of his own. His teeth were small, regular, and white; these, I afterwards found, he took great pains to preserve.[2]

I expected to discover that he had a club, perhaps a *cloven* foot; but it would have been difficult to distinguish one from the other, either in size or in form, though it is true they were not the most symmetrical.

On the whole his figure was manly, and his countenance handsome and prepossessing, and very expressive; and the familiar ease of his conversation soon made me perfectly at home in his society. Our first interview was marked with a cordiality and confidence that flattered while it delighted me; and I felt anxious for the next day, in order that I might repeat my visit.

Medwin's Conversations of Lord Byron, ed. Ernest J. Lovell Jr (Princeton, NJ: Princeton University Press, 1966) pp. 6–10.

When I called on his Lordship at two o'clock, he had just left his bed-room, and was at breakfast, if it could be called one. It consisted of a cup of strong green tea, without milk or sugar, and an egg, of which he ate the yolk raw. I observed the abstemiousness of his meal.

'My digestion is weak; I am too bilious', said he, 'to eat more than once a-day, and generally live on vegetables. To be sure I drink two bottles of wine at dinner, but they form only a vegetable diet. Just now I live on claret and soda-water. . . .'

NOTES

Thomas Medwin (1788–1869) was a second cousin and boyhood friend of Shelley, a life of whom he published in 1847. Leaving Oxford without a degree, he became a lieutenant in the 24th Dragoons and served in India. When he met Byron in November 1821 he was a half-pay officer and had published some volumes of verse. His *Conversations of Lord Byron* was hastily concocted and proved an enormous success: the book went through fifteen editions between 1824 and 1842, and according to Ernest J. Lovell Jr was to a significant extent responsible for Byron's enormous influence throughout Europe. Trelawny called Medwin 'a measureless and unprincipled liar' – a good example of the pot calling the kettle black. See biography by Lovell (Austin, Tex., 1962).

   1. Bertel Thorwaldsen's marble bust of Byron was executed in 1817 and is reproduced in Marchand, opposite p. 844.

   2. 'For this purpose he used tobacco when he first went into the open air; and he told me he was in the habit of grinding his teeth in his sleep, to prevent which he was forced to put a napkin between them.' (Note by Medwin.)

First Impressions V (1822)*

E. J. TRELAWNY

In external appearance Byron realised that ideal standard with which imagination adorns genius. He was in the prime of life, thirty-four; of middle height, five feet eight and a half inches; regular features, without a stain or furrow on his pallid skin, his shoulders broad, chest open, body and limbs finely proportioned. His small highly-finished head and curly hair had an airy and graceful appearance from the

Records of Shelley, Byron, and the Author (London: Pickering, 1878) I, 27–33.

massiveness and length of his throat: you saw his genius in his eyes and lips. In short, Nature could do little more than she had done for him, both in outward form and in the inward spirit she had given to animate it. But all these rare gifts to his jaundiced imagination only served to make his one personal defect (lameness) the more apparent, as a flaw is magnified in a diamond when polished; and he brooded over that blemish as sensitive minds will brood until they magnify a wart into a wen.

His lameness certainly helped to make him sceptical, cynical, and savage. There was no peculiarity in his dress, it was adapted to the climate: a tartan jacket braided – he said it was the Gordon pattern, and that his mother was of that race. A blue velvet cap with a gold band, and very loose nankeen trousers, strapped down so as to cover his feet: his throat was not bare, as represented in drawings. At three o'clock, one of his servants announced that his horses were at the door, which broke off his discussion with Shelley, and we all followed him to the hall. At the outer door we found three or four very ordinary-looking horses; they had holsters on the saddles, and many other superfluous trappings, such as the Italians delight in, and Englishmen eschew. Shelley, and an Irish visitor just announced, mounted two of these sorry jades. I luckily had my own cattle. Byron got into a calèche, and did not mount his horse until we had cleared the gates of the town, to avoid, as he said, being stared at by the 'damned Englishers', who generally congregated before his house on the Arno. After an hour or two of slow riding and lively talk – for he was generally in good spirits when on horseback – we stopped at a small *podere* on the roadside, and dismounting went into the house, in which we found a table with wine and cakes. From thence we proceeded into the vineyard at the back; the servant brought two brace of pistols, a cane was stuck in the ground, and a five-paul piece, the size of a half-a-crown, placed in a slit at the top of the cane. Byron, Shelley, and I fired at fifteen paces, and one of us generally hit the cane or the coin; our firing was pretty equal; after five or six shots each, Byron pocketed the battered money and sauntered about the grounds. We then remounted. On our return homewards, Shelley urged Byron to complete something he had begun. Byron smiled and replied,

'John Murray,[1] my patron and paymaster, says my plays won't act. I don't mind that, for I told him they were not written for the stage – but he adds, my poesy won't sell: that I do mind, for I have an "itching palm". He urges me to resume my old "*Corsair*" style, to please the ladies".'

Shelley indignantly answered,

'That is very good logic for a bookseller, but not for an author: the shop interest is to supply the ephemeral demand of the day. It is not for him but you "to put a ring in the monster's nose" to keep him from mischief.'

Byron smiling at Shelley's warmth, said,

'John Murray is right, if not righteous: all I have yet written has been for women-kind; you must wait until I am forty, their influence will then die a natural death, and I will show the men what I can do.'

Shelley replied,

'Do it now – write nothing but what your conviction of its truth inspires you to write; you should give counsel to the wise, and not take it from the foolish. Time will reverse the judgement of the vulgar. Contemporary criticism only represents the amount of ignorance genius has to contend with.'

I was then and afterwards pleased and surprised at Byron's passiveness and docility in listening to Shelley – but all who heard him felt the charm of his simple, earnest manner; while Byron knew him to be exempt from the egotism, pedantry, coxcombry, and, more than all, the rivalry of authorship, and that he was the truest and most discriminating of his admirers.

Byron looking at the western sky, exclaimed,

'Where is the green your friend the Laker talks such fustian about', meaning Coleridge –

> Gazing on the western sky,
> And its peculiar tint of yellow green.
> > 'Dejection: An Ode'

'Who ever', asked Byron, 'saw a green sky?'

Shelley was silent, knowing that if he replied, Byron would give vent to his spleen. So I said, 'The sky in England is oftener green than blue.'

'Black, you mean', rejoined Byron; and this discussion brought us to his door.

As he was dismounting he mentioned two odd words that would rhyme. I observed on the felicity he had shown in this art, repeating a couplet out of *Don Juan*; he was both pacified and pleased at this, and putting his hand on my horse's crest, observed,

'If you are curious in these matters, look in Swift. I will send you a volume; he beats us all hollow; his rhymes are wonderful.'

And then we parted for that day, which I have been thus particular in recording, not only as it was the first of our acquaintance, but as containing as fair a sample as I can give of his appearance, ordinary habits, and conversation.

A short time after I knew Byron I said to Shelley,

'How very unlike Byron is to what people say of him. I see no mystery about him – he is too free; he says things better not said. I shall take care what I say to him. He reads parts of letters from his London correspondents.' (Mrs Shelley smiled; she knew they cautioned Byron not to risk his popularity by coupling his name with Shelley's.) 'He is as impulsive and jealous as a woman, and may be as changeable.'

'At a subsequent conversation Shelley called Mrs Shelley and said, 'Mary, Trelawny has found out Byron already. How stupid we were – how long it took us.'

'That', she observed, 'is because he lives with the living, and we with the dead.'

I observed,

'Byron asked me if he were like the person I expected. I said, No. He went on: "They know nothing about me. How should they? My poesy is one thing, I am another. I am not such an anthropophagist[2] as they make me. My poetry is a separate faculty. The ideal has no effect on the real character. I can only write when the *estro*[3] is upon me; at all other times I am myself." '

NOTES

Edward John Trelawny (1792–1881), who came of an old Cornish family, arrived in Pisa on 14 January 1822 and called on Byron the following day. He was a self-dramatising character – in David Wright's apt phrase 'more Byronic than Byron' – whose allegedly autobiographical *Adventures of a Younger Son* (1831) has been shown to be a tissue of romancing. Harold Nicolson described him roundly as 'a liar and a cad'. His *Records* represents a reworking of his earlier book *Recollections of the Last Days of Shelley and Byron* (1858), of which there are useful modern editions by J. E. Morpurgo (1952) and David Wright (1973). The extracts in the present volume have been taken from the *Records*, which in some places gives a fuller version and also represents a toning-down of the author's animus towards Byron. Trelawny's admiration for Shelley led him to denigrate Byron and to contrast the two poets as an Ariel and a Caliban. In a letter of 13 June 1870 to Claire Clairmont he wrote, 'Byron and Shelley, what a contrast – the one the incarnation of rank selfishness – the other of a bountiful and loving nature' – *Letters of Edward John Trelawny*, ed. H. Buxton Forman (1910) p. 230. Earlier he had written to Captain Daniel Roberts concerning his *Recollections* that 'the book is brief and to the point and has elevated Shelley and shown Byron as he was' – 19 Sep 1858, *Letters*, p. 214. By 1878 he was prepared to modify some of his earlier judgements: for instance, the statement in Chapter 5 of the *Recollections* that Byron 'was neither just nor generous, and never drew his weapon to redress any wrongs but his own' was dropped, as was a passage in Chapter 14 concerning Byron's meanness over money. There are biographies of Trelawny by H. J. Massingham (1930), Margaret Armstrong (1941), R. Glynn Grylls (1950) and William St Clair (1977).

1. John Murray (1778–1843), publisher, headed the firm founded by his father (also John Murray) in 1768 and published Scott, Southey and other leading authors, as well as the influential *Quarterly Review*. He issued much of Byron's work from *Childe Harold* onwards, corresponded extensively with Byron, and introduced him to Scott. It was in Murray's office that Byron's memoirs were burned shortly after his death (see p. 58).

2. Cannibal.

3. Caprice, fancy (Italian).

First Impressions VI (1823)*

LADY BLESSINGTON

Saw Lord Byron for the first time. The impression of the first few minutes disappointed me, as I had, both from the portraits and descriptions given, conceived a different idea of him. I had fancied him taller, with a more dignified and commanding air; and I looked in vain for the hero-looking sort of person with whom I had so long identified him in imagination. His appearance is, however, highly prepossessing; his head is finely shaped, and the forehead open, high, and noble; his eyes are grey and full of expression, but one is visibly larger than the other; the nose is large and well shaped, but from being a little *too thick*, it looks better in profile than in front-face: his mouth is the most remarkable feature in his face, the upper lip of Grecian shortness, and the corners descending; the lips full, and finely cut. In speaking, he shows his teeth very much, and they are white and even; but I observed that even in his smile – and he smiles frequently – there is something of a scornful expression in his mouth that is evidently natural, and not, as many suppose, affected. This particularly struck me. His chin is large and well shaped, and finishes well the oval of his face. He is extremely thin, indeed so much so that his figure has almost a boyish air; his face is peculiarly pale, but not the paleness of ill-health, as its character is that of fairness, the fairness of a dark-haired person – and his hair (which is getting rapidly grey) is of a very dark brown, and curls naturally: he uses a good deal of oil in it, which makes it look still darker. His countenance is full of expression, and changes with the subject of conversation; it gains on the beholder the more it is seen, and leaves an agreeable impression. I should say that melancholy was its prevailing character, as I observed that when any observation elicited a smile – and they were many, as the conversation was gay and playful – it appeared to linger but for a moment on his lip, which instantly resumed its former expression of seriousness. His whole appearance is remarkably gentlemanlike, and he owes nothing of this to his toilet, as

---

*Lady Blessington's Conversations of Lord Byron, ed. Ernest J. Lovell Jr (Princeton, NJ: Princeton University Press, 1969) pp. 5–7.

his coat appears to have been many years made, is much too large – and all his garments convey the idea of having been purchased ready-made, so ill do they fit him. There is a *gaucherie* in his movements, which evidently proceeds from the perpetual consciousness of his lameness, that appears to haunt him; for he tries to conceal his foot when seated, and when walking, has a nervous rapidity in his manner. He is very slightly lame, and the deformity of his foot is so little remarkable that I am not now aware which foot it is. His voice and accent are peculiarly agreeable, but effeminate – clear, harmonious, and so distinct, that though his general tone in speaking is rather low than high, not a word is lost. His manners are as unlike my preconceived notions of them as is his appearance. I had expected to find him a dignified, cold, reserved, and haughty person, resembling those mysterious personages he so loves to paint in his works, and with whom he has been so often identified by the good-natured world: but nothing can be more different; for were I to point out the prominent defect of Lord Byron, I should say it was flippancy, and a total want of that natural self-possession and dignity which ought to characterise a man of birth and education.

Albaro, the village in which the Casa Saluzzo, where he lives, is situated, is about a mile and a half distant from Genoa; it is a fine old palazzo, commanding an extensive view, and with spacious apartments, the front looking into a court-yard and the back into the garden. The room in which Lord Byron received us was large, and plainly furnished. A small portrait of his daughter Ada,[1] with an engraved portrait of himself, taken from one of his works, struck my eye. Observing that I remarked that of his daughter, he took it down, and seemed much gratified when I discovered the strong resemblance it bore to him. Whilst holding it in his hand, he said, 'I am told she is clever – I hope not; and, above all, I hope she is not poetical: the price paid for such advantages, if advantages they be, is such as to make me pray that my child may escape them.'

NOTES

Marguerite, Countess of Blessington (1789–1849), travelled on the Continent with her husband and Alfred, Count d'Orsay, and met Byron in Genoa on 1 April 1823, having arrived in the city on the previous day. As she wrote in her diary, 'Desirous as I am to see "Genoa the Superb", with its street of palaces, and the treasures of art they contain, I confess that its being the residence of Lord Byron gives it a still greater attraction for me.' Her *Conversations of Lord Byron* was serialised in the *New Monthly Magazine* intermittently from July 1832 to December 1833, and published in volume form in February 1834. 'The instalments were eagerly read, achieving from the very first a success, part genuine popularity and part scandal' – Michael Sadleir, *Blessington–D'Orsay: A Masquerade* (1933) p. 201. Most of what she reports consists not of 'conversations' but of monologues in which Byron is shown holding forth in Johnsonian manner and in language resembling that of an eighteenth-century periodical essayist. Though the substance of what she gives is often confirmed from other sources, her reports cannot be taken as anything approaching an accurate transcription of Byron's words. Sadleir comments (p. 60),

> Undoubtedly [records] were originally kept from day to day, but they were none of them made public until some years after the events described. When their author decided to publish, she not only revised but, one suspects, largely re-wrote the contents of her notebooks. On the one hand discretion, on the other a desire to produce something saleable, made a very thorough refurbishing necessary.

A somewhat different account of her reactions to meeting Byron is given in Lady Blessington's *The Idler in Italy* (1839–40). In this later version her disappointment, and her difficulty in reconciling Byron's lively manner with the authorship of *Childe Harold* and *Manfred*, receive more emphasis: 'I can imagine the man I saw as the author of *Beppo* and *Don Juan*. He is witty, sarcastic, and lively enough for these works, but he does not look like my preconceived notion of the melancholy poet.'

    1. Augusta Ada, Byron's legitimate daughter, born 10 December 1815. Byron's thoughts were with her on his deathbed.

Byron's Snobbery*

JOHN GALT

The pride of rank was indeed one of the greatest weaknesses of Lord Byron, and everything, even of the most accidental kind, which seemed to come between the wind and his nobility,[1] was repelled on the spot. I recollect having some debate with him once respecting a pique of etiquette, which happened between him and Sir William Drummond,[2] somewhere in Portugal or Spain. Sir William was at the time an ambassador (not, however, I believe, in the country where the incident occurred), and was on the point of taking precedence in passing from one room to another, when Byron stepped in before him. The action was undoubtedly rude on the part of his Lordship, even though Sir William had presumed too far on his riband: to me it seemed also

The Life of Lord Byron, pp. 169–70.

wrong; for, by the custom of all nations from time immemorial, ambassadors have been allowed their official rank in passing through foreign countries, while peers in the same circumstances claim no rank at all; even in our own colonies it has been doubted if they may take precedence of the legislative counsellors. But the rights of rank are best determined by the heralds, and I have only to remark, that it is almost inconceivable that such things should have so morbidly affected the sensibility of Lord Byron; yet they certainly did so, and even to a ridiculous degree. On one occasion, when he lodged in St James's Street, I recollect him rating the footman for using a double knock in accidental thoughtlessness.

These little infirmities are, however, at most only calculated to excite a smile; there is no turpitude in them, and they merit notice but as indications of the humour of character. It was his Lordship's foible to overrate his rank, to grudge his deformity beyond reason, and to exaggerate the condition of his family and circumstances. But the alloy of such small vanities, his caprice and feline temper, were as vapour compared with the mass of rich and rare ore which constituted the orb and nucleus of his brilliancy.

NOTES

On Galt, see p. 17.
1. Shakespeare, *Henry IV, Part 1*, I, iii, 45.
2. British ambassador to Naples.

The Effects of Fame*

R. C. DALLAS

I was now [1812] to see Lord Byron in a new point of view. The town was full of company, as usual in the spring. Besides the speech he had made on the Frame-breaking Bill, he again attracted notice on the Catholic Question, which was agitated warmly by the peers in the beginning of April.[1] His name was in every mouth, and his poem[2] in every hand. He converted criticism to adulation, and admiration to love. His stanzas abounded with passages which impressed on the

Recollections of the Life of Lord Byron, pp. 244–9, 295–6.

heart of his readers pity for the miserable feelings of a youth who could express so admirably what he felt; and this pity, uniting with the delight proceeding from his poetry, generated a general affection of which he knew not the value; for while the real fruits of happiness clustered around him, he neglected them, and became absorbed in gratifications that could only tend to injure the reputation he had gained. He professedly despised the society of women, yet female adulation became the most captivating charm to his heart. He had not admitted the ladies of his own family to any degree of intimacy; his aunts, his cousins, were kept at a distance, and even his sister had hitherto shared the like fate. Among the admirers who had paid their tribute in prose or verse to the muse of the Pilgrimage, I have already mentioned one who asked for an acknowledgment of the receipt of her letter. He had treated that letter lightly, and said he would not answer it. He was not able to keep his resolution; and on finding his correspondent to be a fine young woman, and distinguished for eccentric notions, he became so enraptured, so intoxicated, that his time and thoughts were almost entirely devoted to reading her letters and answering them. One morning he was so absorbed in the composition of a letter to her, that he barely noticed me as I entered the room. I said, 'Pray go on'; and sat down at one side of the table at which he was writing, where I looked over a newspaper for some time. Finding that he did not conclude, I looked at him, and was astonished at the complete abstraction of his mind, and at the emanation of his sentiments on his countenance. He had a peculiar smile on his lips; his eyes beamed the pleasure he felt from what was passing from his imagination to his paper; he looked at me and then at his writing, but I am persuaded he did not see me, and that the thoughts with which he teemed prevented his discerning any thing about him. I said, 'I see you are deeply engaged.' His ear was as little open to sound as his eye to vision. I got up; on which he said, 'Pray sit.' I answered that I would return. This roused him a little, and he said, 'I wish you would.' I do not think he knew what passed, or observed my quitting him. This scene gave me great pain. I began to fear that his fame would be dearly bought. Previous to the appearance of *Childe Harold's Pilgrimage*, his mind had gained some important conquests over his senses; and I also thought he had barred his heart against the grosser attacks of the passion of vanity. If these avenues of destruction to the soul were again to be thrown open by the publication of the poem, it were better that it had never been published. I called upon him the next day, when I found him in his usual good-humour. He told me to whom he had been writing, and said he hoped I never thought him rude. I took my usual liberty with him, and honestly warned him against his new dangers. While I was with him the lady's page brought him a new letter. He was a fair-faced delicate boy of thirteen or fourteen years old, whom one might have taken for the lady herself.[3] He was dressed in a scarlet huzzar jacket and pantaloons, trimmed in front in much the same manner with silver buttons, and twisted silver lace, with which the narrow slit cuffs of his jacket were also embroidered. He had light hair curling about his face; and held a feathered fancy hat in his hand, which completed the scenic appearance of this urchin Pandårus.[4] I could not but suspect at the time that it was a disguise. If so, he never disclosed it to me, and as he had hitherto had no reserve with me, the thought vanished with the object of it, and I do not precisely recollect the mode of his exit. I wished it otherwise, but wishing was in vain. . . .

There was something of a pride in him which carried him beyond the common sphere of thought and feeling. And the excess of this characteristic pride bore away, like a whirlwind, even the justest feelings of our nature; but it could not root them entirely from his heart. In vain did he defy his country and hold his countrymen in scorn; the choice he made of the motto for *Childe Harold*[5] evinces that patriotism had taken root in his mind. The visions of an Utopia in his untravelled fancy deprived reality of its charm; but when he awakened to the state of the world, what said he? 'I have seen the most celebrated countries in the world, and have learned to prefer and to love my own'.

NOTES

On Dallas, see p. 10.

1. Byron's maiden speech on 27 February 1812 was on the Frame-breaking Bill. On 21 April of the same year he spoke on the Catholic Claims Bill, and his third and last speech was on 1 June 1813.

2. The first two cantos of *Childe Harold* had been published on 10 March 1812.

3. The 'page' was Lady Caroline Lamb (see p. 20). Marchand reproduces (opposite p. 419) a miniature showing her in page's dress.

4. Pandarus in Shakespeare's *Troilus and Cressida* is the uncle of Cressida and a go-between.

5. The epigraph of *Childe Harold* is a quotation in French consisting of the opening sentences of *Le Cosmopolite, ou le Citoyen du Monde* (1753) by Louise Charles Fougeret de Monbron. The gist of the lines is that the speaker has learned to love his own country by travelling abroad.

'Soothed by Success'*

JOHN GALT

For some time after the publication of *Childe Harold*, the noble author appeared to more advantage than I ever afterwards saw him. He was soothed by success; and the universal applause which attended his poem seemed to make him think more kindly of the world, of which he has too often complained, while it would be difficult to discover, in his career and fortunes, that he had ever received any cause from it to justify his complaint.

At no time, I imagine, could it be said that Lord Byron was one of those men who interest themselves in the concerns of others. He had always too much to do with his own thoughts about himself, to afford time for the consideration of aught that was lower in his affections. But still he had many amiable fits, and at the particular period to which I allude, he evinced a constancy in the disposition to oblige, which proved how little self-control was wanting to have made him as pleasant as he was uniformly interesting. I felt this towards myself in a matter which had certainly the grace of condescension in it, at the expense of some trouble to him. I then lived at the corner of Bridge Street, Westminster, and in going to the House of Lords he frequently stopped to inquire if I wanted a frank.[1] His conversation, at the same time, was of a milder vein, and with the single exception of one day, while dining together at the St Alban's, it was light and playful, as if gaiety had become its habitude.

Perhaps I regarded him too curiously, and more than once it struck me that he thought so. For at times, when he was in his comfortless moods, he has talked of his affairs and perplexities as if I had been much more acquainted with them than I had any opportunity of being. But he was a subject for study, such as is rarely met with – at least, he was so to me; for his weaknesses were as interesting as his talents, and he often indulged in expressions which would have been blemishes in the reflections of other men, but which in him often proved the germs of philosophical imaginings. He was the least qualified for any sort of business of all men I have ever known; so skinless in sensibility as respected himself, and so distrustful in his universal apprehensions of

*The Life of Lord Byron, pp. 192–4.

human nature, as respected others. It was, indeed, a wild, though a beautiful, error of nature, to endow a spirit with such discerning faculties, and yet render it unfit to deal with mankind. But these reflections belong more properly to a general estimate of his character, than to the immediate purpose before me, which was principally to describe the happy effects which the splendid reception of *Childe Harold* had on his feelings; effects which, however, did not last long. He was gratified to the fullness of his hopes; but the adulation was enjoyed to excess, and his infirmities were aggravated by the surfeit. I did not, however, see the progress of the change, as in the course of the summer I went to Scotland , and soon after again abroad. But on my return, in the following spring, it was very obvious.

I found him, in one respect, greatly improved; there was more of a formed character about him; he was evidently, at the first glance, more mannered, or endeavouring to be so, and easier with the proprieties of his rank; but he had risen in his own estimation above the honours so willingly paid to his genius, and was again longing for additional renown. Not content with being acknowledged as the first poet of the age, and a respectable orator in the House of Lords, he was aspiring to the *éclat* of a man of gallantry; so that many of the most ungracious peculiarities of his temper, though brought under better discipline, were again in full activity.

NOTES

On Galt, see p. 17.
1. Signature of person (such as a member of the House of Lords) entitled to send letters free.

'As Playful as a Kitten'*

SIR WALTER SCOTT

[23 Nov 1825.] On comparing notes with Moore I was confirmed in one or two points which I had always laid down in considering poor

The Journal of Sir Walter Scott, ed. W. F. K. Anderson (Oxford: Clarendon Press, 1972) pp. 8–9, 44, 82.

Byron's [peculiarities]. One was that like Rousseau he was apt to be very suspicious, and a plain downright steadiness of manner was the true mode to maintain his good opinion. Will Rose[1] told me that once while sitting with Byron he fixed insensibly his eyes on his feet, one of which it must be remembered was deformed. Looking up suddenly he saw Byron regarding him with a look of concentrated and deep displeasure which wore off when he observed no consciousness or embarrassment in the countenance of Rose. Murray[2] afterwards explained this by telling Rose that Lord Byron was very jealous of having this personal imperfection noticed or attended to. In another point Moore confirmed my previous opinion. Namely that Byron loved mischiefmaking. Moore had written to him cautioning him against the project of establishing the paper called the *Liberal*[3] in communion with such men as P. B. Shelley and Hunt on whom he said the World had set its mark. Byron showed this to the parties. Shelley wrote a modest and rather affecting expostulation to Moore. These two peculiarities of extreme suspicion and love of mischief are both shades of the malady which certainly tinctured some part of the character of this mighty genius and, without some tendency towards which, genius – I mean that kind which depends on the imaginative power – perhaps cannot exist to great extent. The wheels of a machine to play rapidly must not fit with the utmost exactness else the attrition diminishes the Impetus.

Another of Byron's peculiarities was the love of mystifying which indeed may be referred to that of mischief. There was no knowing how much or how little to believe of his narratives. Instance. Mr Bankes[4] expostulating with him upon a dedication which he had written in extravagant terms of praise to Cam Hobhouse, Byron told him that Cam had teased him into the dedication till he had said 'Well; it shall be so – providing you will write the dedication yourself – and affirmed that Cam Hobhouse did write the high-coloured dedication accordingly. I mentioned this to Murray, having the report from Will Rose to whom Bankes had mentioned it. Murray in reply assured me that the dedication was written by Lord Byron himself and showed it me in his own hand. I wrote to Rose to mention the thing to Bankes as it might have made mischief had the story got into the circle.

Byron was disposed to think all men of imagination were addicted to mix fiction or poetry with their prose. He used to say he dared believe the celebrated courtesan of Venice about whom Rousseau makes so piquante a story was if one could see her a draggled tailed wench enough. I believe that he embellished his own amours considerably and that he was in many respects *Le fanfaron des vices qu'il n' avait pas*[5]. He loved to be thought awful mysterious and gloomy and sometimes hinted at strange causes. I believe the whole to have been the creation and sport of a wild and powerful fancy. In the same manner he *crammed* people as it is termed about duels and what [not] which never existed or were much exaggerated.

[21 Dec: Scott recalls a dinner in London in 1815 at which 'Matthews the Comedian' (Charles Matthews) was also present]   .. a most brilliant day we had of it. I never saw Byron so full of fun frolic wit and whim. He was as playful as a kitten.

[9 Feb 1826.] Byron used to kick and frisk more contemptuously against the literary gravity and slang than any one I ever knew who had climbed so high – then it is true I never knew any one climb so high, and before you despise the eminence, carrying people along with you as convinced that you are not playing the fox and grapes, you must be at the top of the eminence. Moore told me two delightful stories of him.

One was that while they stood at the window of Byron's palazzo in Venice looking at a beautiful sun set Moore was naturally led to say something of its beauty when Byron answered in a tone that I can easily conceive 'Ah come d—n me, Tom, don't be poetical.' Another time standing with Moore on the balcony of the same palazzo a gondola passed with two English gentlemen who were easily distinguished by their appearance. They cast a careless look at the balcony and went on. Byron crossed his arms and half stooping over the balcony said 'Ah d—n ye if you had known what two fellows you were staring at you would have taken a longer look at us.'[6] This was the man – quaint capricious and playful with all his immense genius – He wrote from impulse never from effort and therefore I have always reckoned Burns and Byron the most genuine poetical geniuses of my time and a half a century before me. We have however many men of high poetical talent but none I think of that ever gushing and perennial fountain of natural water.

NOTES

Sir Walter Scott (1771–1832), poet and novelist. Byron had read his verse romances and corresponded with him before meeting Scott on 7 April 1815, on which occasion they 'conversed together for nearly two hours' (diary entry by John Murray, who published the work of both writers and introduced them to each other). They met frequently thereafter until Byron's departure from England.

1. William Rose (1775–1843), poet and translator.
2. See p. 27.
3. See p. 22.
4. William Bankes (died 1856), a Trinity friend of Byron's. The reference is presumably to the long dedicatory letter placed at the beginning of Canto IV of *Childe Harold*.
5. One who boasts about vices that he does not possess (French).
6. For Moore's version of these anecdotes, see p. 61 below.

Later Recollections*

SIR WALTER SCOTT

It was in the spring of 1815 that, chancing to be in London, I had the advantage of personal introduction to Lord Byron. Report had prepared me to meet a man of peculiar habits and a quick temper, and I had some doubts whether we were likely to suit each other in society. I was most agreeably disappointed in this respect. I found Lord Byron in the highest degree courteous, and even kind. We met, for an hour or two almost daily, in Mr Murray's drawing-room, and found a great deal to say to each other. We also met frequently in parties and evening society, so that for about two months I had the advantage of a considerable intimacy with this distinguished individual. Our sentiments agreed a good deal, except upon the subjects of religion and politics, upon neither of which I was inclined to believe that Lord Byron entertained very fixed opinions. I remember saying to him, that I really thought, that if he lived a few years he would alter his sentiments. He answered, rather sharply, 'I suppose you are one of those who prophesy I will turn Methodist.' I replied, 'No – I don't expect your conversion to be of such an ordinary kind. I would rather look to see you retreat upon the Catholic faith, and distinguish yourself by the austerity of your penances. The species of religion to which you must, or may, one day attach yourself must exercise a strong power on the imagination.' He smiled gravely, and seemed to allow I might be right.

On politics, he used sometimes to express a high strain of what is now called Liberalism; but it appeared to me that the pleasure it afforded him as a vehicle of displaying his wit and satire against individuals in office was at the bottom of this habit of thinking, rather than any real conviction of the political principles on which he talked. He was certainly proud of his rank and ancient family, and, in that respect, as much an aristocrat as was consistent with good sense and good breeding. Some disgusts, how adopted I know not, seemed to me to have given this peculiar and, as it appeared to me, contradictory cast of mind: but, at heart, I would have termed Byron a patrician on principle.

*Thomas Moore, *The Life of Lord Byron* (London: John Murray, 1847) pp. 280–1.

Lord Byron's reading did not seem to me to have been very extensive either in poetry or history. Having the advantage of him in that respect, and possessing a good competent share of such reading as is little read, I was sometimes able to put under his eye objects which had for him the interest of novelty. I remember particularly repeating to him the fine poem of 'Hardyknute'[1], an imitation of the old Scottish Ballad, with which he was so much affected, that some one who was in the same apartment asked me what I could possibly have been telling Byron by which he was so much agitated. . . .

I think I can add little more to my recollections of Byron. He was often melancholy – almost gloomy. When I observed him in this humour, I used either to wait till it went off of its own accord, or till some natural and easy mode occurred of leading him into conversation, when the shadows almost always left his countenance, like the mist rising from a landscape. In conversation he was very animated. . . .

I think I also remarked in Byron's temper starts of suspicion, when he seemed to pause and consider whether there had not been a secret, and perhaps offensive, meaning in something casually said to him. In this case, I also judged it best to let his mind, like a troubled spring, work itself clear, which it did in a minute or two. I was considerably older, you will recollect, than my noble friend, and had no reason to fear his misconstruing my sentiments towards him, nor had I ever the slightest reason to doubt that they were kindly returned on his part. If I had occasion to be mortified by the display of genius which threw into the shade such pretensions as I was then supposed to possess, I might console myself that, in my own case, the materials of mental happiness had been mingled in a greater proportion.

I rummage my brains in vain for what often rushes into my head unbidden – little traits and sayings which recall his looks, manner, tone, and gestures; and I have always continued to think that a crisis of life was arrived in which a new career of fame was opened to him, and that had he been permitted to start upon it, he would have obliterated the memory of such parts of his life as friends would wish to forget.

NOTE

1. In *The Evergreen* (1724), a collection of traditional Scottish and English songs and ballads, with some material by Ramsay and others. Allan Ramsay (1686–1758) made an important contribution to the revival of Scots vernacular literature.

Life in London*

R. H. GRONOW

I was once [in the autumn of 1815] invited to dinner by Sir James Burges[1] ... I there met, to my great delight, Lord Byron and Sir Walter Scott; and amongst the rest of the company were Lord Caledon, and Croker[2], the Secretary to the Admiralty. . . .

Walter Scott was quite delightful; he appeared full of fire and animation, and told some interesting anecdotes connected with his early life in Scotland. I remember that he proved himself, what would have been called in the olden times he delighted to portray, 'a stout trencher-man'; nor were his attentions confined by any means to the eatables; on the contrary, he showed himself worthy to have made a third in the famous carousal in *Ivanhoe*, between the Black Knight and the Holy Clerk of Copmanhurst.

Byron, whom I had before seen at the shooting-galleries and else-where, was then a very handsome man, with remarkably fine eyes and hair; but was, as usual, all show-off and affectation. I recollect his saying that he disliked seeing women eat, or to have their company at dinner, from a wish to believe, if possible, in their more ethereal nature; but he was rallied into avowing that his chief dislike to their presence at the festive board arose from the fact of their being helped first, and consequently getting all the wings of the chickens, whilst men had to be content with the legs or other parts. Byron, on this occasion, was in great good humour, and full of boyish and even boisterous mirth.

Croker was also agreeable, notwithstanding his bitter and sarcastic remarks upon everything and everybody. The sneering, ill-natured expression of his face, struck me as an impressive contrast to the frank and benevolent countenance of Walter Scott.

I never assisted at a more agreeable dinner. According to the custom of the day, we sat late; the poets, statesmen, and soldiers all drank an immense quantity of wine, and I for one felt the effects of it next day. Walter Scott gave one or two recitations, in a very animated manner, from the ballads that he had been collecting, which delighted his

* *The Reminiscences and Recollections of Captain Gronow, Being Anecdotes of the Camp, Courts, Clubs, and Society, 1810–1860* (London: Nimmo, 1892) I, 149–54. Originally published in 1862.

auditory; and both Lord Byron and Croker added to the hilarity of the evening by quotations from, and criticisms on, the more prominent writers of the period.

LORD BYRON. – I knew very little of Lord Byron personally, but lived much with two of his intimate friends, Scrope Davies[3] and Wedderburn Webster,[4] from whom I frequently heard many anecdotes of him. I regret that I remember so few; and wish that I had written down those told me by poor Scrope Davies, one of the most agreeable men I ever met.

When Byron was at Cambridge, he was introduced to Scrope Davies by their mutual friend, Matthews,[5] who was afterwards drowned in the river Cam. After Matthews's death, Davies became Byron's particular friend, and was admitted to his rooms at all hours. Upon one occasion he found the poet in bed with his hair *en papillote*,[6] upon which Scrope cried, 'Ha, ha! Byron, I have at last caught you acting the part of the Sleeping Beauty.'

Byron, in a rage, exclaimed, 'No, Scrope; the part of a d—d fool, you should have said.'

'Well, then, anything you please; but you have succeeded admirably in deceiving your friends, for it was my conviction that your hair curled naturally.'

'Yes, naturally every night', returned the poet; 'but do not, my dear Scrope, let the cat out of the bag, for I am as vain of my curls as a girl of sixteen.'

When in London, Byron used to go to Manton's shooting-gallery, in Davies Street, to try his hand, as he said, at a wafer. Wedderburn Webster was present when the poet, intensely delighted with his own skill, boasted to Joe Manton that he considered himself the best shot in London. 'No, my Lord,' replied Manton, 'not the best; but your shooting to-day was respectable.' Whereupon Byron waxed wroth, and left the shop in a violent passion.

Lords Byron, Yarmouth, Pollington, Mountjoy, Wallscourt, Blandford, Captain Burges, Jack Bouverie, and myself, were in 1814, and for several years afterwards, amongst the chief and most constant frequenters of this well-known shooting-gallery, and frequently shot at the wafer for considerable sums of money. Manton was allowed to enter the betting list, and he generally backed me. On one occasion I hit the wafer nineteen times out of twenty.

Byron lived a great deal at Brighton, his house being opposite the Pavilion. He was fond of boating and was generally accompanied by a lad, who was said to be a girl in boy's clothes. This report was confirmed to me by Webster, who was then living at Brighton. The vivid description of the page in *Lara*,[7] no doubt, gave some plausibility to this often-told tale. I myself witnessed the dexterous manner in which Byron used to get into his boat; for, while standing on the beach,

I once saw him vault into it with the agility of a harlequin, in spite of his lame foot.

On one occasion, whilst his lordship was dining with a few of his friends in Charles Street, Pall Mall, a letter was delivered to Scrope Davies, which required an immediate answer. Scrope, after reading its contents, handed it to Lord Byron. It was thus worded: –

MY DEAR SCROPE, – Lend me 500*l.* for a few days; the funds are shut for the dividends, or I would not have made this request.

G. BRUMMEL[8]

The reply was:–

MY DEAR BRUMMEL, – All my money is locked up in the funds.

SCROPE DAVIES

This was just before Brummel's escape to the Continent.

I have frequently asked Scrope Davies his private opinion of Lord Byron, and invariably received the same answer – that he considered Lord Byron very agreeable and clever, but vain, overbearing, conceited, suspicious, and jealous. Byron hated Palmerston, but liked Peel, and thought that the whole world ought to be constantly employed in admiring his poetry and himself: he never could write a poem or a drama without making himself its hero, and he was always the subject of his own conversation.

During one of Hobhouse's visits to Byron, at his villa near Genoa, and whilst they were walking in the garden, his lordship suddenly turned upon his guest, and, *apropos* of nothing, exclaimed, 'Now, I know, Hobhouse, you are looking at my foot.' Upon which Hobhouse kindly replied, 'My dear Byron, nobody thinks of or looks at anything but your head.'

NOTES

Rees Howell Gronow (1794–1865) published his memoirs in four series (1862–6). Besides a later two-volume edition (1892) there are abridgements by John Raymond (1964) and Nicolas Bentley (1977).

1. Byron's uncle by marriage. George Ticknor, an American visitor, was present when Sir James one day

came suddenly into the room, and said abruptly, 'My Lord, my lord, a great battle has been fought in the Low Countries, and Bonaparte is entirely defeated.' 'But is it true?' said Lord Byron, – 'is it true?' 'Yes, my lord, it is certainly true; an aide-de-camp arrived in town last night. . . . He says he thinks Bonaparte is in full retreat towards Paris.' After an instant's pause,

Lord Byron replied, 'I am d—d sorry for it'; and then, after another slight pause, he added, 'I didn't know but I might live to see Lord Castlereagh's head on a pole. But I suppose I shan't, now.' And this was the first impression produced on his impetuous nature by the news of the battle of Waterloo.   (*The Life, Letters and Journals of George Ticknor*, ed. F. Greenslet (Boston, Mass., 1909) I, 59).

2. John Wilson Croker (1780–1857), Tory politician and savage critic, remembered for his attack on Keats in the *Quarterly Review*.

3. See p. 8.

4. James Wedderburn Webster (born 1789) may have met Byron at Cambridge and was one of his boon companions during the early years in London, also visiting him at Newstead. Webster married Lady Frances Annesley in 1810 and Byron visited them at Aston Hall in 1813, on which occasion he flirted with his friend's wife in his presence. See also p. 70.

5. Charles Skinner Matthews met Byron at Trinity College in 1806 and they became friends. Matthews had occupied Byron's rooms for a time during his absence and had been delighted by the tutor's admonition 'not to damage any of the movables, for Lord Byron, Sir, is a young man of *tumultuous passions*' (recounted in Byron's letter to John Murray, 19 Nov 1820). It was Matthews who introduced Byron to Davies. Matthews was drowned in a bathing-accident in the Cam on 3 August 1811. A graphic account of his death is given in the *Memoir of the Rev. Francis Hodgson*, I, 182–4. Byron, whose mother had died two days earlier, was much upset by his death, and wrote to Davies (7 Aug 1811), 'My mother lies a corpse in this house; one of my best friends is drowned in a ditch. . . . Come to me Scrope, I am almost desolate.'

6. In curl-papers (French).

7. *Lara* was published in 1814.

8. George Brummell, better known as 'Beau' Brummell (1778–1840), friend of the Prince Regent and celebrated dandy, fled to the Continent to escape his creditors and died in poverty at Caen.

Byron's Marriage and Departure from England*

J. C. HOBHOUSE

[19 Oct 1814.] Found a letter from Byron asking me to stand grooms-man at his marriage.

Recollections of a Long Life, I, 165,194–7, 229, 323, 324, 333, 334–6.

[31 Dec.] We had dinner at six, and had a little jollity upon the signing of the settlements, which was done in the morning. I put my name to a deed which is to provide for the younger children of the marriage; . . .

I talked and talked in the evening, which concluded jollily with a mock marriage, I being Lady B, Noel[1] parsonifying, and Hoare[2] giving me away. Shook hands for New Year.

[1 Jan 1815.] We had not quite so jolly a dinner as yesterday, but fair, considering.

Byron at night said, 'Well, Hobhouse, this is our last night; tomorrow I shall be Annabella's.' (*Absit omen.*)

[2 Jan.] I dressed in full-dress, with white gloves, and found Byron up and dressed, with Noel in canonicals. Lady Milbanke and Sir Ralph soon came, also dressed. Her Ladyship could not make tea, her hand shook.

Miss Milbanke did not appear. The Rev. Wallace came in, also in canonicals. At half-past ten we parted company; Byron and I went into his room, the others upstairs.

In ten minutes we walked up into the drawing-room, and found kneeling-mats disposed for the couple and the others. The two clergymen, the father and mother, and myself, were in waiting when Miss Milbanke came in, attended by her governess, the respectable Mrs Clermont.

She was dressed in a muslin gown trimmed with lace at the bottom, with a white muslin curricle jacket, very plain indeed, with nothing on her head.

Noel was decent and grave. He put them, Byron and Miss Milbanke, on their cushions. Lady Milbanke placed Sir Ralph next to his daughter; I stood next to Sir Ralph; my Lady and Mrs Clermont were rather opposite in the corner.

Wallace read the responses.

Miss Milbanke was as firm as a rock, and, during the whole ceremony, looked steadily at Byron. She repeated the words audibly and well. Byron hitched at first when he said, 'I, George Gordon', and when he came to the words, 'With all my worldly goods I thee endow', looked at me with a half-smile. They were married at eleven.

I shook Lady Byron by the hand after the parson, and embraced my friend with unfeigned delight. He was kissed by my Lady Milbanke. Lady Milbanke and Mrs Clermont were much affected.

Lady Byron went out of the room, but soon returned to sign the register, which Wallace and I witnessed.

She again retired hastily, her eyes full of tears when she looked at her father and mother, and completed her conquest, her innocent conquest.

She came in her travelling-dress soon after, a slate-coloured satin pelisse trimmed with white fur, and sat quietly in the drawing-room. Byron was calm and as usual. I felt as if I had buried a friend.

I put a complete collection of Byron's Poems, bound in yellow morocco, into the carriage for Lady Byron as a wedding gift. It was inscribed thus:

TO THE RIGHT HONOURABLE LADY BYRON.

These volumes, the production of a poet, the admiration of his countrymen, the delight of his associates, and the approved choice of her understanding and her heart, are presented, as a sincere token of congratulation, on her union with his best friend, by her faithful and devoted servant,

JOHN C. HOBHOUSE

At a little before twelve I handed Lady Byron downstairs and into her carriage. When I wished her many years of happiness, she said, 'If I am not happy it will be my own fault.'

Of my dearest friend I took a melancholy leave. He was unwilling to leave my hand, and I had hold of his out of the window when the carriage drove off.

I left Seaham at twelve. Lady Milbanke asked me if she had not behaved well, as if she had been the mother of Iphigenia. It is not wonderful that the marriage of an only daughter and child, born seventeen years after marriage, should cause a pang at parting. . . .

The little bells of Seaham church struck up after the wedding, and half a dozen fired muskets in front of the house.

The couple went to Halnaby, Sir R. Milbanke's estate in Yorkshire.

[1 Apr.] Before I left London on Wednesday I saw [Byron] and his wife. He advises me 'not to marry', though he has the best of wives.

[4 Aug.] Dine at [Sir Francis] Burdett's. . . . Lord Byron tells me he and she have begun a little snubbing on money matters. Marry not, says he.

[25 Nov.] Called on Byron. In that quarter things do not go well. Strong advice against marriage. Talking of going abroad.

[3 Apr 1816.] Rode up to London and settled at Lord Byron's No. 13, Piccadilly Terrace. S. B. Davies and L. Hunt of the *Examiner* dined with us . . . .

[22 Apr.] Rogers came to take leave of Byron . . . . Everything prepared for Byron's departure. All his papers put into my hands . . . .

[23 Apr.] Up at six; breakfasted, but not off till half-past nine. Polidori and I went in Scrope Davies's chaise; Byron and Davies in Byron's new Napoleonic carriage built by Baxter for £500. There was a crowd about the door. . . . Arrived at Dover by half-past eight; dined at the Ship.

In today's *Chronicle* appeared a very sensible paragraph, by Perry[3], I suppose, about Lord Byron, and announcing his departure from the country . . . .

[24 Apr.] This morning Fletcher told me the bailiffs had got into No. 13 and had seized everything. I was in alarm respecting their descent to Dover and the carriage, therefore had it put on board as soon as possible. Wind contrary, from eastwards, and strong.

Dined at five; walked in the evening to the church to see Churchill's[4] tomb. The old sexton took us to an open spot or churchyard without a church, and showed us a green sod with a common head-stone. Byron lay down on the grave and gave the man a crown to fresh turf it . . . .

[25 Apr.] Up at eight, breakfasted; all on board except the company. The Captain said he could not wait, and Byron could not get up a moment sooner. Even the serenity of Scrope was disturbed. However, after some bustle out came Byron, and, taking my arm, walked down to the quay. . . . He got on board a little after nine: the bustle kept Byron in spirits, but he looked affected when the packet glided off. I ran to the end of the wooden pier, and as the vessel tossed by us through a rough sea and contrary wind, I saw him again; the dear fellow pulled off his cap and waved it to me. I gazed until I could not distinguish him any longer. God bless him for a gallant spirit and a kind one.

I shall, fate allowing, join him in two or three months. He sometimes talked of returning in a year or so, at others of being longer away, but told me he felt a presentiment that his absence would be long. Again God bless him.

NOTES

On Hobhouse, see p. 12. Anne Isabella (known as Annabella) Milbanke, who became Lady Byron (1792–1860), was the only daughter of Sir Ralph and Lady Judith Milbanke of Seaham, near Durham. She was brought up quietly and became something of a bluestocking. She saw Byron for the first time on 25 March 1812 and wrote in her diary that evening (quoted in Marchand, p. 333),

His mouth continually betrays the acrimony of his spirit. I should judge him sincere and independent – sincere at least in society as far as he can be, whilst dissimulating the violence of his scorn. He very often hides his mouth with his hand while speaking. . . . It appeared to me that he tried to control his natural sarcasm and vehemence as much as he could, in order not to offend, but at times his lips thickened with disdain, and his eyes rolled impatiently. Indeed the scene [a social gathering at which Byron was besieged by female admirers] was calculated to show human absurdities.

Byron was at the time basking in the success of *Childe Harold*, and, as Miss Milbanke wrote to her mother, was 'the object of universal attention . . . all the women were absurdly courting him, and trying to *deserve* the lash of his Satire'. She refused Byron's first proposal (13 Sep 1812) but accepted his second (9 Sep 1814). The marriage took place on 2 January 1815, their daughter Augusta Ada was born on 10 December, and on 15 January 1816 she returned to her parents' home and never lived with Byron again.

There is an extensive literature relating to Byron's marriage, including Harriet Beecher Stowe, *Lady Byron Vindicated* (Boston, Mass., 1870); Ralph Milbanke, Earl of Lovelace, *Astarte* (1921); Ethel Colburn Mayne, *The Life and Letters of Anne Isabella, Lady Noel Byron* (1929); G. Wilson Knight, *Lord Byron's Marriage* (1957); Malcolm Elwin, *Lord Byron's Wife* (1962). Malcolm Elwin is also the author of *Lord Byron's Family* (1975).

1. The Reverend Thomas Noel, 'Rector of Kirkby Mallory and illegitimate son of Lord Wentworth, Miss Milbanke's maternal uncle, a brisk parson of the better sort' (Hobhouse).

2. 'Confidential counsel and agent of Sir R[alph] M[ilbanke]' (Hobhouse).

3. James Perry, editor of the *Morning Chronicle*.

4. Charles Churchill (1731–64), poet and satirist. Byron's *English Bards and Scotch Reviewers* owes something to Churchill's *Rosciad* (1761).

Travelling with Byron in Europe*

J. W. POLIDORI

[From a letter to his sister Frances, 2 May 1816.] I am very pleased with Lord Byron. I am with him on the footing of an equal, everything alike: at present here we have a suite of rooms between us. I have my sitting-room at one end, he at the other. He has not shown any passion; though we have had nothing but a series of mishaps that have put *me* out of temper though they have not ruffled his. The carriage, the new

The Diary of Dr John William Polidori (1816) Relating to Byron, Shelley, etc., ed. W. M. Rossetti (London: Elkin Matthews, 1911) pp. 211, 66, 213, 97, 111–12, 127–8.

carriage, has had three stoppages. We are at present at Brussels merely to have the carriage-part well looked at and repaired.

[Diary, 4 May.] We rode home together through Soignies forest – black. The twilight made the whole length of the road more pleasing. On reaching home, we found the coach was jogged; so much so that it would not allow us to put confidence in it, etc. At last we gave it into Mr Gordon's hands. My friend has written twenty-six st[anzas][1] to-day – some on Waterloo.

[From a letter to J. C. Hobhouse, written at Coblenz on 11 May.] As we are at last some way on our journey, I take a sheet of paper up, in despair of filling it, to tell you we are both well and hearty. Lord Byron's health is greatly improved, his stomach returning rapidly to its natural state. Exercise and peace of mind, making great advances towards the amendment of his *corps délabré*,[2] leave little for medicine to patch up. His spirits, I think, are also much improved. He blithely carols through the day, 'Here's to you, Tom Brown': and, when he has done, says, 'That's as well as Hobhouse does it.' You and his other friend, Scrope Davies, form a great subject of conversation.

God! here I am at the end of all my thoughts. Oh no! Waterloo was ridden over by my Lord on a Cossack horse, accompanied by myself on a Flemish steed; Lord Byron singing Turkish or Arnaout riding-tunes, and your h[umble] s[ervant] listening. We had a very good day of it.

[Diary, 25 May.] We saw Mont Blanc in the distance; ethereal in appearance, mingling with the clouds; it is more than 60 miles from where we saw it. It is a classic ground we go over. Bonaparte, Joseph, Bonnet, Necker, Staël, Voltaire, Rousseau, all have their villas (except Rousseau). Genthoud, Ferney, Coppet, are close to the road.

We arrived at Sécheron – where L[ord] B[yron], having put his age down as 100, received a letter half-an-hour after from I[nn] K[eeper] – a thing that seems worthy of a novel. It begins again to be the land of the vine. Women, who till the Pays de Vaud were ugly, improving greatly.

[Diary, 1 June.] Rogers[3] the subject: L[or]d B[yron] thinks good poet; malicious. Marquis of Lansdowne being praised by a whole company as a happy man, having all good, R[ogers] said, 'But how horridly he carves turbot!' . . .

On L B's writing a poem to his sister wherein he says, 'And when friends e'en paused and love', etc., Rogers, going to some one, said: 'I don't know what L B means by *pausing*; I called upon him every day.' He did this regularly, telling L B all the bad news with a malignant grin. When L B wrote 'Weep, daughter of a royal line', Rogers came to him one day, and, taking up the *Courier*, said: 'I am sure now you're attacked there; now don't mind them'; and began reading, looking every now and then at L B with an anxious searching eye, till he came to 'that little poet and disagreeable person, Mr Samuel ———' when he tore the paper, and said: 'Now this must be that fellow Croker', and wished L B to challenge him. He talked of going to Cumberland with L B, and asking him how he meant to travel, L B said 'With four horses.' Rogers went to company, and said: 'It is strange to hear a man talking of four horses who seals his letters with a tallow candle.'

[Diary, 18 June.] Shelley and party here. . . . Began my ghost-story after tea.[4] Twelve o'clock, really began to talk ghostly. L[ord] B[yron] repeated some verses of Coleridge's 'Christabel', of the witch's breast;[5] when silence ensued, and Shelley, suddenly shrieking and putting his hands to his head, ran out of the room with a candle. Threw water in his face, and after gave him ether. He was looking at Mrs S[helley], and suddenly thought of a woman he had heard of who had eyes instead of nipples, which, taking hold of his mind, horrified him . . . .

NOTES

John William Polidori (1795–1821), of Anglo-Italian parentage, was educated at Ampleforth College and studied medicine at the University of Edinburgh, graduating at the age of nineteen. Byron engaged him as travelling physician on 28 March 1816 and he was in Byron's party when he left England on 24 April. Vain and quarrelsome, he was dismissed by Byron on 16 September and after travelling in Italy returned to England in 1817. In 1821 he committed suicide on account of gambling-debts. John Murray, Byron's publisher, had offered Polidori £500 for an account of Byron's travels, and Polidori kept a diary from 24 April to 30 June and from 16 September to 30 December 1816. William Michael Rossetti, a nephew of Polidori, edited the diary from a copy made by his aunt Charlotte Polidori, who had destroyed the original and omitted some improper passages from her copy. Polidori published prose and verse during his lifetime, but only *The Vampyre* (see note 4 below) is remembered.

1. As Rossetti comments, 'To write twenty-six stanzas in one day is no small feat; especially if these are the nine-line stanzas of *Childe Harold*, and if the substantial work of the day consisted in riding from Brussels to Waterloo and back, and deliberately inspecting the field of battle.'

2. Body ruined (by dissipation) (French).

3. Samuel Rogers: see p. 19.

4. On the previous day, Polidori had noted that 'The ghost-stories are begun by all but me.' Byron, Shelley, Mary Shelley, Claire Clairmont, and Polidori himself had all agreed to try their hand at writing a ghost-story. Shelley began one based on 'the experiences of his early life' but soon abandoned it, as did Claire Clairmont. Byron described his intended narrative to

the others but gave up after writing a few pages. The most substantial outcome of the enterprise was Mary Shelley's *Frankenstein*, publîshed in 1818. Polidori later published *The Vampyre*, which appeared in 1819 over Byron's name; this does not seem to have been the story begun on the occasion in question, but it probably owes something to Byron's proposed tale. A modern edition of *The Vampyre* (Pasadena, 1968) has a useful introduction by Donald K. Adams.

5. Presumably a reference to lines 252–3:

> Behold! her bosom and half her side –
> A sight to dream of, not to tell!

Italian Travel*

J. C. HOBHOUSE

[10 Oct 1816.] By six o'clock we arrived at our town of Ornavasso. Being in Italy, we took great precautions about luggage, etc. Berger[1] slept in Byron's carriage, the dogs were chained under our chaises, our pistols well-primed in our rooms, and all other warlike preparations made.

[11 Oct.] Before quitting this place we made every arrangement for battle. Pistols were reprimed, swords got ready, Byron's two carbines put into my calash with Joseph. We had four brace of pistols in our carriage, two swords, two sword-sticks, and Byron's dagger. We furnished Springhetti[2] with a brace of pistols, and my postillion – so we had armed men.

Our histories of the late Sesto robbery, and Springhetti's advice to embark on the lake to-day made us think we might have occasion for all our arms, and as much of our courage as might be forthcoming.

We were a little silent, and looked about us on each side of the road. Springhetti did the same. Yet we knew the Jerseys and the Cowpers had just passed safely; but they had luck, and we might have none. I put my napoleons in a secret drawer, which, considering we had resolved to fight, was useless.

We had travelled three-quarters of an hour when we saw a man proceed from some old walls of a vineyard, and then go in again. We took out our pistols, looked at the priming, and went on. Some children made us suspect we might not yet be called upon to use our arms; but passing this spot we saw five or six men running after our last carriage.

Recollections of a Long Life, II, 35–6.

We stopped, holloaed out, and our second coachman saying something about a gun, we were not relieved until we found these fellows were boatmen running to get a fare from us. We did not know we were so close to the Lago Maggiore, coming on which we were at once at ease again.

NOTES

Hobhouse (see p. 12) accompanied Byron when he left England in April 1816. After travelling via Bruges, Ghent, Antwerp, Brussels, Cologne, Bonn, Coblenz, Mannheim, Karlsruhe and Basle, they settled at the Villa Diodati on the shores of Lake Geneva on 10 June. In October they set off again, went up the Rhone Valley to the Simplon Pass, reached Lake Maggiore, and arrived in Venice on 10 November.

1. Byron's Swiss servant.
2. An Italian guide.

Meetings with Byron (1818–21)*

P. B. SHELLEY

[To Mary Shelley, 23 Aug 1818.] At 3 o'clock I called on [Byron]. – He was delighted to see me. . . . Later he took me in his gondola – much against my will for I wanted to return to Claire[1] at Mrs Hoppner's[2] who was anxiously waiting for me – across the laguna to a long sandy island which defends Venice from the Adriatic. When we disembarked, we found his horses waiting for us, and we rode along the sands of the sea talking.[3] Our conversation consisted in histories of his wounded feelings, and questions as to my affairs, and great professions of friendship and regard for me. He said that if he had been in England at the time of the Chancery affair,[4] he would have moved Heaven and Earth to have prevented such a decision. We talked of literary matters, his fourth Canto[5] which he says is very good, and indeed repeated some stanzas of great energy to me, and Foliage[6] which he quizzes immoderately . . . we returned to his palace . . . .

*The Letters of Percy Bysshe Shelley, ed. Frederick L. Jones (Oxford: Clarendon Press, 1964) II, 36–7, 57–8, 316–17, 345.

[To Thomas Love Peacock, 17 or 18 Dec.] I entirely agree with what you say about [the fourth canto of] *Childe Harold*. The spirit in which it is written is, if insane, the most wicked and mischievous insanity that ever was given forth. It is a kind of obstinate and selfwilled folly in which he hardens himself. I remonstrated with him in vain on the tone of mind from which such a view of things alone arises. For its real root is very different from its apparent one, and nothing can be less sublime than the true source of these expressions of contempt and desperation. The fact is, that first, the Italian women are perhaps the most contemptible of all who exist under the moon; the most ignorant, the most disgusting, the most bigoted, the most filthy. Countesses smell so of garlic that an ordinary Englishman cannot approach them. Well, L[ord] B[yron] is familiar with the lowest sort of these women, the people his gondolieri pick up in the streets. He allows fathers and mothers to bargain with him for their daughters, and though this is common enough in Italy, yet for an Englishman to encourage such sickening vice is a melancholy thing. He associates with wretches who seem almost to have lost the gait and physiognomy of man, and who do not scruple to avow practices which are not only not named but I believe seldom even conceived in England. He says he disapproves, but he endures. He is not yet an Italian and is heartily and deeply discontented with himself, and contemplating in the distorted mirror of his own thoughts, the nature and the destiny of man, what can he behold but objects of contempt and despair? But that he is a great poet, I think the address to Ocean proves. And he has a certain degree of candour while you talk to him but unfortunately it does not outlast your departure.

[To Mary Shelley, 7 Aug 1821.] I arrived [in Ravenna] last night at 10 o'clock and sat up last night talking with Lord Byron until 5 this morning. . . .

Lord Byron is very well, and was delighted to see me. He has in fact completely recovered his health, and lives a life totally the reverse of that which he led at Venice. He has a permanent sort of liaison with Contessa Guiccioli, who is now at Florence, and seems from her letters to be a very amiable woman. She is waiting there until something shall be decided as to their emigration to Switzerland or stay in Italy: which is yet undetermined on either side. – She was compelled to escape from the Papal territory in great haste, as measures had already been taken to place her in a Convent where she would have been unrelentingly confined for life. The oppression of the marriage compact, as existing in the laws and opinions of Italy, though less frequently exercised is far severer than that of England. – I tremble to think of what poor Emilia is destined to. – Lord Byron had almost destroyed himself at Venice: his state of debility was such that he was unable to digest any food – he was consumed by hectic fever, and would speedily have perished but for this attachment which reclaimed him from the excesses into which he threw himself from carelessness and pride rather than taste. – Poor fellow – he is now quite well and immersed in politics and literature. He has given me a number of the most interesting details on the former subject – but we will not speak of them in a letter. – Fletcher is here, and as if like a shadow he waxed and waned with the substance of his master, Fletcher also has recovered his good looks and from amidst the unseasonable grey hairs a fresh harvest of flaxen locks put forth. –

We talked a great deal of poetry and such matters last night: and as usual differed and I think more than ever. – He affects to patronise a system of criticism fit only for the production of mediocrity, and although all his fine poems and passages have been produced in defiance of this system: yet I recognise the pernicious effects of it in the 'Doge of Venice',[7] and it will cramp and limit his future efforts however great they may be unless he gets rid of it. I have read only parts of it, or rather he himself read them to me and gave me the plan of the whole. – Allegra,[8] he says, is grown very beautiful: but he complains that her temper is violent and imperious. – He has no intention of leaving her in Italy; indeed the thing is too improper in itself not to carry condemnation along with it. Contessa Guiccioli he says is very fond of her: indeed I cannot see why *she* should not take care of it, if she is to live as his ostensible mistress. – All this I shall know more of soon.

[To Leigh Hunt, 26 Aug 1821.] Before this you will have seen *Adonais*.[9] Lord Byron, I suppose from modesty on account of his being mentioned in it, did not say a word of *Adonais*, though he was loud in his praise of *Prometheus*:[10] and, what you will not agree with him in, censure of the *Cenci*.[11] Certainly, if *Marino Faliero* is a drama, the *Cenci* is not: but that between ourselves. Lord Byron is reformed, as far as gallantry goes, and lives with a beautiful and sentimental Italian lady, who is as much attached to him as may be. I trust greatly to his intercourse with you, for his creed to become as pure as he thinks his conduct is. He has many generous and exalted qualities, but the canker of aristocracy wants to be cut out . . . .

NOTES

Percy Bysshe Shelley (1792–1822) met Byron in Sécheron, near Geneva, on 27 May 1816, and when Byron moved into the Villa Diodati in June he became a near neighbour of the Shelleys and saw them frequently until they set off for England on 28 August. Two years later, on 22 August 1818, Shelley arrived in Venice to visit Byron, and when Byron moved from Ravenna to Pisa in 1821 Shelley joined him there. See C. L. Cline, *Byron, Shelley and their Pisan Circle* (1952); John Buxton, *Byron and Shelley* (1968).

1. Claire or Clare Clairmont (born Mary Jane Clairmont) (1798–1879) was a daughter of William Godwin by his second wife, and hence a step-sister of Mary Shelley. She became involved with Byron in London in 1816 while he was embroiled in the separation from his wife, and soon afterwards travelled to Switzerland with the Shelleys and resumed her relationship with him. Their child Allegra (see note 8 below) was born at the beginning of the following year. For a full account see R. Glynn Grylls, *Claire Clairmont* (1939).

2. Richard Hoppner (1786–1872) and his Swiss wife were residents in Venice, where he was British Consul. They met Byron in 1817 and struck up a friendship with him. Half a century later, Hoppner published an article, 'Byron at Venice', in the *Athenaeum* (22 May 1869, p. 702) in which he writes,

> I don't believe that Lord Byron was naturally of a saturnine disposition, but think the misanthropy that figures as part of his character in his early writings was merely a poetical fiction. His love of pleasure and the eagerness with which he pursued it certainly seem to prove him to have been of anything but a melancholy disposition.

3. This ride is commemorated in Shelley's poem *Julian and Maddalo: A Conversation*, written in 1819 and published posthumously in 1824. The prose preface describes Maddalo (Byron) in the following terms:

> He is a person of the most consummate genius, and capable, if he would direct his energies to such an end, of becoming the redeemer of his degraded country. But it is his weakness to be proud: he derives, from a comparison of his own extraordinary mind with the dwarfish intellects that surround him, an intense apprehension of the nothingness of human life. . . . His ambition preys upon itself, for want of objects which it can consider worthy of exertion . . . .

4. In April 1816, Shelley had lost a suit concerning his inheritance and had gone abroad immediately afterwards.

5. Of *Childe Harold*, published on 28 April 1818.

6. Leigh Hunt's *Foliage* was published in 1818.

7. The subtitle of Byron's drama *Marino Faliero* (1821).

8. Allegra, born 12 January 1817, was the illegitimate daughter of Byron and Claire Clairmont (see note 2 above). She joined Byron in Venice in April or May 1818 and at the age of four was placed in a convent, dying there of fever on 20 April 1822. See Iris Origo, *Allegra* (1935).

9. Shelley had begun his poem, commemorating the death of Keats, in April and had finished it by July.

10. Shelley's 'lyrical drama', *Prometheus Unbound*, published in 1820.

11. Shelley's drama *The Cenci*, published in 1819.

'A Lost Man'*

MARY SHELLEY

[6 Apr 1819.] . . . all goes on as badly there [in Venice] with the noble poet as ever I fear – he is a lost man if he does not escape soon.

[27 Apr.] What a miserable thing it is that he should be lost as he is among the worst inhabitants of Venice.

[11 May 1821.] . . . a man reckless of the ill he does others, obstinate to desperation in the pursuance of his plans or his revenge.

[Dec 1822.] L[ord] B[yron] is to me as kind as ever; . . . he is all professions and politeness. . . . I do not suppose any miracle worked in my favour, or that his defect would not touch me if I touched it, but his purse strings are yet undrawn by me and will remain so, and that you know is the tender point.

[July 1823.] [On] 9 June, . . . I told Lord Byron that I was ready to go, and he promised to provide means. When I talked of going post, it was because he said that I should go so, at the same time declaring that he would regulate all himself. I waited in vain for these arrangements. But, not to make a long story, since I hope soon to be able to relate the details – he chose to transact our negotiation through Hunt, and gave such an air of unwillingness and sense of the obligation he conferred, as at last provoked Hunt to say that there was no obligation, since he owed me £1000.[1]
  Glad of a quarrel, straight I clap the door![2]
  Still keeping up an appearance of amity with Hunt, he has written

---

*The Letters of Mary W. Shelley. ed. Frederick L. Jones (Norman, Okla: University of Oklahoma Press, 1944) I, 67, 70, 140, 208, 229, and II, 61; Mary Shelley's Journal, ed. Frederick L. Jones (Norman, Okla: University of Oklahoma Press, 1947) p. 184.

notes and letters so full of contempt against me and my lost Shelley that
I could stand it no longer, and have refused to receive his still proffered
aid for my journey.

[?8 June 1822?] The last Cantos of Don Juan were written with great
speed – I copied them. There were scarcely any erasures and his chief
delight was in sending them to me, to date the beginning and end with
the name of the same month to prove how quickly they were
composed . . . .

[Journal, 19 Oct 1822.] I do not think that any person's voice has the
same power of awakening melancholy in me as Albè's.[3] I have been
accustomed, when hearing it, to listen and to speak little; another
voice, not mine, ever replied – a voice whose strings are broken. When
Albè ceases to speak, I expect to hear *that other* voice, and when I hear
another instead, it jars strangely with every association. I have seen so
little of Albè since our residence in Switzerland, and, having seen him
there every day, his voice – a peculiar one – is engraved on my
memory with other sounds and objects from which it can never disunite
itself. I have heard Hunt in company and conversation with many,
when my own one was not there. Trelawny, perhaps, is associated in
my mind with Edward [Williams] more than with Shelley. Even our
older friends, Peacock and Hogg,[4] might talk together, or with others,
and their voices would suggest no change to me. But, since incapacity
and timidity always prevented my mingling in the nightly conversations of Diodati,[5] they were, as it were, entirely tête-à-tête between my
Shelley and Albè; and thus, as I have said, when Albè speaks and
Shelley does not answer, it is as thunder without rain – the form of the
sun without heat or light – as any familiar object might be, shorn of its
best attributes; and I listen with an unspeakable melancholy that yet is
not all pain.

The above explains that which would otherwise be an enigma – why
Albè, by his mere presence and voice, has the power of exciting such
deep and shifting emotions within me. For my feelings have no analogy
either with my opinion of him, or the subject of his conversation. With
another I might talk, and not for the moment think of Shelley – at least
not think of him with the same vividness as if I were alone; but, when in
company with Albè, I can never cease for a second to have Shelley in
my heart and brain with a clearness that mocks reality – interfering
even by its force with the functions of life – until, if tears do not relieve
me, the hysterical feeling, analogous to that which the murmur of the
sea gives me, presses painfully upon me.

Well, for the first time for about a month, I have been in company
with Albè for two hours, and, coming home, I write this, so necessary is
it for me to express in words the force of my feelings.

NOTES

Mary Shelley (1797–1851), daughter of William Godwin and second wife of Shelley, left England with Shelley in 1814 and married him in 1816 after his first wife had committed suicide. She published several novels, including *Frankenstein* (1818) (see p. 50) and the autobiographical *Lodore* (1835), which includes a portrait of Byron. In spite of the tone of the above extracts, there is evidence that she was strongly attracted to Byron. Among various studies of Mary Shelley are those by R. Glynn Grylls (1938), Muriel Spark (1951), Janet Harris (1979) and Bonnie R. Neumann (1979). See also E. J. Lovell Jr, 'Byron and Mary Shelley', *Keats – Shelley Journal*, II (1953) 35–49.

1. According to Medwin's account in his *Life of Shelley*, towards the end of 1821 Shelley and Byron made a wager, Byron betting that Lady Noel (formerly Lady Milbanke, and Byron's mother-in-law) would outlive Sir Timothy Shelley (Shelley's father). Lady Noel died shortly afterwards, but the debt was never paid. Perhaps Byron (and Shelley) had not taken the wager seriously, but Mary Shelley and Leigh Hunt certainly did.

2. Quoted from Pope's 'Epistle to Dr Arbuthnot', line 67.

3. Nickname given to Byron by the Shelleys, perhaps derived from the initials LB (Lord Byron), or a short form of Albaneser (Albanian).

4. Thomas Love Peacock (1785–1866), novelist and poet, was Shelley's friend and executor. James Hogg (1770–1835), 'the Ettrick Shepherd', poet, described by Byron as 'of great, though uncouth, powers'.

5. Byron rented the Villa Diodati, in the village of Cologny two miles from Geneva, in June 1816, and during that summer often entertained the Shelleys there.

A Visit from Thomas Moore*

THOMAS MOORE

[7 Oct 1819.] Left Padua at twelve, and arrived at Lord Byron's country house, La Mira, near Fusina, at two. He was but just up and in his bath; soon came down to me; first time we have met these five years; grown fat, which spoils the picturesqueness of his head. . . . Found him in high spirits and full of his usual frolicsome gaiety. . . . He dressed, and we set off together in my carriage for Venice: a glorious sunset when we embarked at Fusina in a gondola, and the view of Venice and the distant Alps (some of which had snow on them, reddening with the last light) was magnificent; but my companion's

*The Journal of Thomas Moore, pp. 32–4.

conversation, which, though highly ludicrous and amusing, was anything but romantic, threw my mind and imagination into a mood not at all agreeing with the scene. . . . [Later, during dinner] Had much curious conversation with him about his wife before Scott arrived. He has written his memoirs,[1] and is continuing them; thinks of going and purchasing lands under the Patriotic Government in South America. Much talk about *Don Juan*; he is writing a third canto; the Duke of Wellington; his taking so much money; gives instances of disinterested men, Epaminondas, etc. etc. down to Pitt himself . . . .

NOTES

Thomas Moore (1779–1852), Irish poet, met Byron in November 1811 at Samuel Rogers's house (see p. 18). They saw each other frequently in London, but met only once, on the occasion described in this extract, after Byron left England. Moore's life of Byron appeared in two volumes in 1830–1.

1. The subsequent history of Byron's memoirs is complex: for full details see Marchand, p. 1245 ff., and Doris Langley Moore, *The Late Lord Byron* (1961) ch. 1. Moore told Hobhouse that, while the first part of the memoirs was innocuous except for isolated passages, the second part 'contained all sorts of erotic adventures'. William Gifford, as John Murray's literary adviser, read them at Murray's request, and reported them 'fit only for a brothel', predicting that, if published, they 'would doom Lord B to everlasting infamy'. Moore, with his projected biography in mind, was eager to publish at any rate a selection of the less offensive portions, but Hobhouse insisted on their wholesale destruction and was supported by Murray. On 17 May 1824, four weeks after Byron's death, they were burned in Murray's office in Albemarle Street, in the presence of Murray, Hobhouse, Moore and other witnesses. Later in the year, reviewing Medwin's *Conversations*, *Blackwood's Magazine*, XVI (Nov 1824) 530, remarked severely, 'Moore has much to answer for – He stands guilty of having violated a sacred trust confided to him by one of the master-spirits of the age'.

Moore Recalls his Visit*

THOMAS MOORE

I was a good deal struck . . . by the alteration that had taken place in his personal appearance. He had grown fatter both in person and face,

*The Life of Lord Byron, pp. 410–12.

and the latter had most suffered by the change – having lost, by the
enlargement of the features, some of that refined and spiritualised look,
that had in other times, distinguished it. The addition of whiskers, too,
which he had not long before been induced to adopt, from hearing that
some one had said he had a *faccia di musico*, as well as the length to
which his hair grew down on his neck, and the rather foreign air of his
coat and cap – all combined to produce that dissimilarity to his former
self I had observed in him. He was still, however, eminently handsome:
and, in exchange for whatever his features might have lost of their high,
romantic character, they had become more fitted for the expression of
that arch, waggish wisdom, that Epicurean play of humour, which he
had shown to be equally inherent in his various and prodigally gifted
nature; while, by the somewhat increased roundness of the contours,
the resemblance of his finely formed mouth and chin to those of the
Belvedere Apollo had become still more striking.

His breakfast, which I found he rarely took before three or four
o'clock in the afternoon, was speedily despatched – his habit being to
eat it standing, and the meal in general consisting of one or two raw
eggs, a cup of tea without either milk or sugar, and a bit of dry biscuit.
Before we took our departure, he presented me to the Countess Guiccioli, who was at this time, as my readers already know, living under
the same roof with him at La Mira; and who, with a style of beauty
singular in an Italian, as being fair-complexioned and delicate, left an
impression upon my mind, during this our first short interview, of
intelligence and amiableness such as all that I have since known or
heard of her has but served to confirm.

We now started together, Lord Byron and myself, in my little
Milanese vehicle, for Fusina – his portly gondolier Tita, in a rich livery
and most redundant mustachios, having seated himself on the front of
the carriage, to the no small trial of its strength, which had already
once given way, even under my own weight, between Verona and
Vicenza. On our arrival at Fusina, my noble friend, from his familiarity with all the details of the place, had it in his power to save me both
trouble and expense in the different arrangements relative to the
custom-house, remise, etc.; and the good-natured assiduity with which
he bustled about in despatching these matters, gave me an opportunity
of observing, in his use of the infirm limb, a much greater degree of
activity than I had ever before, except in sparring, witnessed.

As we proceeded across the Lagoon in his gondola, the sun was just
setting, and it was an evening such as Romance would have chosen for
a first sight of Venice, rising 'with her tiara of bright towers' above the
wave; while, to complete, as might be imagined, the solemn interest of
the scene, I beheld it in company with him who had lately given a new
life to its glories, and sung of that fair City of the Sea thus grandly: –

I stood in Venice on the Bridge of Sighs;
A palace and a prison on each hand:
I saw from out the wave her structures rise
As from the stroke of the enchanter's wand:
A thousand years their cloudy wings expand
Around me, and a dying glory smiles
O'er the far times, when many a subject land
Look'd to the winged lion's marble piles,
Where Venice sat in state, throned in her hundred isles.[1]

But, whatever emotions the first sight of such a scene might, under other circumstances, have inspired me with, the mood of mind in which I now viewed it was altogether the very reverse of what might have been expected. The exuberant gaiety of my companion, and the recollections – any thing but romantic – into which our conversation wandered, put at once completely to flight all poetical and historical associations; and our course was, I am almost ashamed to say, one of uninterrupted merriment and laughter till we found ourselves at the steps of my friend's palazzo on the Grand Canal. All that had ever happened, of gay or ridiculous, during our London life together – his scrapes and my lecturings, – our joint adventures with the Bores and Blues, the two great enemies, as he always called them, of London happiness . . . all was passed rapidly in review between us, and with a flow of humour and hilarity, on his side, of which it would have been difficult, even for persons far graver than I can pretend to be, not to have caught the contagion.

He had all along expressed his determination that I should not go to any hotel, but fix my quarters at his house during the period of my stay; and, had he been residing there himself, such an arrangement would have been all that I most desired. But, this not being the case, a common hotel was, I thought, a far readier resource; and I therefore entreated that he would allow me to order an apartment at the Gran Bretagna, which had the reputation, I understood, of being a comfortable hotel. This, however, he would not hear of; and, as an inducement for me to agree to his plan, said that, as long as I chose to stay, though he should be obliged to return to La Mira in the evenings, he would make it a point to come to Venice every day and dine with me. As we now turned into the dismal canal, and stopped before his damp-looking mansion, my predilection for the Gran Bretagna returned in full force; and I again ventured to hint that it would save an abundance of trouble to let me proceed thither. But 'No – no,' he answered – 'I see you think you'll be very uncomfortable here; but you'll find that it is not quite so bad as you expect.'

As I groped my way after him through the dark hall, he cried out,

'Keep clear of the dog'; and before we had proceeded many paces farther, 'Take care, or that monkey will fly at you'; – a curious proof, among many others, of his fidelity to all the tastes of his youth, as it agrees perfectly with the description of his life at Newstead, in 1809, and of the sort of menagerie which his visitors had then to encounter in their progress through his hall.[2] Having escaped these dangers, I followed him up the staircase to the apartment destined for me. All this time he had been despatching servants in various directions – one, to procure me a *laquais de place*; another, to go in quest of Mr Alexander Scott,[3] to whom he wished to give me in charge; while a third was sent to order his Segretario to come to him. 'So then, you keep a Secretary?' I said. 'Yes,' he answered, 'a fellow who *can't write*[4] – but such are the names these pompous people give to things.'

When we had reached the door of the apartment it was discovered to be locked, and, to all appearance, had been so for some time, as the key could not be found; – a circumstance which, to my English apprehension, naturally connected itself with notions of damp and desolation, and I again sighed inwardly for the Gran Bretagna. Impatient at the delay of the key, my noble host, with one of his humorous maledictions, gave a vigorous kick to the door and burst it open; on which we at once entered into an apartment not only spacious and elegant, but wearing an aspect of comfort and habitableness which to a traveller's eye is as welcome as it is rare. 'Here,' he said, in a voice whose every tone spoke kindness and hospitality – 'these are the rooms I use myself, and here I mean to establish you.'

He had ordered dinner from some Trattoria, and while waiting its arrival – as well as that of Mr Alexander Scott, whom he had invited to join us – we stood out on the balcony, in order that, before the daylight was quite gone, I might have some glimpses of the scene which the Canal presented. Happening to remark, in looking up at the clouds, which were still bright in the west, that 'what had struck me in Italian sunsets was that peculiar rosy hue – ' I had hardly pronounced the word 'rosy', when Lord Byron, clapping his hand on my mouth, said, with a laugh, 'Come, d—n it, Tom *don't* be poetical.' Among the few gondolas passing at the time, there was one at some distance, in which sat two gentlemen, who had the appearance of being English; and, observing them to look our way, Lord Byron putting his arms a-kimbo, said with a sort of comic swagger, 'Ah! if you, John Bulls, knew who the two fellows are now standing up here, I think you *would* stare!' – I risk mentioning these things, though aware how they may be turned against myself, for the sake of the otherwise indescribable traits of manner and character which they convey. After a very agreeable dinner, through which the jest, the story, and the laugh were almost uninterruptedly carried on, our noble host took leave of us to return to La Mira . . . .

NOTES

The extract presents Moore's considerably expanded version, written some ten years after the event, of the meeting described in the previous extract.

1. The opening stanza of Canto IV of *Childe Harold*.

2. On Byron's 'menagerie', compare Medwin's account in his *Conversations of Lord Byron*, p. 3:

> His travelling equipage was rather a singular one . . . :seven servants, five carriages, nine horses, a monkey, a bull-dog and a mastiff, two cats, three pea-fowls and some hens (I do not know whether I have classed them in order of rank) formed part of his live stock; and all his books, consisting of a very large library of modern works (for he bought all the best that came out), together with a vast quantity of furniture.

3. An Englishman of independent means who resided in Venice and became friendly with Byron during this period.

4. Byron's joke: as Moore explains in a note, 'The title of *Segretario* is sometimes given, as in this case, to a head servant or house-steward.'

'A Thoroughly Spoilt Man'*

E. J. TRELAWNY

The Pilgrim moved about like a Pasha, with a host of attendants, and all that he and they required on the journey. So far as I could learn from Fletcher, his yeoman bold – and he had been with him from the time of his first leaving England – Byron, wherever he was, so far as it was practicable, pursued the same lazy, dawdling habits he continued during the time I knew him. He was seldom out of his bed before noon, when he drank a cup of very strong green tea, without sugar or milk. At two he ate a biscuit and drank soda-water. At three he mounted his horse and sauntered along the road – and generally the same road, – if alone, racking his brains for fitting matter and rhymes for the coming poem; he dined at seven, as frugally as anchorites are said in story-books to have done; at nine he visited the family of Count Gamba; on his return home he sat reading or composing until two or three o'clock in the morning, and then to bed, often feverish, restless, and exhausted – to dream, as he said, more than to sleep.

Records of Shelley, Byron, and the Author, pp. 37–41, 44–5, 52–9, 69–77.

Something very urgent, backed by the importunity of those who had influence over him, could alone induce him to break through the routine I have described, for a day, and it was certain to be resumed on the next – he was constant in this alone.

His conversation was anything but literary except when Shelley was near him. The character he most commonly appeared in was of the free and easy sort, such as had been in vogue when he was in London, and George IV was Regent; and his talk was seasoned with anecdotes of the great actors on and off the stage, boxers, gamblers, duellists, drunkards, etc., etc., appropriately garnished with the slang and scandal of that day. Such things had all been in fashion, and were at that time considered accomplishments by gentlemen; and of this tribe of Mohawks[1] the Prince Regent was the chief, and allowed to be the most perfect specimen. Byron, not knowing the tribe was extinct, still prided himself on having belonged to it; at nothing was he more indignant than at being treated as a man of letters, instead of as a Lord and a man of fashion: this prevented foreigners and literary people from getting on with him, for they invariably so offended. His long absence had not effaced the mark John Bull brands his children with; the instant he loomed above the horizon, on foot or horseback, you saw at a glance he was a Britisher. He did not understand foreigners, nor they him; and, during the time I knew him, he associated with no Italians except the family of Count Gamba. He seemed to take an especial pleasure in making a clean breast to all new-comers, as if to mock their previous conceptions of him, and to give the lie to the portraits published of him.

> The lunatic, the lover, and the poet
> Are of imagination all compact[2]

says our greatest Poet; and the Stoic philosophers denounced all poetry as lies. Men of genius are not to be measured by the ordinary standard of men; their organisation is different; they stand higher and see farther; we hope to see the diviner part of human nature exemplified in the life of a pre-eminent poet. Byron disenchanted me. He saw it, and said, as we were riding together alone, shortly after I knew him,

'Now, confess, you expected to find me a "Timon of Athens", or a "Timur the Tartar":[3] or did you think I was a mere sing-song driveller of poesy, full of what I heard Braham[4] at a rehearsal call "*Entusamusy*"; and are you not mystified at finding me what I am – a man of the world – never in earnest – laughing at all things mundane?' . . .

What Byron says of the world, that it will, perhaps, do Shelley justice when he can be no better for it, is far more applicable to himself. If the world erred, they did so in ignorance; Shelley was a myth to them. Byron had no such plea to offer.

Talking of the distinguishing quality of the humans,

TRE.: Shelley says it is superstition – Landor, that we have the worst of all the animals and the best of none.

BYRON: Man is a two-legged reptile, crafty and venomous. – After a pause, coming close to me, and smiling cynically, Everybody hates everybody.

TRE.: That's in his way.

He took no notice of this; he urged his horse, and we trotted a mile or two, then resumed our talk.

BYRON: I wrote thirty-five lines of *Don Juan* last night, or rather this morning; was stopped for a rhyme. It was in my head, there it stuck; strong waters could not loosen it, trotting has. I read it in a magazine, an old one, years ago, in a couplet quoted from Swift. He beat all the craft; he could find a rhyme for any word. To-night I shall write thirty more lines, and that will finish a canto – a thousand guineas. Murray now says pounds: I won't be stinted of my sizings. Murray told Tom Moore he was no judge of the morality; but sermons did not sell, and the *Don* had a 'devil of a sale'. I must make him a sinner, but he shall reform and end as a saint. . . .

TRE.: Shelley says he finds it far more irksome to write prose for publication than poetry.

BYRON: So do I. All this morning I was in labour at a letter to John Murray. It will be made public in his back parlour, where the rooks meet and will caw over it. They complain of my showing letters; mine go a regular circuit.

TRE.: Why do your London friends treat Shelley so cavalierly? they rarely notice him. He is as well born and bred as any of them. What are they afraid of?

BYRON, leeringly: He is not a Christian.

TRE.: Are they?

BYRON: Ask them.

TRE.: If I met the Devil at your table, I should treat him as a friend of yours.

Byron, scanning me keenly to see if I was jeering, said, 'The Devil is a Royal personage.' . . .

The next day, resuming the talk regarding Shelley –

BYRON: They don't dislike or fear Shelley; they are afraid of each other, and of poor innocent me. They spy a taint in my late writings, and think that I have fallen into bad hands. They say my orthodoxy is verging on heterodoxy. Their impression is, my popularity is declining. Cain,[5] they opine, is a suggestion of Shelley. (Turning to me) You are the only one of my visitors they approve of. You saved Rogers from a stumbling horse and a savage dog.

The dog story is this. On my nearing the passage leading to Byron's study, where Moretto[6] was as a sentinel to give notice to his master of any stranger's approach, I heard the dog's low growl, and a voice trying to quiet him, and evidently terrified. I hastened up, and found Rogers in a fix. The dog knew me, and so I convoyed the old poet through the pass. Byron was in the billiard-room, and I saw by his sinister look he had heard the row, knew it was Rogers, and maliciously enjoyed his visitor's terror. He advanced briskly towards him, saying, 'My dear Rogers, glad to see you; didn't know it was you', went on bantering him, saying to me, 'Excuse us for five minutes', took Rogers by the arm and led him into his *sanctum sanctorum*. He told me after that on hearing Rogers's voice in the passage he was giving the finishing touches to the most savage satire on him that he had ever written, repeating the last lines. 'I had only time to put it under the sofa, and he sat on it.'

Byron's malice was caused by a London correspondent accusing Rogers as the author of scandalous stories relating to Byron. Rogers was a silent, cautious, and excessively timid man, and had the reputation of saying, in his quiet way, sarcastic things. If a man acquires this reputation, he is debited with all the ill-natured scandal that society gloats on. Byron believing this (I did not; there was no proof), he should have been on his guard in his talk. On the contrary, it excited the poet, like a perverse child, to what he designated mystifying him. This game of equivocation – i.e. lying – had been in fashion with the young swells in Byron's time; to me it seemed simply perplexing people with exaggerated falsehoods. In this way Byron, to astonish and shock the demure and moral Rogers, and stock his budget, plied him with a highly-coloured catalogue of his delinquencies, glancing at me to mark his mystifications. Rogers was a good listener: his face expressed nothing, and he said nothing. My conviction was he believed nothing he had heard. Byron's intimates smiled at his vaunting of his vices, but comparative strangers stared, and noted his sayings to retail to their friends, and that is the way many scandals got abroad. George IV had made it the fashion, and the men about town were ashamed of being thought virtuous, and bragged of their profligacy. Byron, in his splenetic moods, if any one uttered moral or sentimental commonplace twaddle, sneered and scoffed, and denounced it as cant. The great poet, in the words of the greatest, 'Gave his worst of thoughts the worst of words'.[7] Under the same provocation, I and others have done the same. Byron's words were not lost, but noted and circulated, ours forgotten. The nicknames given us in our youth are generally appropriate. Byron was designated 'Baby Byron'; it fitted him to a T – wayward, capricious, lured by glitter and false lights and his vivid imagination, ever screaming after new toys and then picking them to pieces to see what they were made of, with nothing satisfied.

Byron on one occasion said 'What book is that?'

TRE.: The Life of a Poet.

He looked at the last chapter, saying 'If there is nothing in that, it's not worth reading.'

TRE.: There is a birth, marriage, and death; a eulogy on the author's genius and tedious criticisms on his works; nothing of the individuality of the man.

BYRON: Literary lives are compiled for the bibliopolists, as puffs to sell their wares; they are nothing. When I die you will see mine, written by myself.

TRE.: Will it be published as you have written it?

BYRON: Yes; I leave it in safe hands – Tom Moore's. He is pledged to publish, and omit words, but not garble facts. I have good security – he always wants money; my memoirs will bring it.

The poet could not forecast that Moore would get the money and not publish the book; that his bibliopolist's compilation – all puff and laudation to sell his stock – would be substituted – a lifeless life, giving no notion of the author, nothing told as Byron told it, and, excepting the letters it contains, unreadable and unread. Byron could not escape the poet's fate – his true life suppressed, and a bookish, elaborate eulogy of his poetry to sell his works substituted. Tom Moore, by his keen wit and continual practice, had perfected himself in the art of flattery; in his hands it was a fine art, and pleased all tastes. He deluded Byron into the belief that he was a thoroughly fearless and independent man; that he cared nothing for the world, its censure or praise; whereas Moore was the slave of forms, ceremony, and etiquette, excessively tenacious, and spoke of the big houses he frequented as if he controlled them. Moore's life is published: a sorry catalogue of lords, ladies, their dinners and parties. Where are they all? Vanished as shadows on the wall, 'alms for oblivion',[8] Moore will be remembered for his Irish melodies and his treachery in suppressing Byron's vindication of himself, particularly as he had read and approved of it and recommended the publication as necessary to prevent the fictitious slanders that might be spread after his death and that had been circulated during his life, and to set at rest the principal questions concerning his life. There was nothing in the memoirs that should have been omitted but the names of some people then living and some passages disconnected with his life. To these suggestions Byron readily assented.

What men say when two or three are gathered together in familiar talk I take no note of; they do not represent a man's deliberate sentiments. Byron never argued, said he could not. He admitted nothing and doubted everything; he had not made up his mind on any subject. His talk was in short sentences, generally in opposition. Mrs Shelley quoting with approval a sentiment from an Italian writer, Byron dissented, with sneers, and jibes, and irony. His reckless audacity and startling opinions made Mrs Shelley stare. Shelley, absorbed in thought, said little, and when they left Byron she reproached her husband for not advocating his own opinions. She said,

'Could Byron mean what he said?'

Shelley answered,

'No, certainly not; Byron never is in earnest except in the morning, when he is talking to one person, with whom he is at his ease. I was with him at one o'clock. He told me he had been writing all night, and had had no food but biscuits for three days, but had taken strong stimulants. The long-continued strain on his nerves and brain, intensified by his capricious way of life, disorders his mind. He wants food and rest; he is feverish, and that makes him fitful.'

Mrs Shelley: 'Great wit to madness nearly is allied'.[9]

In company Byron talked in Don Juan's vein; with a companion with whom he was familiar he thought aloud; with strangers, as others do, but not at his ease. I have said enough to show him as he was, a thoroughly spoilt man. . . .

Byron has been accused of drinking deeply. Our universities, certainly, did turn out more famous drinkers than scholars. In the good old times, to drink lustily was the characteristic of all Englishmen, just as tuft-hunting is now. Eternal swilling, and the rank habits and braggadocio manners which it engendered, came to a climax in George IV's reign. Since then, excessive drinking has gone out of fashion, but an elaborate style of gastronomy has come in to fill up the void; so there is not much gained. Byron used to boast of the quantity of wine he had drunk. He said, 'We young Whigs imbibed claret, and so saved our constitutions: the Tories stuck to port, and destroyed theirs and their country's.'

He bragged, too, of his prowess in riding, boxing, fencing, and even walking; but to excel in these things feet are as necessary as hands. In the water a fin is better than a foot, and in that element he did well; he was built for floating – with a flexible body, open chest, broad beam, and round limbs. If the sea were smooth and warm, he would stay in it for hours; but as he seldom indulged in this sport, and when he did, over-exerted himself, he suffered severely; which observing, and knowing how deeply he would be mortified at being beaten, I had the magnanimity when contending with him to give in.

He had a misgiving in his mind that I was trifling with him; and one day as we were on the shore, and the *Bolivar*[10] at anchor, about three miles off, he insisted on our trying conclusions; we were to swim to the yacht, dine in the sea alongside of her, treading water the while, and then to return to the shore. It was calm and hot, and seeing he would not be fobbed off, we started. I reached the boat a long time before he did; ordered the edibles to be ready, and floated until he arrived. We ate our fare leisurely, from off a grating that floated alongside, drank a bottle of ale, and I smoked a cigar, which he tried to extinguish – as he never smoked. We then put about, and struck off towards the shore. We had not got a hundred yards on our passage, when he retched violently, and, as that is often followed by cramp, I urged him to put his hand on my shoulder that I might tow him back to the schooner.

'Keep off, you villain, don't touch me. I'll drown ere I give in.'

I answered as Iago did to Roderigo,

'A fig for drowning! drown cats and blind puppies.'[11] I shall go on board and try the effects of a glass of grog to stay my stomach.'

'Come on,' he shouted, 'I am always better after vomiting.'

With difficulty I deluded him back; I went on board, and he sat on the steps of the accommodation-ladder, with his feet in the water. I handed him a wine-glass of brandy, and screened him from the burning sun. He was in a sullen mood, but after a time resumed his usual tone. Nothing could induce him to be landed in the schooner's boat, though I protested I had had enough of the water.

'You may do as you like', he called out, and plumped in, and we swam on shore.

He never afterwards alluded to this event, nor to his prowess in swimming, to me, except in the past tense. He was ill, and kept his bed for two days afterwards.

He said abruptly to me one day,

'I have been reading of men's sufferings after a wreck; they were nothing to what I have gone through in a country house, imprisoned with a family of Puritans, the only divertissement prayers and discourses on propriety and morality. A wreck must stir the blood, mine stagnated.' . . .

To return to his drinking propensities, after this digression about his gymnastic prowess: I must say, that of all his vauntings, it was, luckily for him, the emptiest – that is, after he left England and his boon companions, as I know nothing of what he did there. From all that I heard or witnessed of his habits abroad, he was and had been exceedingly abstemious in eating and drinking. When alone, he drank a glass or two of small claret or hock, and when utterly exhausted at night a single glass of grog; which when I mixed it for him I lowered to what sailors call 'water bewitched', and he never made any remark. I once, to try him, omitted the alcohol; he then said, 'Tre, have you not forgotten the creature comfort?' I then put in two spoonfuls, and he was satisfied. This does not look like an habitual toper. His English acquaintances in Italy were, he said in derision, all milksops. On the rare occasions of any of his former friends visiting him; he would urge them to have a carouse with him, but they had grown wiser. He used to say that little Tommy Moore was the only man he then knew who stuck to the bottle and put him on his mettle, adding, 'But he is a native of the damp isle, where men subsist by suction.'

Byron had not damaged his body by strong drinks, but his terror of getting fat was so great that he reduced his diet to the point of absolute starvation. He was of that soft, lymphatic temperament which it is almost impossible to keep within a moderate compass, particularly as in his case his lameness prevented his taking exercise. When he added to his weight, even standing was painful, so he resolved to keep down to eleven stone, or shoot himself. He said everything he swallowed was instantly converted into tallow and deposited on his ribs.

He was the only human being I ever met with who had sufficient self-restraint and resolution to resist this proneness to fatten: he did so; and at Genoa, where he was last weighed, he was ten stone and nine pounds, and looked much less. This was not from vanity about his personal appearance, but from a better motive; and as, like Justice Greedy, he was always hungry, his merit was the greater. Occasionally he relaxed his vigilance, when he swelled apace.

I remember one of his old friends saying, 'Byron, how well you are looking!' If he had stopped there it had been well, but when he added, 'You are getting fat', Byron's brow reddened, and his eyes flashed – 'Do you call getting fat looking well, as if I were a hog?' and, turning to me, he muttered, 'The beast, I can hardly keep my hands off him.' The man who thus offended him was the husband of the lady addressed as 'Genevra', and the original of his 'Zuleika', in *The Bride of Abydos*.[12] I don't think he had much appetite for his dinner that day, or for many days, and never forgave the man who, so far from wishing to offend, intended to pay him a compliment.

Byron said he had tried all sorts of experiments to stay his hunger, without adding to his bulk. 'I swelled', he said , 'at one time to fourteen stone, so I clapped the muzzle on my jaws, and, like the hibernating animals, consumed my own fat.'

He would exist on biscuits and soda-water for days together, then, to allay the eternal hunger gnawing at his vitals, he would make up a horrid mess of cold potatoes, rice, fish, or greens, deluged in vinegar, and swallow it like a famished dog. Either of these unsavoury dishes, with a biscuit and a glass or two of Rhine wine, he cared not how sour, he called feasting sumptuously. Upon my observing he might as well have fresh fish and vegetables, instead of stale, he laughed and answered,

'I have an advantage over you – I have no palate; one thing is as good as another to me.'

'Nothing', I said, 'disagrees with the natural man, he fasts and gorges, his nerves and brains don't bother him; but if you wish to live –'

'Who wants to live?' he replied, 'not I. The Byrons are a short-lived race on both sides, father and mother: longevity is hereditary: I am nearly at the end of my tether. I don't care for death a damn: it is her sting I can't bear – pain.'

His habits and want of exercise damaged him, not drink. It must be borne in mind, moreover, that his brain was always working at high pressure. The consequences resulting from his way of life were low or intermittent fevers; these last had fastened on him in his early travels in the Levant; and there is this peculiarity in malaria fevers, that if you have once had them, you are ever after peculiarly susceptible to a renewal of their attacks if within their reach, and Byron was hardly ever out of it. Venice and Ravenna are belted in with swamps, and fevers are rife in the autumn. By starving his body Byron kept his brains clear; no man had brighter eyes or a clearer voice; and his resolute bearing and prompt replies, when excited, gave his body an appearance of muscular power that imposed on strangers. I never doubted, for he was indifferent to life, and prouder than Lucifer, that if he had drawn his sword in Greece, or elsewhere, he would have thrown away the scabbard.

NOTES

On Trelawny see p. 27.

1. Mohawks (also spelt Mohocks) were upper-class rowdies who created disturbances in the London streets.

2. Shakespeare, *A Midsummer Night's Dream*, V.i.7–8.

3. Timon of Athens is the misanthropic hero of Shakespeare's tragedy of that name. Timur the Tartar, also known as Tamerlane (died 1405), was a ruthless conqueror and is the subject of Marlowe's play.

4. John Braham (?1774–1856), a tenor associated with Drury Lane Theatre from 1805 (Byron was for a time a member of the theatre's Sub-Committee of Management).

5. Byron's tragedy *Cain* was published in 1821.

6. Byron's bulldog.

7. Adapted from Shakespeare's *Othello*, III.iii.132–3.

8. Shakespeare's *Troilus and Cressida*, III.iii.146.

9. Misquoted from Dryden's *Absalom and Achitophel*, I.164 ('Great Wits are sure to Madness near allied').

10. Byron's schooner, named after the South American patriot Simon Bolivar (1783-1830).

11. A confusion of two separate quotations in *Othello*, I.iii: 'Virtue! a fig!' (line 323), and 'Come, be a man: drown thyself! drown cats and blind puppies' (lines 339–40).

12. The reference is to James Wedderburn Webster (see p. 43), who visited Byron in Genoa in the autumn of 1822. Webster had by this time separated from his wife, who is said to have been in Byron's mind when he wrote *The Bride of Abydos* (1813), the original title of which was *Zuleika*.

'A Most Eccentric Character'*

ANONYMOUS

Whilst Lord Byron remained at Ancona . . . he was returning into the city after nine o'clock in the evening, and was stopped at the Levant Gate by the guard, who, considering him from his dress a wine-mountaineer or Ragusan peasant, demanded of him his passport. He refused to show one, and would give no account of himself, so that they had him conveyed in a '*carshal*', or spring-cart, opposite the 'Spread Eagle Hotel' (the Austrian arms), where he beckoned to the attendants whom he saw standing at the gate. The cart was stopped, and he got out. The guard then began to be alarmed, fearing they had made some grand mistake; but, having enjoyed his joke, and been satisfied that his *queer dress* had deceived the penetration of the guard, and occasioned them no little surprise and confusion, he laughed heartily at the joke, and paid them well for the trouble he had given them.

On another occasion, his Lordship and Captain Crawley having been out sporting, were allowed to pass into Zante after sunset free of toll, '*not having the appearance of gentlemen!*' Such, however, were the expressions of the collector as he let them pass, and his Lordship was never more delighted than when 'appearances were against him', and 'the knowing ones were taken in'. . . .

Lord Byron patronised a little female singer of the Opera-house at Venice, named Henriette; she was far from being a favourite, but his Lordship's notice made her popular, particularly amongst the English, although she met few of them in Lord Byron's company. This lady applied for an engagement during the absence of his Lordship, and met with a positive refusal. When he returned she was performing at the Ancona theatre. His Lordship presently resolved to lower the crest of the manager, and he threw three rooms in the old palace of Gordoni into one, which he fitted up for the reception of musical parties. He engaged four of the best singers, and most of the principal dancers, to

*The Life, Writings, Opinions and Times of . . . Lord Byron . . . by an English Gentleman, in the Greek Military Service, and Comrade of his Lordship (London, 1825) I, 367-74.

perform there, and tickets were disposed of amongst his numerous connections, and still more numerous admirers, at six zeleemes each, the whole of the receipts being for the benefit of Signora Henriette. The consequence of this opposition was nearly the ruin of the Opera-house; all the rank and fashion of Venice attended, it becoming quite the rage. The manager of the Opera-house humbled himself in vain during two whole seasons, out of which the Opera-house had been closed *fifty-nine* nights for want of audiences; the scheme was then abandoned, not in mercy to the manager, but because the Signora Henriette was married to a Lieutenant in the Navy – now Captain J —, and relinquished performing altogether. That officer was well aware of her former character, and though (from Lord Byron's patronage) she had amassed a pretty considerable fortune, he did not stand in need of it, as he had an independence besides his commission; he married her, therefore, as she sang – *con amore*. It was for a long time believed that many of the songs composed for this opposition theatre were written by Lord Byron; but the fact was he never wrote a line of them, though to this hour they appear in Venice with his name attached to them. His punishment of the poor manager, who would not engage a second-rate singer at a first-rate salary, was severe; and his Lordship seldom evinced so much spleen on any other occasion; but it was eccentric, energetic, and effectual; in a word – *à la Byron*.

Lord Byron's aquatic excursions, the ardour with which he sought out all manner of strange characters, and the report of his liberality to merit or enterprise of every kind, produced many strange adventures, and were a teeming source of amusement to him. Every one was eager for the honour of attending him, and there was not a gondolier in Venice, or a mariner in the Adriatic, who did not look upon the *English Lord* as one of their own *fraternity*, and would have run any risk to oblige or serve him. He was very partial to the island of Sabioncello, which lies in the neighbourhood of the city of Ragusa. He generally went thither in a four-oared gondola, in company with the Marchioness G[uiccioli], and two or three friends. His writing materials he took care never to be without, and the lady took her sketch-book: she had a good taste for landscape painting. A curious incident once occurred on one of these voyages: there are several small islands on the way, and they often touched at them to refresh, shoot, or fish, for a few hours. The Lesser Grossa is a rock barely covered with verdure, and not more than half a mile long, and about as much in breadth. Early one day they all landed on it; and as there is a fine spring near its centre, where the only shelter from the sun can be found under some bushes, they resolved to dine near that spot. The gondoliers were set to work, lighting a fire, and cooking fish, and all the party for two hours enjoyed themselves without reflection or care. When they thought on embarking, lo! the boat, which was slightly made fast to the rocks, had drifted out to sea, and they beheld her the sport of the waves, full two leagues from land. They were twenty miles from Sabioncello, and the islands nearer were not inhabited. His Lordship laughed heartily at the dreadful visages of his companions; but it was really no laughing matter, as boats or vessels very seldom came near the place. They had guns, ammunition, and fishing-tackle in plenty, and some provisions; but in the boat there was store for a week, for which they might now sigh in vain. They began by erecting a flag-staff, on which they hoisted a white silk cloak belonging to the lady, as a signal of distress, and by the means of cloaks spread over the bushes, they formed a kind of tent; and had no alternative but to wait patiently until they should be starved to death by cold or hunger, or relieved by some chance vessel observing their signal, and hearing their guns, which they fired at intervals. The weather was fine, and the tent being occupied by the lady, the gentle-men slept around, like Bedouin Arabs in an encampment. Whilst their spirits and wine held out they were not much depressed; but two nights passed in this situation put them all into a state of alarm, and they began to think of making a raft, but not a stick thicker than a man's thumb grew on the place; to swim from isle to isle was impracticable, and even Lord Byron began to look despondingly, when a Venetian, nicknamed *Cyclops*, from being blind of one eye, suggested a plan, and at once, stimulated by the greatness of the reward held out to him, and by his own sense of danger, proceeded to put it into immediate execution. Sabioncello was ill supplied with water, and they had brought a cask to fill at this spring; this cask they contrived to cut through with their knives, and with a couple of sticks for paddles, Cyclops placed himself in a tub composed of one half of the cask, and to their great joy it floated with him very well. With a little spirits to comfort him, he launched out to sea in this novel bark, and rolled along at a tolerable rate for an hour, when, getting into a current of great rapidity, he was hurried out of sight. As the current set in for the main land, they doubted not that he would be able to get assistance, and they were right; for on the following morning, before day, Cyclops returned, to their inexpressible joy, in a six-oared galley, with ample store of fruits and wine to recruit their drooping and exhausted natures. He had been carried in his tub beyond the island of Sabioncello, and landed at the town of Macarlisa, not far from Ragusa; having made a voyage of thirty miles in six hours, in such a vehicle as never man before floated so far in. Lord Byron paid Cyclops liberally, and when they returned to Venice, purchased him a new gondola, and called her *The Tub*, in memory of his exploit, of which he was justly proud and vain-glorious. The boat which had drifted from the rock was picked up four leagues off at sea, by a Venetian trader, and carried to Venice. The papers on board, and other things, were all known to belong to Lord Byron; the boat was recognised by the gondoliers' wives and families, and most alarming reports were in circulation relative to the fate of the whole party. His Lordship's friends sent out boats on the search, and the general opinion was, that they had been taken by pirates, who, knowing the value of their prisoners, had abandoned the boat as of no consequence. His Lordship had never told any one whither he was going, as was usual with him on such excursions, or much trouble and anxiety might have been spared to all his friends at Venice on this occasion. The party proceeded to Ragusa, where a second boat and supplies being obtained, they all landed, as originally intended, at Sabioncello. Lord Byron did not even think of writing to Venice, not having any idea of the consternation that prevailed there concerning them; for they had not a thought of their boat having been preserved, and carried into its port of destination. . . .

Talking of gondoliers, as one of that fraternity was one day rowing an English gentleman along one of the canals of Venice, Lord Byron and his party passed in another gondola. 'There goes your great countryman', said the gondolier to his passenger. 'What great country-man?' – 'Lord Byron, the great poet.' 'He is a most eccentric charac-ter, I have heard.' 'He is so, Signor; but as good a bit of stuff as ever was put together. Heaven knows best, to be sure, why it made him a *lord* and a *poet*; but, by Santa Maria! it spoiled a good *gondolier* by so doing.'

NOTE

This gossipy three-volume work, which offered the titbit of 'copious recollec-tions of the lately destroyed memoirs', was published anonymously and has been ascribed to Matthew Iley.

Teresa Guiccioli*

THOMAS MEDWIN

Calling on Lord Byron one evening after the opera, we happened to talk of *Cavalieri Serventi*,[1] and Italian women; and he contended that much was to be said in excuse for them, and in defence of the system.

'We will put out of the question', said he, 'a *Cavalier Serventeism*; that

---

Medwin's Conversations of Lord Byron, pp. 22–4.

1. Byron at Harrow (1801), pencil sketch, signed T. W.

2. Byron and Robert Rushton (1808), by George Sanders.

3. Portrait of Byron (1813), by Richard Westall.

4. Byron in Albanian dress (1814), by Thomas Phillips.

5. Byron aged 26 (1814), by Thomas Phillips.

6. Byron at Pisa (1822), engraving by C. Turner based on a painting by W. C. West.

7. 'A Noble Poet Scratching up his Ideas', cartoon (1823).

8. 'The Burning of Shelley's Body' (1889), by L. E. Fournier.

is only another term for prostitution, where the women get all the money they can, and have (as is the case in all such contracts) no love to give in exchange. – I speak of another, and of a different service.'

'Do you know how a girl is brought up here?' continued he. 'Almost from infancy she is deprived of the endearments of home, and shut up in a convent till she has attained a marriageable or marketable age. The father now looks out for a suitable son-in-law. As a certain portion of his fortune is fixed by law for the dower of his children, his object is to find some needy man of equal rank, or a very rich one, the older the better, who will consent to take his daughter off his hands, under the market price. This, if she happen to be handsome, is not difficult of accomplishment. Objections are seldom made on the part of the young lady to the age, and personal or other defects of the intended, who perhaps visits her once in the parlour as a matter of form or curiosity. She is too happy to get her liberty on any terms, and he her money or her person. There is no love on either side. What happiness is to be expected, or constancy, from such a *liaison*? Is it not natural, that in her intercourse with a world, of which she knows and has seen nothing, and unrestrained mistress of her own time and actions, she should find somebody to like better, and who likes her better, than her husband? The Count Guiccioli, for instance, who is the richest man in Romagna, was sixty when he married Teresa; she sixteen.[2] From the first they had separate apartments, and she always used to call him *Sir*. What could be expected from such a preposterous connection? For some time she was an Angiolina, and he a Marino Faliero,[3] a good old man; but young women, and your Italian ones too, are not satisfied with your good old men. Love is not the same dull, cold, calculating feeling here as in the North. It is the business, the serious occupation of their lives; it is a want, a necessity. Somebody properly defines a woman, "a creature that loves". They die of love; particularly the Romans: they begin to love earlier, and feel the passion later than the Northern people. When I was at Venice, two dowagers of sixty made love to me. – But to return to the Guiccioli. The old Count did not object to her availing herself of the privileges of her country; an *Italian* would have reconciled him to the thing: indeed for some time he winked at our intimacy, but at length made an exception against me, as a foreigner, a heretic, an Englishman, and, what was worse than all, a liberal.

'He insisted – the Guiccioli was as obstinate; her family took her part. Catholics cannot get divorces. But, to the scandal of all Romagna, the matter was at length referred to the Pope, who ordered her a separate maintenance, on condition that she should reside under her father's roof. All this was not agreeable, and at length I was forced to smuggle her out of Ravenna, having disclosed a plot laid with the sanction of the Legate for shutting her up in a convent for life, which she narrowly escaped. . . .'

NOTES

On Medwin see p. 24. On Teresa Guiccioli, see the notes to the next extract.

1. Acknowledged lovers of married women (Italian).

2. The date of her birth is not known for certain, but it seems likely that at the time of the marriage she was eighteen and her husband fifty-seven. See Iris Origo, *The Last Attachment* (1949) p. 493.

3. The reference is to Byron's drama *Marino Faliero* (1821).

'The Handsomest of Men'*

TERESA GUICCIOLI

The Almighty has created beings of such harmonious and ideal beauty that they defy description or analysis. Such a one was Lord Byron. His wonderful beauty of expression has never been rendered either by the brush of the painter or the sculptor's chisel. It summed up in one magnificent type the highest expression of every possible kind of beauty. If his genius and his great heart could have chosen a human form by which they could have been well represented, they could not have chosen another! Genius shone in his very looks. All the effects and emotions of a great soul were therein reflected as well as those of an eminently good and generous heart, and indeed contrasts were visible which are scarcely ever united in one and the same person. His eyes seized and betrayed the sentiments which animated him, with a rapidity and transparency such as called forth from Sir Walter Scott the remark, that the fine head of his young rival 'was like unto a beautiful alabaster vase lightened up by an interior lamp'. To see him, was to understand thoroughly how really false were the calumnies spread about as to his character . The mass, by their obstinacy in identifying him with the imaginary types of his poems, and in judging him by a few eccentricities of early youth, as well as by various bold thoughts and expressions, had represented to themselves a factitious Byron, totally at variance with the real man. Calumnies, which unfortunately he passed over in disdainful silence, have circulated as acknowledged facts. Time has destroyed many, but it would not be correct to say that they have all entirely been destroyed. Lord Byron was silent, because he depended upon time to silence his calumniators.

* My Recollections of Lord Byron, and Those of Eye-witnesses of his Life (New York: Harper, 1869) pp. 58–69.

All those who saw him must have experienced the charm which surrounded him as a kind of sympathetic atmosphere, gaining all hearts to him. What can be said to those who never saw him? Tell them to look at the pictures of him which were painted by Saunders, by Phillips, by Holmes, or by Westall?[1] All these, although the works of great artists, are full of faults. Saunders's picture represents him with thick lips, whereas his lips were harmoniously perfect: Holmes almost gives him a large instead of his well-proportioned and elegant head! In Phillips's picture the expression is one of haughtiness and affected dignity, never once visible to those who ever saw him.

'These portraits', says Dallas, 'will certainly present to the stranger and to posterity that which it is possible for the brush to reproduce so far as the features are concerned, but the charm of speech and the grace of movement must be left to the imagination of those who have had no opportunity to observe them. No brush can paint these.'

The picture of Byron by Westall is superior to the others, but does not come up to the original. As for the copies and engravings which have been taken from these pictures, and circulated, they are all exaggerated, and deserve the appellation of caricatures.

Can his portrait be found in the descriptions given by his biographers? But biographers seek far more to amuse and astonish, in order that their writings may be read, than to adhere to the simple truth.

It can not be denied, however, that in the portraits which several, such as Moore, Dallas, Sir Walter Scott, Disraeli in London, the Countess Albrizzi at Venice, Beyle (Stendhal) at Milan, Lady Blessington and Mrs Shelley in Italy, have drawn of Lord Byron there is much truth, accompanied by certain qualifications which it is well to explain. I shall therefore give in their own words (preferring them to my own impressions) the unanimous testimony of those who saw him, be they friends or beings for whom he was indifferent. Here are Moore's words: – 'Of his face, the beauty may be pronounced to have been of the highest order, as combining at once regularity of features with the most varied and interesting expression.

'His eyes, though of a light grey, were capable of all extremes of expression, from the most joyous hilarity to the deepest sadness, from the very sunshine of benevolence to the most concentrated scorn or rage. But it was in the mouth and chin that the great beauty as well as expression of his fine countenance lay.

'His head was remarkably small, so much so as to be rather out of proportion with his face. The forehead, though a little too narrow, was high, and appeared more so from his having his hair (to preserve it, as he said) shaved over the temples. Still the glossy dark-brown curls, clustering over his head, gave the finish to its beauty. When to this is added that his nose, though handsomely was rather thickly shaped, that his teeth were white and regular, and his complexion colourless, as good an idea perhaps as it is in the power of mere words to convey may be conceived of his features.

'In height he was, as he himself has informed us, five feet eight inches and a half, and to the length of his limbs he attributed his being such a good swimmer. His hands were very white, and, according to his own notions of the size of hands as indicating birth, aristocratically small.'

'What I chiefly remember to have remarked', adds Moore, 'when I was first introduced to him, was the gentleness of his voice and manners, the nobleness of his air, his beauty, and his marked kindness to myself. Being in mourning for his mother, the colour as well of his dress, as of his glossy, curling and picturesque hair, gave more effect to the pure, spiritual paleness of his features, in the expression of which, when he spoke, there was a perpetual play of lively thought, though melancholy was their habitual character when in repose.'

When Moore saw him again at Venice, some eight years after the first impressions which Byron's beauty had produced upon him in London (1812), he noted a change in the character of that beauty.

'He had grown fatter both in person and face, and the latter had most suffered by the change – having lost by the enlargement of the features some of that refined and spiritualised look that had in other times distinguished it. . . . He was still, however, eminently handsome, and in exchange for whatever his features might have lost of their high romantic character, they had become more fitted for the expression of that arch, waggish wisdom, that Epicurean play of humour, which he had shown to be equally inherent in his various and prodigally gifted nature; while by the somewhat increased roundness of the contours the resemblance of his finely-formed mouth and chin to those of the Belvedere Apollo had become still more striking.' . . .

Here is the portrait of him which another lady (the Comtesse Albrizzi of Venice) has drawn, notwithstanding her wounded pride at the refusal of Lord Byron to allow her to write a portrait of him and to continue her visits to him at Venice: –

'What serenity on his forehead! What beautiful auburn, silken, brilliant, and naturally curled hair! What variety of expression in his sky-blue eyes! His teeth were like pearls, his cheeks had the delicate tint of a pale rose; his neck, which was always bare, was of the purest white. His hands were real works of art. His whole frame was faultless, and many found rather a particular grace of manner than a fault in the slight undulation of his person on entering a room. This bending of the body was, however, so slight that the cause of it was hardly ever inquired into.'

As I have mentioned the deformity of his foot, even before quoting other testimonies to his beauty, I shall tarry a while and speak of this defect, the only one in so pre-eminently favoured a being. What was this defect, since all becomes illustrious in an illustrious man? Was it visible? Was it true that Lord Byron felt this imperfection so keenly? Here is the truth.

No defect existed in the formation of his limbs; his slight infirmity was nothing but the result of weakness of one of his ankles.

His habit of ever being on horseback had brought on the emaciation of his legs, as evinced by the post-mortem examination; besides which, the best proof of this has been lately given in an English newspaper much to the following effect: –

'Mrs Wildman (the widow of the colonel who had bought Newstead) has lately given to the Naturalist Society of Nottingham several objects which had belonged to Lord Byron, and among others his boot and shoe trees. These trees are about nine inches long, narrow, and generally of a symmetrical form. They were accompanied by the following statement of Mr Swift, bootmaker, who worked for his lordship from 1805 to 1807. Swift is still alive, and continues to reside at Southwell. His testimony as to the genuineness of the trees, and to the nature of Lord Byron's deformity, of which so many contradictory assertions have circulated, is as follows: –

William Swift, bootmaker at Southwell, Nottinghamshire, having had the honour of working for Lord Byron when residing at Southwell from 1805 to 1807, asserts that these were the trees upon which his lordship's boots and shoes were made, and that the last pair delivered was on 10 May 1807. He, moreover, affirms that his lordship had not a club foot, as has been said, but that both his feet were equally well formed, one, however, being an inch and a half shorter than the other. The defect was not in the foot but in the ankle, which, being weak, caused the foot to turn out too much. To remedy this his lordship wore a very light and thin boot, which was tightly laced just under the sole, and, when a boy, he was made to wear a piece of iron with a joint at the ankle, which passed behind the leg and was tied behind the shoe. The calf of this leg was weaker than the other, and it was the left leg.

(Signed)   WILLIAM SWIFT'

This, then, is the extent of the defect of which so much has been said, and which has been called a deformity. As to its being visible, all those who knew him assert that it was so little evident that it was even impossible to discover in which of the legs or feet the fault existed. To the testimonies already quoted I must add another: –

'His defect', says Mr Galt, 'was scarcely visible. He had a way of walking which made it appear almost imperceptible, and indeed entirely so. I spent several days on board a ship with him without discovering this defect; and, in truth, so little perceptible was it that a doubt always existed in my mind whether it might not be the effect of a temporary accident rather than a natural defect.'

All those who knew him being therefore agreed in this opinion, that of people who were not acquainted with him is of no value. But if, in the material appreciation of a defect, they have not been able to err, several have erred in their moral appreciation of the fact by pretending that Lord Byron, for imaginary reasons, was exceedingly sensible of this defect. This excessive sensibility was a pure invention on the part of his biographers. When he did experience it (which was never but to a very moderate extent), it was only because, physically speaking, he suffered from it. Under the sole of the weak foot he at times experienced a painful sensation, especially after long walks.

'Once, at Genoa,' says Mme G, 'he walked down the hill of Albaro to the seaside with me, by a rugged and rough path. When we had reached the shore he was very well and lively. But it was an exceedingly hot day, and the return home fatigued him greatly. When home I told him I thought he looked ill. "Yes," said he, "I suffer greatly from my foot; it can hardly be conceived how much I suffer at times from that pain", and he continued to speak to me about this defect with great simplicity and indifference.'

He used often even to laugh at it, so superior was he to that weakness. 'Beware,' said Count Gamba to him on one occasion while riding with him, and on reaching some dangerous spot, 'beware of falling and breaking your neck.' 'I should decidedly not like it', said Byron; 'but if this leg of which I don't make much use were to break, it would be the same to me, and perhaps then I should be able to procure myself a more useful one.'

The sensitiveness, therefore, which he was said to experience, and which would have been childish in him, was in reality only the occasional experience of a physical pain which did not, however, affect his strength, nor the grace of his movements, in all those physical exercises to which he was so much attached. It in no wise altered his good looks, and, as a proof of this, I shall again bring testimonies, giving first that of MN, who was at Constantinople when Byron arrived there for the first time, and who thus describes him in a review which he wrote of him after Byron's death: –

'A stranger then entered the bazaar. He wore a scarlet cloak, richly embroidered with gold in the style of an English aide-de-camp's dress uniform. He was attended by a janissary attached to the English Embassy and by a cicerone: he appeared to be about twenty-two. His features were of so exquisite a delicacy, that one might almost have given him a feminine appearance, but for the manly expression of his fine blue eyes. On entering the inner shop he took off his hat, and showed a head of curly auburn hair, which improved in no small degree the uncommon beauty of his face. The impression his whole appearance made upon my mind, was such that it has ever remained most deeply engraven on it; and although fifteen years have since gone by, the lapse of time has not in the least impaired the freshness of the recollection.' Then, speaking of his manner, he goes on to say: 'There was so irresistible an attraction in his manner, that only those who have been so fortunate as to be admitted to his intimacy can have felt its power.'

Moore once asked Lady Holland whether she believed that Lady Byron had ever really loved Lord Byron. 'Could it be otherwise?' replied Lady Holland. 'Was it possible not to love so lovable a creature? I see him there now, surrounded as it were by that great light: oh, how handsome he was!'

One of the most difficult things to define was the colour of his eyes. It was a mixture of blue, grey, and violet, and these various colours were each uppermost according to the thought which occupied his mind or his heart. 'Tell me, dear,' said the little Eliza [Smith] to her sister, whose enthusiasm for Byron she shared, 'tell me what is the colour of his eyes?' 'I can not say; I believe them to be dark,' answered Miss Eliza, 'but all I know is that they have quite a supernatural splendour.' And one day, having looked at them with greater attention in order to ascertain their colour, she said, 'They are the finest eyes in the world, but not dark, as I had at first believed. Their hue is that of the eyes of Mary Stuart, and his long, black eye-lashes make them appear dark. Never did I before, nor ever again shall I, see such eyes! As for his hands, they are the most beautiful hands, for a man, I ever saw. His voice is a sweet melody.'

Sir Walter Scott was enchanted when he could dilate on the extraordinary beauty of Byron. One day, at Mr Home Drummond's, he exclaimed: – 'As for poets, I have seen the best that this country has produced, and although Burns had the finest eyes that can be imagined, I never thought that any man except Byron could give an artist the exact idea of a poet. His portraits do not do him the least justice; the varnish is there, but the ray of sunshine is wanting to light them up. The beauty of Byron', he added 'is one which makes one dream.'

Colonel Wildman, his colleague at Harrow, and his friend, was always wont to say, 'Lord Byron is the only man among all those I have seen, who may be called, without restriction, a really handsome man.'

Disraeli, in his novel entitled *Venetia*[1837], speaks thus of the beauty of Hubert (who is Lord Byron) when Venetia finds his portrait: –

'That being of supernatural beauty is her father. Young as he was, command and genius, the pride of noble passions, all the glory of a creative mind, seemed stamped upon his brow. With all his marvellous beauty he seemed a being born for greatness. . . . Its reality exceeded the wildest dreams of her romance, her brightest visions of grace and loveliness and genius seemed personified in this form. He was a man in the very spring of sunny youth and of radiant beauty. He was above the middle height, yet with a form that displayed exquisite grace. . . . It was a countenance of singular loveliness and power. The lips and the moulding of the chin resembled the eager and impassioned tenderness of the shape of Antinous; but instead of the effeminate sullenness of the eye, and the narrow smoothness of the forehead, shone an expression of profound and piercing thought. On each side of the clear and open brow descended, even to the shoulders, the clustering locks of golden hair; while the eyes large and yet deep, beamed with a spiritual energy, and shone like two wells of crystalline water that reflect the all-beholding heavens.'

M Beyle (Stendhal) writes to Mr Swanton Belloc: – 'It was in the autumn of the year 1816 that I met Lord Byron at the theatre of the Scala, at Milan, in the box of the Bremen Minister. I was struck with Lord Byron's eyes at the time when he was listening to a sestetto in Mayer's opera of *Elena*. I never in my life saw any thing more beautiful or more expressive. Even now, when I think of the expression which a great painter should give to genius, I always have before me that magnificent head. I had a moment of enthusiasm.' And further, he adds that one day he saw him listening to Monti while the latter was singing his first couplet in the *Mascheroniana*. 'I shall never forget', said he, 'the divine expression of his look; it was the serene look of genius and power.'

I might multiply these testimonies of people who have seen him, and fill many pages; their particular character is their uniform resemblance. This proves the soundness of the ground on which their truth is based. I will add one more testimony to the others, that of Mrs Shelley, which is even nearer the truth, and condenses all the others: – 'Lord Byron', said this distinguished woman, 'was the first genius of his age and the handsomest of men.' . . .

This inability on the part of artists and biographers to render exactly Byron's features and looks, is not to be wondered at, for although perfectly regular, his features derived their principal beauty from the life which his soul instilled into them. The emotions of his heart, the changes of his thoughts, appeared so variously upon his countenance, and gave the latter so changeable a cast, that it sufficed not for the artist who had to portray him, to gaze at and study him, as one generally does less gifted or elevated organisations. The reality was more likely to be well interpreted when it stood a prey to the various emotions of the soul; in his leisure hours, in the full enjoyment of life and love, he was satisfied with the knowledge that he was young, handsome, beloved, and admired. Then it was that his beauty became, as it were, radiant and brilliant like a ray of sunshine.

The time to see him was when, under the influence of genius, his soul was tormented with the desire of pouring out the numberless ideas and thoughts which flooded his mind: at such moments one scarcely dared approach him, awed, as it were, by the feeling of one's own nothingness in comparison with his greatness. Again, the time to see him was when, coming down from the high regions to which a moment before he had soared, he became once more the simple child adorned with goodness and every grace; taking an interest in all things, as if he were really a child. It was impossible then to refrain from the contemplation of this placid beauty, which, without taking away in the least from the admiration which it inspired, drew one toward him, and made him more accessible to one, and more familiar by lessening a little the distance which separated one from him. But, above all, he should have been seen during the last days of his stay in Italy, when his soul had to sustain the most cruel blows; when heroism got the better of his affections, of his worldly interests, and even of his love of ease and tranquillity; when his health, already shaken, appeared to fail him each day more and more, to the loss of his intellectual powers. Had one seen him then as we saw him, it would scarcely have been possible to paint him as he looked. Does not genius require genius to be its interpreter? Thorwaldsen alone has, in his marble bust of him, been able to blend the regular beauty of his features with the sublime expression of his countenance. Had the reader seen him, he would have exclaimed with Sir Walter Scott, 'that no picture is like him'.

NOTES

Teresa Guiccioli, born Teresa Gamba Ghiselli, came of an aristocratic family of Ravenna, and was born in about 1799. Shortly after leaving the convent school where she was educated, she married (1818) the wealthy Count Alessandro Guiccioli, who was about three times her age. A few days after her marriage she met Byron for the first time, and they became lovers in 1819. The Pope granted her a decree of separation in 1820, and she and Byron lived happily together until his departure for Greece. She visited England in 1832 and subsequently remarried and settled in Paris. Her book *Lord Byron Jugé par les Témoins de sa Vie* was published in Paris in 1868, and a translation by H. E. H. Jerningham appeared in London in the same year. She also wrote a still largely unpublished book, *Vie de Lord Byron en Italie*. Teresa died in 1879. See Austin K. Gray, *Teresa: The Story of Byron's Last Mistress* (1948); Iris Origo, *The Last Attachment* (1949).

1. George Sanders, a fashionable painter, executed several portraits of Byron; the earliest of them (about 1807) is reproduced in Marchand, opposite p. 162. Thomas Phillips painted Byron three times and was responsible for the well-known portrait of Byron in Albanian dress (1814), now in the National Portrait Gallery (Plate 4). James Holmes painted a miniature of Byron in 1816 (Marchand, opposite p. 556), and Richard Westall a portrait in about 1813, also in the National Portrait Gallery (Plate 3).

Life at Pisa I*

EDWARD E. WILLIAMS

[2 Dec 1821.] Walk with Jane in the evening and meet Lord B's party – with whom we shoot. Lord B hit, at the distance of 14 yards, the bull's eye four times, and a half-crown piece three. The last shot struck the piece of money so exactly in the centre that it was afterwards found with the ball enclosed within it – the sides being drawn to the centre like a three-cornered cocked hat.

[9 Jan 1822.] Dined with Lord B — He told me that during the composition of his *Corsair* he was in a very low state of mind, turning night into day, the sight of which he could not endure. He lived chiefly upon biscuits and soda water, and completed the poem in ten nights – and almost without correcting a line. *The Bride of Abydos* he wrote in three days, – but *Lara* cost him a longer time than any of his others, having been composed on his return from several parties, balls etc. during a very gay part of his life when the allied powers were in England. – return very late.

[12 Mar.] Dined with Lord B — It is a singular circumstance that this personage should be so insensible to his real merit. During dinner S[helley] repeated some of the finest lines of *Childe Harold*, and Lord B after listening to a stanza – cried 'Heavens! Shelley, what infinite nonsense are you quoting?'

[24 Mar – 3 Apr.] Went to dine at [the] S[helley]s and after sitting for a considerable time waiting for their return home I was surprised at the lateness of the evening – Trelawny at length came in and told us that Lord B's party consisting of himself, Shelley, Captain Hay,[1] Count Gamba (the son), Taaffe,[2] and the Countess [Guiccioli] with Mrs S[helley] behind in the carriage when a mounted dragoon dashed through their party, and touched Taaffe's Horse as he passed in an insolent and defying manner – Lord B put spurs to his horse saying –

Maria Gisborne and Edward E. Williams: Shelley's Friends: Their Journals and Letters, ed. Frederick L. Jones (Norman, Okla: University of Oklahoma Press, 1951) pp. 116, 124, 133, 136–41, 162–3.

that he should give some account of such insolence – S[helley]'s horse however was the fleetest and coming up to the Dragoon he crossed and stopped him till the party arrived, but they had now reached the gate, where a guard was stationed, and finding himself so well supported, he drew his sword and after abusing them all as cursed English (*male detto Inglese*) began to cut and slash to the right and left – saying he arrested them all – and what signified it to him if he had the blood of all the English [?] – Do that if you can said Lord B and dashed through the Guard with young Count G[amba] and reached home to bring arms for what he expected would turn to a serious scuffle – The Dragoon finding the rest of the party intended to force their way, made a desperate cut at Shelley who took off his cap and warding the blow from the sharp part of the sabre the hilt struck his head and knocked him from his horse, the fellow was repeating a cut at S[helley] while down, when Captain Hay parried with a cane he held in hand, but the sword cut it in two, and struck Captain H's face across the nose – a violent scene now took place and the dragoon tried to get into the town and escape, when Lord B arrived, and half drawing a sword stick to show that he was armed the fellow put up his sword – and begged of Lord B to do the same – It was now dark and after walking a few paces with Lord B he put his horse into a gallop, and endeavoured to get off, but on passing Lord B's House, a servant had armed himself with a pitch fork, and speared him as he passed – He fell from his horse and was carried to the hospital – the wound is in the abdomen –

Trelawny had finished his story when Lord B came in – the Countess fainting on his arm – S[helley] sick from the blow – Lord B and the young Count foaming with rage – Mrs S[helley] looking philosophically upon this interesting scene – and Jane and I wondering what the Devil was to come next – A surgeon came in, and Lord B took him with the Countess home – where she was bled and soon came round – Taaffe next entered, and after having given his deposition at the Police, returned to us with a long face saying that the Dragoon could not live out the night – All soon again sallied forth to be the first to accuse, and according to Italian policy not wait to be accused – All again return mutually recriminated and recriminating.

9 o'clock – The report already in circulation about Pisa is that a party of peasants having risen in insurrection made an attack upon the guard headed by some Englishmen – that the guard maintained their ground manfully against an awful number of the armed insurgents – that they were at length defeated – one Englishman whose name was Trelawny left dead at the gate, and Lord B mortally wounded, who is now telling me the tale–and T drinking brandy and water by his side–

10 [o']clock. How the attack ought to have been conducted is now agitating – all appear to me to be wrong. 11 o'clock – disperse to our separate homes.

Monday, 25 March. Cloudy. At 7 this morning an officer from the Police called here demanding my name – country – Profession – and requesting to have an account of my actions between the hours of 6 and 8 yesterday evening – My servants told him I was then asleep, but that they could inform him, that I was engaged in a very bloody scene between those hours – Then he must come to the Police Office – Ask him said I if I am to bring the *scene* with me – or the whole play as far as I have written – 12 o'clock. S[helley] calls. The wounded dragoon much worse – Hear that the Soldiers are confined to their barracks, but they swear to be revenged on some of us – The Countess G[uiccioli] better as well as Captain Hay. A report is now abroad that Taaffe is the assassin and is now confined in Lord B's house guarded by bulldogs etc. to avoid the Police – This he overheard himself while walking down the Lung'Arno – S[helley] and T[relawny] think it necessary to go armed – a skaite strap is therefore substituted for a pistol belt and my pistols so slung to T's waist.

2 [o'clock]. Sallied forth – very much stared and pointed at – Called on Lord B — heard that extreme unction had been administered to the Dragoon whose wound is considered mortal – A deposition is drawn up and sent with all the signatures concerned to the Police –

The Grand Duke expected tonight –

4 o'clock. The Dragoon dying – 1/2 past 4 all armed with swordsticks – pistols etc. mount as usual, amidst a great crowd that surround the door. Nothing new on their return except a great crowd *to see them dismount.*

10 o'clock. S[helley] called here after having been with Lord B. The Dragoon much worse – The Grand Duke arrived –

Tuesday, 26 March. Cloudy. Shelley calls to Breakfast – He received a note from a lady last night desiring him not to venture near her House after dark for the friends of the Dragoon were on the look-out for him, although they did not consider him as most to blame.

The young Gamba joined a party of gossips that had collected round a *Spezeria* and joining the conversation as if he had been unconcerned in the business, saying it was a pity that the man was so dangerously wounded – 'Ah! the only pity is' said a fellow 'that in ten days the affair will be forgotten and the cursed English will go abroad as secure as ever.'

Jane's music master comes, and informs us that the report is, the Dragoon is better, but raves like a madman against the English –

11 o'clock. Called on S[helley] previous to going to Captain Hay's – met there Vaccà[3] who had just quitted his patient the Dragoon – V thinks him better but not out of danger. The man's story is that he was held by one of Lord B's servants while the other stabbed him – and that he should never have drawn his sword had he not been horse-whipped by some one of the party – this was strongly denied by us to V who seems to view the thing in a most unfavourable light – and

declares that in any court of justice he could swear conscientiously that the wound was given with a stiletto – having 3 sides like a bayonet.

Called on Captain Hay with S[helley] – found him doing well but his face is much cut and bruised – On our mentioning to him what we considered a falsehood in the Dragoon's having said he was struck, Hay confirmed the fact by saying the young Count Gamba cut him with his whip as he passed – The affair consequently takes a serious turn in the man's favour.

3 o'clock. Called on Lord B. The Police had only proceeded so far as to require the evidence of his Courier – Suspicion as to the person who really stabbed the Dragoon is much excited – nothing else new – They ride as usual –

7 o'clock. The wound neither better nor worse – Trelawny dined with us and Mary passed the evening. It is a singular circumstance that an affair of a similar nature occurred to one of this man's brothers – and having been cured of a wound which he had received in a scuffle he awaited concealed for the person whom he suspected – stabbed him to the heart and flung him into the river! –

Wednesday, 27 March. Fine. The man better than yesterday and hopes are entertained – It is S[helley]'s opinion that on recovery this man will demand the *satisfaction of a gentleman* – and some of the *most respectable* Italians think that it ought not to be refused to him – S breakfasted here, and we afterwards went to the Post together – A letter from Roberts[4] to T[relawny] informs us that the boat will not be finished in less than 12 or 14 days –

On our way met the young Count Gamba with a deposition from a gentleman of the name of Crawfurd who from a balcony [had] seen Lord B return – He says that Lord B did not dismount from his horse but called to the servants from the door; that they brought him a walking stick with which he returned to meet the dragoon, who on seeing him, put out his hand which Lord B accepted, demanding his name – At this moment one of Lord B's servants interposed and pushed the Dragoon from his master's side, and on the Dragoon's putting his horse into a gallop, he observed a man rush at him with a pole and nearly thrust him from his horse, from which he fell shortly afterwards. Lord B seemed collected, and on requiring of the Dragoon some explanation of his conduct – he replied 'This is not the place' – and spurred onward when he met the fatal blow from the pitchfork.

12 o'clock. Walked with T[relawny] – met S[helley] and sailed up the River with him –

4 o'clock. Went with S[helley] to Lord B's – The man remains in the same state. Taaffe who during the affair could not be found and who has since talked so greatly of his valour on the occasion has been named by Jane *False Taaffe*. Walked with Mary and Jane and met the Countess G[uiccioli] who accompanied us –

At 9 p.m. Trelawny and S[helley] called – went to Lord B's together

– found him engaged in a letter to the British Ambassador. His servants Tita and Vincenzo had been examined and Vincenzo acquitted, when the silly fellow accompanied Tita back to make his deposition, who though innocent was mad enough to go into Court armed with a stiletto and a brace of pistols – They were consequently both imprisoned and remain confined in separate cells. Left Lord B at 11 – during our stay th[ere] his Secretary was sent for by the Police and examined but nothing transpired.

Thursday, 28 March. Fine. Vaccá, who is prejudiced, says the man is neither better nor worse, and is further convinced of the wound having been given with a stiletto, as it passed through the Dragoon's swordbelt and left a mark or hole that he could not mistake. Todd's[5] opinion is, that the man is bett[er]. [A] report in Pisa is, that Lord B and all his servants with 4 English gentlemen were taken in Lord B's house last night, after a desperate resistance – that 40 brace of pistols were discovered, stilettos etc. – and at Leghorn they have it, that the party returning home Sunday evening attacked a division [of] Dragoons, and after being taken [pr]isoners stabbed 3 of them in the [ba]ck, and that Lord B and all the [o]thers had fled to Lucca –

12 o'clock. Man as before – [no]thing new –

4 o'clock. Walked with Mary and Jane – all quiet –

5 [o'clock]. Say a party of dragoons on [the] bridge watching Lord B's party as it passed –

7 [o'clock]. Mary dined. Antonio the Countess G[uiccioli]'s servant confined with the others.

Went to the Theatre –

Friday, 29 March. Fine. The Dragoon much better, and likely to do well. It is singular that Vaccá who has been so forward to instigate the police should have pronounced the man out of danger 3 days ago.

10 [o'clock]. Walked with Jane to the Botanical Garden, a place fitted for the improvement of the young students – but nothing to the advancement of the science. There is a fossil museum and other curiosities here, but nothing worthy any particular notice that I saw.

1 o'clock. Called on Captain Hay – found him doing well. He had heard that my name had been substituted for his in the affair – that my nose had been cut off, and that Lord B and myself had left Pisa with as many horses as could be put to the carriage.

2 o'clock. Vincenzo and another man liberated. Strong suspicions on Antonio the Countess's man – Called on Lord B. He had received an answer from Mr Dawkins the Chargé d' Affaires at Florence offering every assistance, but speaking very lightly of the affair – Nothing new, excepting that a law officer from Florence arrives to take the several depositions.

Taafe['s] conduct highly blamable – but his very deposition damns him.

7 [o'clock]. Trelawny dined – and passed the Evening.

Saturday, 30 March. Fine. Shelley breakfasted. The dragoon considerably recovered and doing well. – Nothing new – At Florence the
reports are favourable to us –

Wrote a few lines. Walked with Mary and Jane. Called on the
Countess – Wrote to Roberts at Genoa about a House. Passed the
evening with [the] S[helley]s.

Sunday, 31 March. Cloudy. Strong wind. All well – the man yet in
confinement – Sailed with Trelawny up the Arno – Called on Lord B –
played at billiards till 5 – Dined with Mary – and passed the evening.

Monday, 1 April. Cloudy – and piercing cold – strong wind –
Walked with Jane to the Botanical Garden – Called on Trelawny –
and walked with him. Heard from Roberts about the boat – Called on
Lord B – The dragoon is recovering fast but swears to be revenged
when he gets on his legs again . . . .

Tuesday, 2 April. Cloudy – April showers at intervals – At 1/2 past
nine went with Jane to Leghorn. . . .

Trelawny wrote to Lord B acquainting him with certain information
he had received relative to Mr Taaffe's conduct in the late affair – Lord
B and the party therefore requested me to wait on Taaffe and make
certain enquiries of him. This was done rather to the satisfaction of the
party – T having exculpated himself from most of the charges. Called
on Lord B and returned at 12.

Wednesday, 3 April. Fine. Walked with Jane – Called on Taaffe to
learn further of the business – on Lord B acquainting him with it –
Lord B willing to give his hand to Taaffe as usual – all right again –
Mrs B[eauclerc?] wrote to Lord B requesting his interference with
Trelawny and enclosing all the notes that had passed between them –
devil of an affair – all parties quarrelling – and everybody defaming
everybody –

[6 July 1822.] In Lord B's family all is confusion – The cutthroats he
is so desirous to have about him have involved him in a second affair,
and although the present banishment of the Gambas from Tuscany is
attributed to the first affair of the Dragoon, the continued disturbances
among his and their servants is I am sure a principal cause for its being
carried into immediate effect. Four days, (commencing from the day of
our arrival at Leghorn) were only given them to find another retreat –
and as Lord B considers this a personal though tacit attack upon
himself he chooses to follow their fortunes in another country – Genoa
was first selected, but of that Government they could have no hope –
Geneva was then proposed and this proved as bad, if not worse. Lucca
is now the choice and Trelawny was despatched last night to feel their
way with the Governor to whom he carried letters. All this time Hunt is
shuffled off from day to day; and now Heaven only knows how or when
it will end – Lord B's reception of Mrs H was, as S[helley] tells me,

most shameful – She came into his house sick and exhausted, and he scarcely deigned to notice her – was silent and scarcely bowed – This conduct cut H to the soul . . . .

NOTES

Edward Ellerker Williams (1793-1822) settled in Italy after serving in India and became a friend of Byron and Shelley. Shelley introduced him to Byron on 5 November 1821. His wife Jane is commemorated in several of Shelley's poems. Williams began his journal on 21 October 1821 and continued it until 4 July 1822, during which period he saw Byron frequently. For his drowning, see p. 97. An earlier edition of the *Journal* (1902) has an introduction by Richard Garnett but presents an unreliable text.

   1. Captain John Hay arrived in Pisa in January 1822. Byron had known him earlier in England: at Brighton in 1808 Byron had bet him 100 guineas that he (Byron) would never marry.
   2. John Taaffe, an Irishman who had settled in Italy, met Byron in November 1821.
   3. Dr Vaccá, a surgeon and friend of the Shelleys.
   4. Captain Daniel Roberts supervised the building of boats for Byron and Trelawny.
   5. Dr John Todd, an English physician.

Life at Pisa II*

LEIGH HUNT

Upon seeing Lord Byron, I hardly knew him, he was grown so fat; and he was longer in recognising me, I had grown so thin. He was dressed in a loose nankeen jacket and white trousers, his neckcloth open, and his hair in thin ringlets about his throat; altogether presenting a very different aspect from the compact, energetic, and curly-headed person, whom I had known in England.

He took me into an inner-room, and introduced me to a young lady in a state of great agitation. Her face was flushed, her eyes lit up, and her hair (which she wore in that fashion) looking as if it streamed in

Lord Byron and Some of his Contemporaries, pp. 16–17, 39, 43–6.

disorder. This was the daughter of Count Gamba, wife of the Cavaliere Guiccioli, since known as Madame, or the Countess, Guiccioli, – all the children of persons of that rank in Italy bearing the title of their parents. The Conte Pietro, her brother, came in presently, also in a state of agitation, and having his arm in a sling. I then learned, that a quarrel having taken place among the servants, the young Count had interfered, and been stabbed. He was very angry; Madame Guiccioli was more so, and would not hear of the charitable comments of Lord Byron, who was for making light of the matter. Indeed there was a look in the business a little formidable; for, though the stab was not much, the inflicter of it threatened more, and was at that minute keeping watch under the portico with the avowed intention of assaulting the first person that issued forth. I looked out of window, and met his eyes glaring upward, like a tiger. The fellow had a red cap on, like a sans-culotte, and a most sinister aspect, dreary and meagre, a proper caitiff. Thus, it appeared, the house was in a state of blockade; the nobility and gentry of the interior all kept in a state of impossibility by a rascally footman.

How long things had continued in this state I cannot say; but the hour was come when Lord Byron and his friends took their evening ride, and the thing was to be put an end to somehow. Fletcher, the valet, had been despatched for the police, and was not returned. It was wondered, among other things, how I had been suffered to enter the house with impunity. Somebody conceived, that the man might have taken me for one of the constituted authorities; a compliment which few Englishmen would be anxious to deserve, and which I must disclaim any pretensions to. At length we set out, Madame Guiccioli earnestly entreating 'Bairon' to keep back, and all of us waiting to keep in advance of Conte Pietro, who was exasperated. It was a curious moment for a stranger from England. I fancied myself pitched into one of the scenes in *The Mysteries of Udolpho*,[1] with Montoni and his tumultuous companions. Every thing was new, foreign, and violent. There was the lady, flushed and dishevelled, exclaiming against the *scelerato*;[2] the young Count, wounded and threatening; the assassin, waiting for us with his knife; and last, not least in the novelty, my English friend, metamorphosed, round-looking, and jacketed, trying to damp all this fire with his cool tones, and an air of voluptuous indolence. He had now, however, put on his loose riding-coat of mazarin blue, and his velvet cap, looking more lordly than before, but hardly less foreign. It was an awkward moment for him, not knowing what might happen; but he put a good face on the matter; and as to myself, I was so occupied with the novelty of the scene, that I had not time to be frightened. Forth we issue at the door, all squeezing to have the honour of being the boldest, when a termination is put to the tragedy by the vagabond's throwing himself on a bench, extending his arms, and bursting into tears. His cap was half over his eyes; his face gaunt, ugly, and unshaved; his appearance altogether more squalid and miserable than an Englishman would conceive it possible to find in such an establishment. This blessed figure reclined weeping and wailing, and asking pardon for his offence; and to crown all, he requested Lord Byron to kiss him.

The noble Lord conceived this excess of charity superfluous. He pardoned him, but said he must not think of remaining in his service; and the man continued weeping, and kissing his hand. I was then amused with seeing the footing on which the gentry and their servants stand with each other in Italy, and the good-nature with which the fiercest exhibitions of anger can be followed up. . . .

Our manner of life was this. Lord Byron, who used to sit up at night, writing *Don Juan* (which he did under the influence of gin and water), rose late in the morning. He breakfasted; read; lounged about, singing an air, generally out of Rossini, and in a swaggering style, though in a voice at once small and veiled; then took a bath, and was dressed; and coming downstairs, was heard, still singing, in the courtyard, out of which the garden ascended at the back of the house. The servants at the same time brought out two or three chairs. My study, a little room in a corner, with an orange tree peeping in at the window, looked upon this courtyard. I was generally at my writing when he came down, and either acknowledged his presence by getting up and saying something from the window, or he called out, 'Leontius!'[3] and came halting up to the window with some joke, or other challenge to conversation. (Readers of good sense will do me the justice of discerning where anything is spoken of in a tone of objection, and where it is only brought in as requisite to the truth of the picture.) His dress, as at Monte-Nero, was a nankeen jacket, with white waistcoat and trousers, and a cap, either velvet or linen, with a shade to it. In his hand was a tobacco-box, from which he helped himself like unto a shipman, but for a different purpose; his object being to restrain the pinguefying impulses of hunger. Perhaps also he thought it good for the teeth. We then lounged about, or sat and talked, Madame Guiccioli with her sleek tresses descending after her toilet to join us. . . .

When the heat of the day declined, we rode out, either on horseback or in a barouche, generally towards the forest. He was a good rider, graceful, and kept a firm seat. He loved to be told of it, and being true, it was a pleasure to tell him. Good God! what homage might not that man have received, and what love and pleasure reciprocated, if he could have been content with the truth, and had truth enough of his own to think a little better of his fellow-creatures! But he was always seeking for uneasy sources of satisfaction. The first day we were going out on horseback together, he was joking upon the bad riding of this and that acquaintance of his. He evidently hoped to have the pleasure of adding me to the list; and finding, when we pushed forward, that there was nothing particular in the spectacle of my horsemanship, he said in a tone of disappointment, 'Why, Hunt, you ride very well!' Trelawny sometimes went with us, on a great horse, smoking a cigar. We had blue frock-coats, white waistcoats and trousers, and velvet caps *à la Raphael*; and cut a gallant figure. Sometimes we went as far as a vineyard, where he had been accustomed to shoot at a mark, and where the brunette lived, who came into his drawing-room with the basket of flowers. The father was an honest-looking man, who was in trouble with his landlord, and heaved great sighs; the mother a loud swarthy woman, with hard lines in her face. There was a little sister, delicate-looking and melancholy, very different from the confident though not unpleasing countenance of the elder, who was more handsome. They all, however, seemed good-humoured. We sat under an arbour, and had figs served up to us, the mother being loud in our faces, and cutting some extraordinary jokes, which made me any thing but merry. Upon the whole, I was glad to come away. . . .

Of an evening I seldom saw him. He recreated himself in the balcony, or with a book; and at night, when I went to bed, he was just thinking of setting to work with *Don Juan*. His favourite reading was history and travels. I think I am correct in saying that his favourite authors were Bayle[4] and Gibbon. . . .

Lord Byron's collection of books was poor, and consisted chiefly of new ones. . . . He was anxious to show you that he possessed no Shakespeare and Milton; 'because', he said, 'he had been accused of borrowing from them!' He affected to doubt whether Shakespeare was so great a genius as he has been taken for, and whether fashion had not a great deal to do with it; an extravagance, of which none but a patrician author could have been guilty. . . . Spenser he could not read; at least he said so. All the gusto of that most poetical of the poets went with him for nothing. I lent him a volume of *The Faerie Queene* and he said he would try to like it. Next day he brought it to my study-window, and said, 'Here, Hunt, here is your Spenser. I cannot see anything in him'; and he seemed anxious that I should take it out of his hands, as if he was afraid of being accused of copying so poor a writer. That he saw nothing in Spenser is not very likely; but I really do not think that he saw much. Spenser was too much out of the world, and he too much in it. It would have been impossible to persuade him, that Sandys's Ovid was better than Addison's and Croxall's.[5] He wanted faith in the interior of poetry, to relish it, unpruned and unpopular. Besides, he himself was to be mixed up somehow with every thing, whether to approve it or disapprove. When he found Sandys's Ovid among my books, he said, 'God! what an unpleasant recollection I have of this book! I met with it on my wedding-day; I read it while I was waiting to go to church.' Sandys, who is any thing but an anti-bridal poet, was thenceforward to be nobody but an old fellow who had given him an unpleasant sensation. The only great writer of pastimes, whom he read with avowed satisfaction, was Montaigne . . . .

NOTES

On Leigh Hunt, see p. 22. There are, again, some interesting variations of tone between the account given here and that offered much later in Hunt's *Autobiography* (see p. 22): for instance, in the description of the fracas in Byron's household, the reference to Byron's behaviour ('trying to damp all this fire with his cool tones, and an air of voluptuous indolence') was modified to 'Nobody, however, could have put a better face on the matter than Lord Byron did – composed, and endeavouring to compose . . . .'

    1. Mrs Radcliffe's novel, published in 1794, had enjoyed a great success and is one of the few examples of 'Gothic' fiction still remembered.

    2. Scoundrel, villain.

    3. Facetious Latinising of 'Leigh Hunt'.

    4. Pierre Bayle (1647-1706), French *Philosophe*, author of the *Dictionnaire historique et critique* (1697–1702).

    5. George Sandys's translation of Ovid's *Metamorphoses* was published in 1621–6. Joseph Addison and Samuel Croxall both contributed to Garth's *Ovid's Metamorphoses Translated* (1717).

The Cremation of Williams and Shelley*

E. J. TRELAWNY

We walked along the shore to the grave, where Byron and Hunt soon joined us; they, too, had an officer and soldiers from the tower of Migliarino, an officer of the Health Office, and some dismounted dragoons, so we were surrounded by soldiers; but they kept the ground clear, and readily lent their aid. There was a considerable gathering of spectators from the neighbourhood, and many ladies richly dressed were amongst them. The spot where the body lay was marked by the gnarled root of a pine tree.

    A rude hut, built of young pine-tree stems, and wattled with their branches, to keep the sun and rain out, and thatched with reeds, stood

*Records of Shelley, Byron, and the Author, I, 206–14.

on the beach to shelter the look-out man on duty. A few yards from this was the grave, which we commenced opening – the Gulf of Spezia and Leghorn at equal distances of twenty-two miles from us. As to fuel I might have saved myself the trouble of bringing any, for there was an ample supply of broken spars and planks cast on the shore from wrecks, besides the fallen and decaying timber in a stunted pine forest close at hand. The soldiers collected fuel whilst I erected the furnace, and then the men of the Health Office set to work, shovelling away the sand which covered the body, while we gathered round, watching anxiously. The first indication of their having found the body was the appearance of the end of a black silk handkerchief – I grubbed this out with a stick, for we were not allowed to touch anything with our hands – then some shreds of linen were met with, and a boot with the bone of the leg and the foot in it. On the removal of a layer of brushwood, all that now remained of my lost friend was exposed – a shapeless mass of bones and flesh. The limbs separated from the trunk on being touched.

'Is that a human body?' exclaimed Byron; 'why, it's more like the carcase of a sheep, or any other animal, than a man: this is a satire on our pride and folly.'[1]

I pointed to the letters EEW on the black silk handkerchief.

Byron looking on, muttered, 'The entrails of a worm hold together longer than the potter's clay of which man is made. Hold! let me see the jaw', he added, as they were removing the skull, 'I can recognise any one by the teeth, with whom I have talked. I always watch the lips and mouth: they tell what the tongue and eyes try to conceal.'

I had a boot of Williams's with me; it exactly corresponded with the one found in the grave. The remains were removed piecemeal into the furnace.

'Don't repeat this with me', said Byron; 'let my carcase rot where it falls.'

The funereal pyre was now ready; I applied the fire, and the materials being dry and resinous the pine-wood burnt furiously, and drove us back. It was hot enough before, there was no breath of air, and the loose sand scorched our feet. As soon as the flames became clear, and allowed us to approach, we threw frankincense and salt into the furnace, and poured a flask of wine and oil over the body. The Greek oration was omitted, for we had lost our Hellenic bard. It was now so insufferably hot that the officers and soldiers were all seeking shade.

'Let us try the strength of these waters that drowned our friends', said Byron, with his usual audacity. 'How far out do you think they were when their boat sank?'

'If you don't wish to be put into the furnace, you had better not try; you are not in condition.'

He stripped, and went into the water, and so did I and my companion. Before we got a mile out, Byron was sick, and persuaded to return to the shore. My companion, too, was seized with cramp, and reached the land by my aid. At four o'clock the funereal pyre burnt low, and when we uncovered the furnace, nothing remained in it but dark-coloured ashes, with fragments of the larger bones. Poles were now put under the red-hot furnace, and it was gradually cooled in the sea. I gathered together the human ashes, and placed them in a small oak-box, bearing an inscription on a brass plate, screwed it down, and placed it in Byron's carriage. He returned with Hunt to Pisa, promising to be with us on the following day at Viareggio. I returned with my party in the same way we came, and supped and slept at the inn. On the following morning we went on board the same boats, with the same things and party, and rowed down the little river near Viareggio to the sea, pulled along the coast towards Massa, then landed, and began our preparations as before.

Three white wands had been stuck in the sand to mark the Poet's grave, but as they were at some distance from each other, we had to cut a trench thirty yards in length, in the line of the sticks, to ascertain the exact spot, and it was nearly an hour before we came upon the grave.

In the meantime Byron and Leigh Hunt arrived in the carriage, attended by soldiers, and the Health Officer, as before. The lonely and grand scenery that surrounded us so exactly harmonised with Shelley's genius, that I could imagine his spirit soaring over us. The sea, with the islands of Gorgona, Capraja, and Elba, was before us; old battlemented watch-towers stretched along the coast, backed by the marble-crested Apennines glistening in the sun, picturesque from their diversified outlines, and not a human dwelling was in sight. As I thought of the delight Shelley felt in such scenes of loneliness and grandeur whilst living, I felt we were no better than a herd of wolves or a pack of wild dogs, in tearing out his battered and naked body from the pure yellow sand that lay so lightly over it, to drag him back to the light of day; but the dead have no voice, nor had I power to check the sacrilege – the work went on silently in the deep and unresisting sand, not a word was spoken, for the Italians have a touch of sentiment, and their feelings are easily excited into sympathy. Byron was silent and thoughtful. We were startled and drawn together by a dull hollow sound that followed the blow of a mattock; the iron had struck a skull, and the body was soon uncovered. Lime had been strewn on it; this, or decomposition, had the effect of staining it of a dark and ghastly indigo colour. Byron asked me to preserve the skull for him; but remembering that he had formerly used one as a drinking-cup,[2] I was determined Shelley's should not be so profaned. The limbs did not separate from the trunk, as in the case of Williams's body, so that the corpse was removed entire into the furnace. I had taken the precaution of having more and larger pieces of timber, in consequence of my experience of the day before of the difficulty of consuming a corpse in the open air with our apparatus. After the fire was well kindled we repeated the ceremony of the previous day; and more wine was poured over Shelley's dead body than he had consumed during his life. This with the oil and salt made the yellow flames glisten and quiver. The heat from the sun and fire was so intense that the atmosphere was tremulous and wavy. The corpse fell open and the heart was laid bare. The frontal bone of the skull, where it had been struck with the mattock, fell off; and, as the back of the head rested on the red-hot bottom bars of the furnace, the brains literally seethed, bubbled, and boiled as in a cauldron, for a very long time.

Byron could not face this scene, he withdrew to the beach and swam off to the *Bolivar*. Leigh Hunt remained in the carriage. The fire was so fierce as to produce a white heat on the iron, and to reduce its contents to grey ashes. The only portions that were not consumed were some fragments of bones, the jaw, and the skull; but what surprised us all was that the heart remained entire. In snatching this relic from the fiery furnace, my hand was severely burnt; and had any one seen me do the act I should have been put into quarantine.

After cooling the iron machine in the sea, I collected the human ashes and placed them in a box, which I took on board the *Bolivar*. Byron and Hunt retraced their steps to their home, and the officers and soldiers returned to their quarters. I liberally rewarded the men for the admirable manner in which they behaved during the two days they had been with us.

As I undertook and executed this novel ceremony, I have been thus tediously minute in describing it. A sage critic remarks that I performed this cremation in a bungling manner, that I should have used a gas retort. My answer is that neither gas nor retorts were then known in Italy. He further remarks that bodies washed on shore were obliged to be burnt; that is an error. Bodies washed on shore were buried in the sand above the wash of the sea, and as the Inquisition no longer burnt heretics, I followed the practice of the Hindus in using a funereal pyre.

In all cases of death from suffocation the heart is gorged with blood; consequently it is the more difficult to consume, especially in the open air.

Byron's idle talk during the exhumation of Williams's remains did not proceed from want of feeling, but from his anxiety to conceal what he felt from others. When confined to his bed and racked by spasms, which threatened his life, I have heard him talk in a much more unorthodox fashion, the instant he could muster breath to banter. He had been taught during his town-life that any exhibition of sympathy or feeling was maudlin and unmanly, and that the appearance of daring and indifference denoted blood and high breeding.

NOTES

On Trelawny, see p. 27. Shelley and Williams set off from Leghorn in the sailing-boat *Don Juan* on 8 July 1822 and were never seen alive again. Their bodies were found washed ashore on 16 and 18 July and were promptly buried on the beach in accordance with local health regulations. That of Williams was exhumed and cremated on 15 August and that of Shelley on the following day. Trelawny wrote at least a dozen accounts of the episode, the first almost immediately afterwards (see note 1), the last in 1878. See Leslie A. Marchand, 'Trelawny on the Death of Shelley', *Keats–Shelley Memorial Bulletin*, IV (1952) 9–34. In his *Journal*, under the date 12 July 1828 (p. 178), Thomas Moore describes Byron's premonition of Shelley's death: according to Moore's informant, Byron had told him that he had seen Shelley 'walking into a little wood at Lerici, when it was discovered afterwards that Shelley was at that time in quite another direction. "This", said Byron, in a sort of awe-struck voice, "was about ten days before his death."'

1. Compare the version given by Trelawny more than half a century earlier in a letter dated 15 August 1822 (*Letters of Edward John Trelawny*, p. 8):

Lord B looking at it said – 'Are we all to resemble that? – why it might be the carcase of a sheep for all I can see' – and pointing to the black handkerchief – said 'an old rag retains its form longer than a dead body – what a nauseous and degrading sight!'

2. In 1808, when a human skull was unearthed at Newstead Abbey, Byron had it set in silver at a cost of 17 guineas and made into a drinking-cup. See his poem written at that time, 'Lines Inscribed upon a Cup Formed from a Skull'. Hamlet holding a skull is a favourite pictorial subject, and the invitation to regard him as a Hamlet-figure was probably conscious on Byron's part.

A Clergyman Visits Lord Byron*

ANONYMOUS

It was [in Genoa] that I had an introduction to the extraordinary man, who at this moment forms the topic of conversation in every circle, and whose recent death will now be sincerely regretted, as having happened at the early age of 37, when he was exerting himself in the glorious cause of Greece, and when he was really turning his great talents to a noble and useful purpose. The first and only time that I ever had an opportunity of conversing with Lord Byron, was at Genoa; and however one may differ in opinion, with such restless spirits as himself who figure in the world, and occupy an unusual portion of its

*Blackwood's Magazine, XV (June 1824) 696–701.

regards, rather from the abuse and perversion of their powers of mind, than from a right application of them; yet it would argue a curious taste, to be indifferent to the accident which throws us in their way. For my own part, I shall value as one of the most interesting in my life, the short interval which I passed with the greatest poet of his age, and I have been turning to my diary, to refer to every particular of an interview, which I carefully noted down on the day in which it took place, while every impression was yet fresh upon my mind. . . .

Lord Byron had been residing some weeks at or near Genoa, when I arrived in that city; many English families were there at the same time, and the eccentric bard was the subject of general conversation. From some of my countrymen I learnt that his lordship was to be seen every night at the opera; from others, that he frequently rode through the streets on horseback, with a party of his friends, armed with swords by their sides, and pistols at their holsters; and from all, that he avoided an Englishman with comtempt and detestation. Such were the reports, but it never fell to my lot to converse with anybody who could speak from personal observation, to the truth of either of these accounts; and I afterwards discovered that they were totally incorrect. . . .

The next day, my friend called upon me at my hotel, and inquired if I had any wish to be introduced to Lord Byron. I signified my surprise at having the option offered to me, as I had been informed that Lord Byron carefully avoided his countrymen. 'The inquisitive and the impertinent,' said he, 'but not others; and I am sure you will have no reason to regret the interview.'

A day was appointed, that Lord Byron might be apprised of the intended introduction, and when it came, Mr —— and I set out from Genoa together, and walked to Albaro, where the noble poet was then residing. . . .

The approach to the part of Albaro where the noble poet dwelt, is by a narrow lane, and on a steep ascent. The palace is entered by lofty iron gates that conduct into a court-yard, planted with venerable yew trees, cut into grotesque shapes. After announcing our arrival at the portal, we were received by a man of almost gigantic stature, who wore a beard hanging down his breast to a formidable length. . . .[1]

By this Goliath of valets we were ushered through a spacious hall, accommodated with a billiard-table, and hung round with portraits, into his Lordship's receiving-room, which was fitted up in a complete style of English comfort. It was carpeted and curtained; a blazing log crackled in the grate, a hearth-rug spread its soft and ample surface before it, a small reading-table, and lounging-chair, stood near the fire-place; and not far from them, an immense oval-table groaned under the weight of newly published quartos and octavos, among other books, which lay arranged in nice order upon it.

In a few seconds after we entered, Lord Byron made his appearance from a room which opened into this; he walked slowly up to the fire-place, and received me with that unreserved air, and good-humoured smile, which made me feel at ease at once, notwithstanding all my prognostications to the contrary. This first impression made upon me was this – that the person who stood before me, bore the least possible resemblance to any bust, portrait, or profile, that I had ever seen, professing to be his likeness; nor have I since examined any which I could consider a perfect resemblance. The portrait in possession of Mr Murray,[2] from which most of the prints seem to be taken, does not strike me as one in which the features of the original are to be recognised at first sight, which perhaps may be owing to the affected position, and studied air and manner, which Lord B assumed when he sat for it. Neither is the marble bust by Bartolini[3] a performance, with whose assistance I should pronounce the lines and lineaments of the Bard could be distinguished at a glance.

It struck me that Lord Byron's countenance was handsome and intellectual, but without being so remarkably such as to attract attention, if it were not previously known whom he was. His lips were full and of a good colour; the lower one inclined to a division in the centre: and this, with what are called gap-teeth (in a very slight degree), gave a peculiar expression to his mouth. I never observed the play of features, or the characteristics of physiognomy, more narrowly than I did Lord Byron's, during the whole period of a very animated conversation, which lasted nearly two hours, and I could not but feel all my Lavaterian[4] principles staggered, by discovering so few indications of violent temper, or of strong tastes and distastes. I could scarcely discern any of the traits for which I searched, and should decide either that he had a powerful command over the muscles of his face, and the expression of his eye, or that there was less of that fiery temperament than what has been ascribed to him. In short, I never saw a countenance more composed and still, and, I might even add, more sweet and prepossessing, than Lord Byron's appeared upon this occasion.

His hair was beginning to lose the glossiness, of which, it is said, he was once so proud, and several grey strangers presented themselves, in spite of his anxiety to have them removed. His figure too, without being at all corpulent or rotund, was acquiring more fullness than he liked; so much so, that he was abstemiously refusing wine and meat, and living almost entirely upon vegetables.

The reserve of a first introduction was banished in a moment, by Mr ——'s starting a subject, which at once rendered Lord Byron as fluent of words as I could have wished to find him: He mentioned the manifesto of the Spanish Cortes, in answer to the declaration of the Holy Alliance,[5] and an animated conversation followed between the two, which, as I was anxious to hear Lord Byron's sentiments, I was in no hurry to interrupt.

Among other things, Lord Byron observed upon the manifesto, that he was particularly pleased with the dry Cervantes humour that it contained. 'It reminds me', said he, 'of the answer of Leonidas to Xerxes, when the Persian demanded his arms – "Come and take them."' He evidently calculated more upon Spanish resistance and courage, than the event justified; and he proceeded to describe, with a great deal of spirit and correctness, the nature of the country which the enemy would have to encounter before they could strike a decisive blow. – 'Spain', he added, 'is not a plain, across which the Russians and Austrians can march at their pleasure, as if they had nothing to do but to draw a mathematical straight line from one given point to another.'

There were several other pretty conceits, as we should call them, in the noble poet's discourse; but when he attempted to enlarge upon any subject, he was evidently at a loss for a good train of reasoning. He did not seem to be able to follow the thread, even of an argument of his own, when he was both opponent and respondent, and was putting a case in his own way.

From the cause of the Spaniards, the conversation directed itself to that of the Greeks, and the state paper of the Holy Alliance upon this subject also was brought upon the carpet. Lord Byron and Mr ——— both ridiculed the idea that was broached in that notable specimen of imperial reasoning, of the *insurrectionary movements* in the east (as it was pleased to style the noblest struggle for liberty, that an oppressed people ever made) being connected with the attempts at revolution in Western Europe, and of a correspondence existing between the reformers of different countries. 'If such a formidable concert as this existed, I suppose', said Lord Byron, smiling, and addressing Mr ——— , 'that two such notorious Radicals as ourselves, ought to be affronted for not being permitted to take some share in it.' Cobbett's[6] name was introduced, and the aristocratic poet's observation was too striking to be forgotten – 'I should not like to see Cobbett presiding at a revolutionary green table, and to be examined by him; for, if he were to put ten questions to me, and I should answer nine satisfactorily, but were to fail in the tenth – for that tenth, he would send me to the lantern.'[7]

Lord Byron then turned to me, and asked, 'Are you not afraid of calling upon such an excommunicated heretic as myself? If you are an ambitious man, you will never get on in the church after this.'

I replied, that he was totally mistaken, if he fancied that there was any such jealous or illiberal spirit at home, and he instantly interrupted me, by saying, 'Yes, yes, you are right – there is a great deal of liberal sentiment among churchmen in England, and that is why I prefer the Established Church of England to any other in the world. I have been intimate, in my time, with several clergymen, and never considered that our difference of opinion was a bar to our intimacy. They say, I am no Christian, but I am a Christian.' I afterwards asked Mr —— what his lordship meant by an assertion so much in contradiction with his writings, and was told that he often threw out random declarations of that kind, without any meaning.

Lord Byron took an opportunity of complaining, that some of his poems had been treated unfairly, and assailed with a degree of virulence they did not deserve. They are not intended, he remarked, to be theological works, but merely works of imagination, and as such, ought not to be examined according to the severe rules of polemical criticism.

I mentioned a late production of a Harrow man, in which *Cain* had been noticed. 'I hope', said Lord B, 'he did not abuse me personally, for that would be too bad, as we were school-fellows, and very good friends.'

Upon my informing him that the strictures were only fair and candid observations, upon what the author considered his Lordship's misstatements, he rejoined, 'It is nothing more than fair and just to examine my writings argumentatively, but nobody has any business to enter the lists with a dagger for my throat, when the rules of the combat allow him to play with tilts only.'

Lord Byron and Mr —— scrupulously avoided touching upon any subject in a manner that was likely to be irksome to me, but once or twice, when their peculiar opinions were betrayed in the course of conversation, I did not choose to lose the opportunity of declaring my own sentiments upon the same subjects, as explicitly as the nature of the conversation would admit. Among other things, I suggested the danger there must be of offending Omniscient Wisdom, by arraigning what we could not always understand, and expressed my belief, that the Supreme Being expects humility from us, in the same manner as we exact deference from our inferiors in attainments or condition. Lord Byron and Mr —— thought otherwise, and the former expressed himself in the celebrated lines of Milton –

> Will God incense his ire
> For such a petty tresspass, and not praise
> Rather your dauntless virtue, whom the pain
> Of death denounced, whatever thing death be,
> Deterred not from achieving what might lead
> To happier life.
>
> *Paradise Lost*, IX. 692–7.

I ventured to reply that his Lordship's sentiments were not unlike those expressed in the Virgilian line – 'Flectere si nequeo Superos, Acheronta movebo.'[8]

During the whole interview, my eyes were fixed very earnestly upon the countenance of the extraordinary man before me. I was desirous of examining every line in his face, and of judging from the movements of his lips, eyes, and brow, what might be passing within his bosom. Perhaps he was not unaware of this, and determined to keep a more steady command over them. A slight colour occasionally crossed his cheeks; and once, in particular, when I inadvertently mentioned the name of a lady, who was formerly said to take a deep interest in his Lordship, and related an anecdote told me of her by a mutual friend – 'I have often been very foolish,' said her ladyship 'but never wicked.' At hearing this, a blush stole over the noble bard's face, and he observed, 'I believe her.'

Once, and once only, he betrayed a slight degree of vanity. He was speaking of a narrow escape that he had lately had in riding through a torrent. His mare lost her footing, and there was some danger of her being unable to recover herself. 'Not, however', said he, 'that I should have been in any personal hazard, for it would not be easy to drown me.' He alluded to his swimming, in which he certainly surpassed most men.

Once also he seemed to think he had spoken incautiously, and took pains to correct himself. He was alluding to an invitation to dinner that had been given to him by an English gentleman in Genoa. 'I did not go, for I did not wish to make any new – I did not feel that I could depart from a rule I had made, not to dine in Genoa.' . . .

When I took my leave of Lord Byron, he surprised me by saying, 'I hope we shall meet again, and perhaps it will soon be in England.' For though he seemed to have none of that prejudice against his native country that has been laid to his charge, yet there was a want of ingenuousness in throwing out an intimation of what was not likely to take place. Upon the whole, instead of avoiding any mention of England, he evidently took an interest in what was going on at home, and was glad, when the conversation led to the mention of persons and topics of the day, by which he could obtain any information, without directly asking for it.

Such was my interview with one of the most celebrated characters of the present age, in which, as is generally the case, most of my anticipations were disappointed. There was nothing eccentric in his manner – nothing beyond the level of ordinary clever men in his remarks or style of conversation, and certainly not anything to justify the strange things that have been said of him by many, who, like the French rhapsodist, would describe him as half angel and half devil.

NOTES

The anonymously-published *Life, Writings, Opinions and Times of . . . Lord Byron . . . by an English Gentleman* (see p. 74) states (III, 46) that the author of this article is 'the Rev. Mr Johnson, a natural son of Lord Hampden', and that he was accompanied on his visit to Byron by Colonel Aaron Burr, 'formerly Vice President of the United States' (Burr had held office 1801–5, had killed Alexander Hamilton, Secretary of the Treasury, in a duel in 1804, and had subsequently been disgraced). The *Life* adds (p. 39) that the account 'gained universal credit at the time of its publication' but that it is incorrect in some respects. Among the corrections are the following:

> The reverend gentleman accuses Lord Byron of wanting ingenuousness, in throwing out a hint that they might probably meet in England – surely this is undeserved; no one could be acquainted with his Lordship's intentions on that point, and he never pledged himself to abandon his native country for ever; he never spoke of it but with enthusiasm, and has often been heard to say, 'If ever I go back to England I will do so and so'. . . . The conversation about the Christian religion is so much unlike him, that it must have been brought up by the parson himself, anxious to know his Lordship's senti- ments, and his Lordship probably laughed in his sleeve at sending his impertinence away puzzled. His Lordship's slight defence of his poems, where he is made to say, 'They are not intended to be theological works', smells so strongly of the pulpit. I think the reverend gentleman only *wished* his Lordship had said so, for he (even in his best moods) assumed a reserved air, if not a determined silence, when any one started as a subject for discussion the merits of his writings . . . .

1. Byron's servant Tita (see p. 154).
2. Perhaps the well-known portrait of Byron in Albanian dress (Plate 4).
3. Lorenzo Bartolini executed busts of Byron and Teresa Guiccioli in 1822. Byron said that he had been made to look like 'a superannuated Jesuit'; according to Marchand (p. 958) he was 'shocked to see his own physical deterioration recorded in stone'.
4. Johann Lavater (1741–1801), Swiss physiognomist.
5. Document signed in 1815 by the monarchs of Russia, Prussia and Austria.
6. William Cobbett (1763–1835), English Radical journalist and author.
7. Scaffold (from the phrase 'À la lanterne', popular during the French Revolution).
8. Virgil *Aeneid*, VII. 312.

Byron's Conversation I: On Books and Authors

SHAKESPEARE AND POPE*

Talking of Shakespeare, Byron said, that he owed one half of his popularity to his low origin, which, like charity, covereth a multitude of sins with the multitude, and the other half, to the remoteness of the time at which he wrote from our own days. 'All his vulgarisms', continued Byron, 'are attributed to the circumstances of his birth and breeding depriving him of a good education; hence they are to be excused, and the obscurities with which his works abound are all easily explained away by the simple statement, that he wrote about 200 years ago, and that the terms then in familiar use are now become obsolete. With two such good excuses, as want of education, and having written above 200 years before our time, any writer may pass muster; and when to these is added the being a sturdy hind of low degree, which to three parts of the community in England has a peculiar attraction, one ceases to wonder at his supposed popularity; I say supposed, for who goes to see his plays, and who, except country parsons, or mouthing, stage-struck, theatrical amateurs, read them?' I told Byron what really was, and is, my impression, that he was not sincere in his depreciation of our immortal bard; and I added, that I preferred believing him insincere, than incapable of judging works, which his own writings proved he must, more than most other men, feel the beauties of. He laughed, and replied, 'That the compliment I paid to his writings was so entirely at the expense of his sincerity, that he had no cause to be flattered; but that, knowing I was one of those who worshipped Shakespeare, he forgave me, and would only bargain that I made equal allowance for his worship of Pope.' I observed, 'That any comparison between the two was as absurd as comparing some magnificent feudal castle, surrounded by mountains and forests, with foaming cataracts, and boundless lakes, to the pretty villa of Pope, with its sheen lawn, artificial grotto, stunted trees, and trim exotics.' He said that my simile was more ingenious than just, and hoped that I was prepared to admit that Pope was the greatest of all modern poets, and a philosopher as

*Lady Blessington's Conversations of Lord Byron, pp. 202–4.

well as a poet. I made my peace by expressing my sincere admiration of Pope, but begged to be understood as refusing to admit any comparison between him and Shakespeare; and so the subject ended. Byron is so prone to talk for effect, and to assert what he does not believe, that one must be cautious in giving implicit credence to his opinions. My conviction is, that, in spite of his declarations to the contrary, he admires Shakespeare as much as most of his countrymen do; but that, unlike the generality of them, he sees the blemishes that the freedom of the times in which the great poet lived led him to indulge in in his writings, in a stronger point of view, and takes pleasure in commenting on them with severity, as a means of wounding the vanity of the English. I have rarely met with a person more conversant with the works of Shakespeare than was Byron. I have heard him quote passages from them repeatedly; and in a tone that marked how well he appreciated their beauty, which certainly lost nothing in his delivery of them, as few possessed a more harmonious voice or a more elegant pronunciation than did Byron. Could there be a less equivocal proof of his admiration of our immortal bard than the tenacity with which his memory retained the finest passages of all his works? When I made this observation to him he smiled, and affected to boast that his memory was so retentive that it equally retained all that he read; but as I had seen many proofs of the contrary, I persevered in affirming what I have never ceased to believe, that, in despite of his professions to the reverse, Byron was in his heart a warm admirer of Shakespeare.

DR JOHNSON*

It was a jest between us, that the only book that was a thorough favourite on both sides, was Boswell's *Life of Johnson*. I used to talk of Johnson when I saw him disturbed, or when I wished to avoid other subjects. He asked me one day how I should have felt in Johnson's company. I said it was difficult to judge; because, living in other times, and one's character being modified by them, I could not help thinking of myself as I was now, and Johnson as he was in times previous: so that it appeared to me that I should have been somewhat 'Jacobinical' in his company, and not disposed to put up with his *ipse dixit*. He said that 'Johnson would have awed him, he treated lords with so much respect.' The reader, after what I have lately said, will see what was at the bottom of these remarks on both sides. Had the question been asked me now, I should have said, that I loved Johnson, and hope I should have shown him all due homage; though I think I should have

*Leigh Hunt, *Autobiography*, pp. 352–3.

been inclined sometimes to contest his conclusions more than they are contested by his interlocutors in Boswell. Lord Byron liked to imitate Johnson, and say, 'Why, sir', in a high mouthing way, rising, and looking about him. His imitation was very pleasant.

JOHNSON AND POPE*

'I have been reading Johnson's *Lives*, a book I am very fond of. I look upon him as the profoundest of critics, and had occasion to study him when I was writing to Bowles.

'Of all the disgraces that attach to England in the eye of foreigners, who admire Pope more than any of our poets (though it is the fashion to under-rate him among ourselves) the greatest perhaps is, that there should be no place assigned to him in Poet's Corner. I have often thought of erecting a monument to him at my own expense in Westminster Abbey, and hope to do so yet. But he was a Catholic, and, what was worse, puzzled Tillotson and the Divines. That accounts for his not having any national monument. Milton, too, had very nearly been without a stone; and the mention of his name on the tomb of another was at one time considered a profanation to a church. The French, I am told, lock up Voltaire's tomb. Will there never be an end to this bigotry? Will men never learn that every great poet is necessarily a religious man? – so at least Coleridge says.'

'Yes', replied Shelley; 'and he might maintain the converse – that every truly religious man is a poet; meaning by poetry the power of communicating intense and impassioned impressions respecting man and Nature.'

VOLTAIRE†

[18 Sep 1822.] Passed the evening with Byron, who declaimed against Shakespeare, and Dante, and Milton, and said Voltaire was worth a thousand such.

MADAME DE STAËL‡

Talking of literary women, Lord Byron said that Madame de Staël was certainly the cleverest, though not the most agreeble woman he had

---

Medwin's Conversations of Lord Byron, p. 198.
†J. C. Hobhouse, *Recollections of a Long Life*, III, 6.
‡*Lady Blessington's Conversations of Lord Byron*, pp. 22–3.

ever known. 'She declaimed to you instead of conversing with you,' said he, 'never pausing except to take breath; and if during that interval a rejoinder was put in, it was evident that she did not attend to it, as she resumed the thread of her discourse as though it had not been interrupted.' This observation from Byron was amusing enough, as we had all made nearly the same observation on him, with the exception that he listened to, and noticed, any answer made to his reflections. 'Madame de Staël', continued Byron, 'was very eloquent when her imagination warmed (and a very little excited it); her powers of imagination were much stronger than her reasoning ones, perhaps owing to their being much more frequently exercised; her language was recondite, but redundant; and though always flowery, and often brilliant, there was an obscurity that left the impression that she did not perfectly understand what she endeavoured to render intelligible to others. She was always losing herself in philosophical disquisition, and once she got entangled in the mazes of the labyrinth of metaphysics; she had no clue by which she could guide her path – the imagination that led her into her difficulties could not get her out of them; the want of a mathematical education, which might have served as a ballast to steady and help her into the port of reason, was always visible, and though she had great tact in concealing her defeat, and covering a retreat, a tolerable logician must have always discovered the scrapes she got into. Poor dear Madame de Staël! I shall never forget seeing her one day, at table with a large party, when the busk (I believe you ladies call it) of her corset forced its way through the top of the corset, and would not descend though pushed by all the force of both hands of the wearer, who became crimson from the operation. After fruitless efforts, she turned in despair to the valet de chambre behind her chair, and requested him to draw it out, which could only be done by his passing his hand from behind over her shoulder, and across her chest, when, with a desperate effort, he unsheathed the busk. Had you seen the faces of some of the English ladies of the party, you would have been like me, almost convulsed; while Madame remained perfectly unsconscious that she had committed any solecism on *la décence Anglaise* . . .'

SIR WALTER SCOTT*

[1] When I entered the room, Lord Byron was devouring, as he called it, a new novel of Sir Walter Scott's.

'How difficult it is', said he, 'to say any thing new!' Who was that

---

*(1)*Medwin's Conversations of Lord Byron*, pp. 199–200; (2)*Lady Blessington's Conversations of Lord Byron*, p. 44.

voluptuary of antiquity, who offered a reward for a new pleasure? Perhaps all nature and art could not supply a new idea.

'This page, for instance, is a brilliant one; it is full of wit. But let us see how much of it is original. This passage, for instance, comes from Shakespeare; this *bon mot* from one of Sheridan's Comedies; this observation from another writer (naming the author); and yet the ideas are new-moulded – and perhaps Scott was not aware of their being plagiarisms. It is a bad thing to have too good a memory.'

'I should not like to have you for a critic', I observed.

' "Set a thief to catch a thief" ', was the reply.

'I never travel without Scott's Novels', said he: 'they are a library in themselves – a perfect literary treasure. I could read them once a-year with new pleasure.'

I asked him if he was certain about the Novels being Sir Walter Scott's?

'Scott as much as owned himself the author of *Waverley* to me in Murray's shop', replied he. 'I was talking to him about the novel, and lamented that its author had not carried back the story nearer to the time of the Revolution. Scott, entirely off his guard, said, "Ay, I might have done so, but" – There he stopped. It was in vain to attempt to correct himself: he looked confused, and relieved his embarrassment by a precipitate retreat.

'On another occasion I was to dine at Murray's; and being in his parlour in the morning, he told me I should meet the author of *Waverley* at dinner. He had received several excuses, and the party was a small one; and, knowing all the people present, I was satisfied that the writer of that novel must have been, and could have been, no other than Walter Scott.

'He spoiled the fame of his poetry by his superior prose. He has such extent and versatility of powers in writing, that, should his Novels ever tire the public, which is not likely, he will apply himself to something else, and succeed as well. . . .'

[2] During dinner he was as usual gay, spoke in terms of the warmest commendation of Sir Walter Scott, not only as an author, but as a man, and dwelt with apparent delight on his novels, declaring that he had read and reread them over and over again, and always with increased pleasure. He said that he quite equalled, nay, in his opinion surpassed, Cervantes. In talking of Sir Walter's private character, goodness of heart, etc., Lord Byron became more animated than I had ever seen him; his colour changed from its general pallid tint to a more lively hue, and his eyes became humid; never had he appeared to such advantage, and it might easily be seen that every expression he uttered proceeded from his heart. Poor Byron! – for poor he is even with all his genius,

rank, and wealth – had he lived more with men like Scott, whose openness of character and steady principle had convinced him that they were in earnest in *their goodness*, and not *making believe*, (as he always suspects good people to be,) his life might be different and happier.

WORDSWORTH*

'Wordsworth, though occasionally a writer for the nursery masters and misses, . . . now and then expressed ideas worth imitating; but, like brother Southey, he had his price; and since he is turned tax-gatherer, is only fit to rhyme about asses and waggoners.' [The reference is to Wordsworth's poems 'Peter Bell' (1819) and 'The Waggoner' (1819).]

SOUTHEY AND LANDOR†

'It is difficult (said Byron) when one detests an author not to detest his works. There are some that I dislike so cordially, that I am aware of my incompetency to give an impartial opinion of their writings. Southey, *par exemple*, is one of these. When travelling in Italy, he was reported to me as having circulated some reports much to my disadvantage, and still more to that of two ladies of my acquaintance; all of which, through the kind medium of some good-natured friends, were brought to my ears; and I have vowed eternal vengeance against him, and all who uphold him; which vengeance has been poured forth, in phials of wrath, in the shape of epigrams and lampoons, some of which you shall see. When any one attacks me, on the spur of the moment I sit down and write all the *méchanceté* that comes into my head; and, as some of these sallies have merit, they amuse me, and are too good to be torn or burned, and so are kept, and see the light long after the feeling that dictated them has subsided. All my malice evaporates in the effusions of my pen: but I dare say those that excite it would prefer any other mode of vengeance. At Pisa, a friend told me that Walter Savage Landor had declared he either would not, or could not, read my works. I asked my officious friend if he was sure which it was that Landor said, as the *would not* was not offensive, and the *could not* was highly so. After some reflection, he, of course *en ami*, chose the most disagreeable signification; and I marked down Landor in the tablet of memory as a

---

*Medwin's Conversations of Lord Byron, p. 194.
†Lady Blessington's Conversations of Lord Byron, pp. 156–7.

person to whom a *coup-de-pat* must be given in my forthcoming work, though he really is a man whose brilliant talents and profound erudition I cannot help admiring as much as I respect his character – various proofs of the generosity, manliness, and independence of which has [*sic*] reached me; so you see I can render justice (*en petite comité*) even to a man who says he could not read my works; this, at least, shows some good feeling, if the *petit* vengeance of attacking him in my work cannot be defended; but my attacking proves the truth of the observation made by a French writer – that we don't like people for the merit we discover in them, but for that which they find in us.'

THOMAS MOORE*

'Moore is one of the few writers who will survive the age in which he so deservedly flourishes. He will live in his *Irish Melodies*; they will go down to posterity with the music; both will last as long as Ireland, or as music and poetry.'

LEIGH HUNT†

'Hunt would have made a fine writer, for he has a great deal of fancy and feeling, if he had not been spoiled by circumstances. He was brought up at the Blue-coat foundation, and had never till lately been ten miles from St Paul's. What poetry is to be expected from such a course of education? He has his school, however, and a host of disciples. . . . But *Rimini* has a great deal of merit. There never were so many fine things spoiled as in *Rimini*.'

SHELLEY‡

'A man who means to be a poet should do, and should have done all his life, nothing else but make verses. There's Shelley has more poetry in him than any man living; and if he were not so mystical, and would not write Utopias and set himself up as a Reformer, his right to rank as a poet, and very highly too, could not fail of being acknowledged. I said what I thought of him the other day; and all who are not blinded by

---

*Medwin's Conversations of Lord Byron, p. 240.
†*Medwin's Conversations of Lord Byron, p. 254.*
‡*Medwin's Conversations of Lord Byron, pp. 235–6.*

bigotry must think the same. The works he wrote at seventeen are much more extraordinary than Chatterton's at the same age.'

A question was started, as to which he considered the easiest of all metres in our language.

'Or rather,' replied he, 'you mean, which is the least difficult? I have spoken of the fatal facility of the octo-syllabic metre. The Spenser stanza is difficult, because it is like a sonnet, and the finishing line must be good. The couplet is more difficult still, because the last line, or one out of two, must be good. But blank-verse is the most difficult of all, because every line must be good.'

SHELLEY AND OTHER CONTEMPORARIES*

As a woman, I felt proud of the homage he paid to the genius of Mrs Hemans, and as a passionate admirer of her poetry, I felt flattered, at finding that Lord Byron fully sympathised with my admiration. He has, or at least expresses, a strong dislike to the Lake school of poets, never mentions them except in ridicule, and he and I nearly quarrelled to-day because I defended poor Keats.

On looking out from the balcony this morning with Byron, I observed his countenance change, and an expression of deep sadness steal over it. After a few minutes' silence he pointed out to me a boat anchored to the right, as the one in which his friend Shelley went down, and he said the sight of it made him ill. – 'You should have known Shelley', said Byron, 'to feel how much I must regret him. He was the most gentle, most amiable, and *least* worldly-minded person I ever met; full of delicacy, disinterested beyond all other men, and possessing a degree of genius, joined to a simplicity, as rare as it is admirable. He had formed to himself a *beau idéal* of all that is fine, high-minded, and noble, and he acted up to this ideal even to the very letter. He had a most brilliant imagination, but a total want of worldly-wisdom. I have seen nothing like him, and never shall again, I am certain. I never can forget the night that his poor wife rushed into my room at Pisa, with a face pale as marble, and terror impressed on her brow, demanding, with all the tragic impetuosity of grief and alarm, where was her husband! Vain were all our efforts to calm her; a desperate sort of courage seemed to give her energy to confront the horrible truth that awaited her; it was the courage of despair. I have seen nothing in tragedy on the stage so powerful, or so affecting, as her appearance, and it often presents itself to my memory. I knew nothing then of the catastrophe, but the vividness of her terror communicated itself to me,

*Lady Blessington's Conversations of Lord Byron, pp. 52–3.

and I feared the worst, which fears were, alas! too soon fearfully realised.

'Mrs Shelley is very clever, indeed it would be difficult for her not to be so; the daughter of Mary Wollstonecraft and Godwin, and the wife of Shelley, could be no common person.'

Byron talked to-day of Leigh Hunt, regretted his ever having embarked in the *Liberal*, and said that it had drawn a nest of hornets on him; but expressed a very good opinion of the talents and principle of Mr Hunt, though, as he said, 'our tastes are so opposite, that we are totally unsuited to each other. He admires the Lakers, I abhor them; in short, we are more formed to be friends at a distance, than near.'

Byron's Conversation II: On Other Topics

AMBITION AND AUTHORSHIP*

Byron had two points of ambition – the one to be thought the greatest poet of his day, and the other a nobleman and man of fashion, who could have arrived at distinction without the aid of his poetical genius. This often produced curious anomalies in his conduct and sentiments, and a sort of jealousy of himself in each separate character, that was highly amusing to an observant spectator. If poets were talked of or eulogised, he referred to the advantages of rank and station as commanding that place in society by right, which was only accorded to genius by sufferance; for, said Byron, 'Let authors do, say, or think what they please, they are never considered as men of fashion in the circles of *haut ton*, to which their literary reputations have given them an *entrée*, unless they happen to be of high birth. How many times have I observed this in London; as also the awkward efforts made by authors to trifle and act the fine gentleman like the rest of the herd in society. Then look at the *faiblesse* they betray in running after great people. Lords and ladies seem to possess, in their eyes, some power of attraction that I never could discover; and the eagerness with which they crowd to balls and assemblies, where they are as *déplacés* as *ennuyés*, all conversation at such places being out of the question, might lead one to think that they sought the heated atmospheres of such scenes as hot-beds to nurse their genius.' If men of fashion were praised, Byron

*Lady Blessington's Conversations of Lord Byron, pp. 97–9.

dwelt on the futility of their pursuits, their ignorance *en masse*, and the necessity of talents to give lustre to rank and station. In short, he seemed to think that the bays of the author ought to be entwined with a coronet to render either valuable, as, singly, they were not sufficiently attractive; and this evidently arose from *his* uniting, in his own person, rank and genius. I recollect once laughingly telling him that he was fortunate in being able to consider himself a poet amongst lords, and a lord amongst poets. He seemed doubtful as to how he should take the parody, but ended by laughing also. . . .

Of his own works, with some exceptions, he always spoke in derision, saying he could write much better, but that he wrote to suit the false taste of the day; and that if now and then a gleam of true feeling or poetry was visible in his productions, it was sure to be followed by the ridicule he could not suppress. Byron was not sincere in this, and it was only said to excite surprise, and show his superiority over the rest of the world. It was this same desire of astonishing people that led him to depreciate Shakespeare, which I have frequently heard him do, though from various reflections of his in conversation, and the general turn of his mind, I am convinced that he had not only deeply read, but deeply felt the beauties of our immortal poet.

LOVE, FRIENDSHIP AND MARRIAGE*

Talking of love and friendship, Byron said, that 'friendship may, and often does, grow into love, but love never subsides into friendship', I maintained the contrary, and instanced the affectionate friendship which replaces the love of married people; a sentiment as tender, though less passionate, and more durable than the first. He said, 'You should say more *enduring*; for, depend on it, that the good-natured passiveness, with which people submit to the conjugal yoke, is much more founded on the philosophical principle of what can't be cured must be endured, than the tender friendship you give them credit for. Who that has felt the all-engrossing passion of love (continued he) could support the stagnant calm you refer to for the same object? No, the humiliation of discovering the frailty of our own nature, which is in no instance more proved than by the short duration of violent love, has something so painful in it, that, with our usual selfishness, we feel, if not a repugnance, at least an indifference to the object that once charmed, but can no longer charm us, and whose presence brings mortifying recollections; nay, such is our injustice, that we transfer the blame of the weakness of our own natures to the person who had not power to retain our love, and discover blemishes in her to excuse our

*Lady Blessington's Conversations of Lord Byron, pp. 108–11.

inconstancy. As indifference begets indifference, vanity is wounded at both sides; and though good sense may induce people to support and conceal their feelings, how can an affectionate friendship spring up like a phœnix, from the ashes of extinguished passion? I am afraid that the friendship, in such a case, would be as fabulous as the phœnix, for the recollection of burnt-out love would remain too mortifying a memento to admit the successor, friendship.' I told Byron that this was mere sophistry, and could not be his real sentiments; as also that, a few days before, he admitted that passion subsides into a better, or at least a more durable feeling. I added, that persons who had felt the engrossing love he described, which was a tempestuous and selfish passion, were glad to sink into the refreshing calm of milder feelings, and looked back with complacency on the storms they had been exposed to, and with increased sympathy to the person who had shared them. The community of interest, of sorrows, and of joys added new links to the chain of affection, and habit, which might wear away the gloss of the selfish passion he alluded to, gave force to friendship, by rendering the persons every day more necessary to each other. I added, that dreadful would be the fate of persons, if, after a few months of violent passion, they were to pass their lives in indifference, merely because their new feelings were less engrossing and exciting than the old. 'Then (said Byron), if you admit that the violent love does, or must, subside in a few months, and, as in coursing, that we are mad for a minute to be melancholy for an hour, would it not be wiser to choose the friend, I mean the person most calculated for friendship, with whom the long years are to be spent, than the idol who is to be worshipped for some months, and then hurled from the altar we had raised to her, and left defaced and disfigured by the smoke of the incense she had received? I maintained that as the idols are chosen nearly always for their personal charms, they are seldom calculated for friendship; hence the disappointment that ensues, when the violence of passion has abated, and the discovery is made that there are no solid qualities to replace the passion that has passed away with the novelty that excited it. When a man chooses a friend in a woman, he looks to her powers of conversation, her mental qualities, and agreeability; and as these win his regard the more they are known, love often takes the place of friendship, and certainly the foundation on which he builds is more likely to be lasting; and, in this case, I admit that affection, or, as you more prettily call it, tender friendship, may last for ever.' I replied that I believe the only difference in our opinions is, that I denied that friendship could not succeed love, and that nothing could change my opinion. 'I suppose (said Byron) that a woman, like

A man, convinced against his will
Is of the same opinion still

so that all my fine commentaries on my text have been useless; at all events I hope you give me credit for being *ingenious*, as well as *ingenuous* in my defence. Clever men (said Byron) commit a great mistake in selecting wives who are destitute of abilities; I allow that *une femme savante* is apt to be a bore, and it is to avoid this that people run into the opposite extreme, and condemn themselves to pass their lives with women who are incapable of understanding or appreciating them. Men have an idea that a clever woman must be disputative and dictatorial, not considering that it is only pretenders who are either, and that this applies as much to one sex as the other. Now, my *beau idéal* would be a woman with talent enough to be able to understand and value mine, but not sufficient to be able to shine herself. All men with pretensions desire this, though few, if any, have courage to avow it; I believe the truth is, that a man must be very conscious of superior abilities to endure the thought of having a rival near the throne, though that rival was his wife; and as it is said that no man is a hero to his valet-de-chambre, it may be concluded that few men can retain their position on the pedestal of genius *vis-à-vis* to one who has been behind the curtain, unless that one is unskilled in the art of judging, and consequently admires the more because she does not understand. Genius, like greatness, should be seen at a distance, for neither will bear a too close inspection. Imagine the hero of a hundred fights in his cotton night-cap, subject to all the infirmities of human nature, and there is an end of his sublimity – and see a poet whose works have raised our thoughts above this sphere of common everyday existence, and who, Prometheus-like, has stolen fire from heaven to animate the children of clay – see him in the throes of poetic labour, blotting, tearing, re-writing the lines that we suppose him to have poured forth with Homeric inspiration, and, in the intervals, eating, drinking and sleeping, like the most ordinary mortal, and he soon sinks to a level with them in our estimation. I am sure (said Byron) we can never justly appreciate the works of those with whom we have lived on familiar terms. I have felt this myself, and it applies to poets more than all other writers. They should live in solitude, rendering their presence more desired by its rarity; never submit to the gratification of the animal appetite of eating in company, and be as distinct in their general habits, as in their genius, from the common herd of mankind.'

RELIGION*

It is difficult to judge, from the contradictory nature of his writings, what the religious opinions of Lord Byron really were. Perhaps the conversations I held with him may throw some light upon a subject

*Medwin's Conversations of Lord Byron, pp.77–81.

that cannot fail to excite curiosity. On the whole, I am inclined to think
that if he were occasionally sceptical, and thought it, as he says,

> A pleasant voyage, perhaps, to float,
> Like Pyrrho, on a sea of speculation
> [*Don Juan*, IX, 18]

yet his wavering never amounted to a disbelief in the divine Founder of
Christianity.

'I always took great delight', observed he, 'in the English Cathedral
service. It cannot fail to inspire every man, who feels at all, with
devotion. Notwithstanding which, Christianity is not the best source of
inspiration for a poet. No poet should be tied down to a direct
profession of faith. Metaphysics open a vast field; Nature, and anti-
Mosaical speculations on the origin of the world, a wide range, and
sources of poetry that are shut out by Christianity.'

I advanced Tasso and Milton.

'Tasso and Milton', replied he, 'wrote on Christian subjects, it is
true; but how did they treat them? The *Jerusalem Delivered* deals little in
Christian doctrines, and the *Paradise Lost* makes use of the heathen
mythology, which is surely scarcely allowable. Milton discarded pa-
pacy, and adopted no creed in its room; he never attended divine
worship.

'His great epics, that nobody reads, prove nothing. He took his text
from the Old and New Testaments. He shocks the severe apprehensions of the Catholics, as he did those of the divines of his day, by too
great a familiarity with Heaven, and the introduction of the Divinity
himself; and, more than all, by making the Devil his hero, and deifying
the dæmons.

'He certainly excites compassion for Satan, and endeavours to make
him out an injured personage – he gives him human passions too,
makes him pity Adam and Eve, and justify himself much as Prometheus does. Yet Milton was never blamed for all this. I should be very
curious to know what his real belief was. The *Paradise Lost* and *Regained*
do not satisfy me on this point. One might as well say that Moore is a
fire-worshipper, or a follower of Mokanna, because he chose those
subjects from the East; or that I am a Cainist.'

Another time he said: 'One mode of worship yields to another; no
religion has lasted more than two thousand years. Out of the eight
hundred millions that the globe contains, only two hundred millions
are Christians. Query – What is to become of the six hundred millions
that do not believe, and of those incalculable millions that lived before
Christ?

'People at home are mad about Missionary Societies, and missions to
the East. I have been applied to, to subscribe, several times since, and
once before I left England. The Catholic priests have been labouring

hard for nearly a century; but what have they done? Out of eighty millions of Hindus, how many proselytes have been made? Sir J. Malcolm said at Murray's before several persons, that the Padres, as he called them, had only made six converts at Bombay during his time, and that even this black little flock forsook their shepherds when the rum was out. Their faith evaporated with the fumes of the arrack. Besides, the Hindus believe that they have had nine incarnations: the Missionaries preach, that a people whom the Indians only know to despise, have had one. It is nine to one against them, by their own showing.

'Another doctrine can never be in repute among the Solomons of the East. It cannot be easy to persuade men who have had as many wives as they pleased, to be content with one; besides, a woman is old at twenty in that country. What are men to do? They are not all St Anthonys. – I will tell you a story. A certain Signior Antonio of my acquaintance married a very little round fat wife, very fond of waltzing, who went by the name of the *Tentazione di Sant' Antonio*. There is a picture, a celebrated one, in which a little woman not unresembling my description plays the principal rôle, and is most troublesome to the Saint, most trying to his virtue. Very few of the modern saints will have his forbearance, though they may imitate him in his martyrdom.

'I have been reading', said he one day, 'Tacitus' account of the siege of Jerusalem, under Titus. What a sovereign contempt the Romans had for the Jews! Their country seems to have been little better than themselves.

'Priestley denied the original sin, and that any would be damned. Wesley, the object of Southey's panegyric [in his *Life of Wesley* (1820)], preached the doctrines of election and faith, and, like all the sectarians, does not want texts to prove both.

'The best Christians can never be satisfied of their own salvation. Dr Johnson died like a coward, and Cowper was near shooting himself; Hume went off the stage like a brave man, and Voltaire's last moments do not seem to have been clouded by any fears of what was to come. A man may study any thing till he believes in it. Creech died a Lucretian, Burckhardt and Browne were Mohammedans. Sale, the translator of the Koran, was suspected of being an Islamite, but a very different one from you, Shiloh (as he sometimes used to call Shelley).

'You are a Protestant – you protest against all religions. There is Taaffe will traduce Dante till he becomes a Dantist. I am called a Manichæan: I may rather be called an Any-chæan, or Anything-arian. How do you like my sect? The sect of Anything-arians sounds well, does it not?'

Calling on him the next day, we found him, as was sometimes the case, silent, dull, and sombre. At length he said:

'Here is a little book somebody has sent me about Christianity, that has made me very uncomfortable: the reasoning seems to me very strong, the proofs are very staggering. I don't think you can answer it, Shelley; at least I am sure I can't, and what is more, I don't wish it.'

Speaking of Gibbon, he said: 'Long Baillie thought the question set at rest in the *History of the Decline and Fall*, but I am not so easily convinced. It is not a matter of volition to unbelieve. Who likes to own that he has been a fool all his life – to unlearn all that he has been taught in his youth? or can think that some of the best men that ever lived have been fools? I have often wished I had been born a Catholic. That purgatory of theirs is a comfortable doctrine; I wonder the reformers gave it up, or did not substitute something as consolatory in its room. It is an improvement on the transmigration, Shelley, which all your wiseacre philosophers taught.

'You believe in Plato's three principles; – why not in the Trinity? One is not more mystical than the other. I don't know why I am considered an enemy to religion, and an unbeliever. I disowned the other day that I was of Shelley's school in metaphysics, though I admired his poetry; not but what he has changed his mode of thinking very much since he wrote the Notes to *Queen Mab*, which I was accused of having a hand in. I know, however, that I am considered an infidel. My wife and sister, when they joined parties, sent me prayer-books. There was a Mr Mulock, who went about the Continent preaching orthodoxy in politics and religion, a writer of bad sonnets, and a lecturer in worse prose – he tried to convert me to some new sect of Christianity. He was a great anti-materialist, and abused Locke.'

DEATH*

Byron never wished to live to be old; on the contrary, I have frequently heard him express the hope of dying young; and I remember his quoting Sir William Temple's opinion – that life is like wine; who would drink it pure must not draw it to the dregs – as being his way of thinking also. He said, it was a mistaken idea that passions subsided with age, as they only changed, and not for the better, Avarice usurping the place vacated by Love, and Suspicion filling up that of Confidence. 'And this', continued Byron, 'is what age and experience brings us. No; let me not live to be old; give me youth, which is the fever of reason, and not age, which is the palsy. I remember my youth, when my heart overflowed with affection towards all who showed any symptom of liking towards me; and now, at thirty-six, no very advanced period of life, I can scarcely, by raking up the dying embers of

*Lady Blessington's Conversations of Lord Byron, pp. 102–4, 128.

affection in that same heart, excite even a temporary flame to warm my chilled feelings.' Byron mourned over the lost feelings of his youth, as we regret the lost friends of the same happy period; there was something melancholy in the sentiment, and the more so, as one saw that it was sincere. He often talked of death, and never with dread. He said that its certainty furnished a better lesson than all the philosophy of the schools, as it enabled us to bear the ills of life, which would be unbearable were life of unlimited duration. He quoted Cowley's lines– [from 'Life and Fame', here misquoted]

> O Life! thou weak-built isthmus, which doth proudly rise
> Up betwixt two eternities!

as an admirable description, and said they often recurred to his memory. He never mentioned the friends of whom Death had deprived him without visible emotion: he loved to dwell on their merits, and talked of them with a tenderness as if their deaths had been recent, instead of years ago. Talking of some of them, and deploring their loss, he observed, with a bitter smile, 'But perhaps it is as well that they are gone: it is less bitter to mourn their deaths than to have to regret their alienation; and who knows but that, had they lived, they might have become as faithless as some others that I have known. Experience has taught me that the only friends that we can call our own – that can know no change – are those over whom the grave has closed: the seal of death is the only seal of friendship. No wonder, then, that we cherish the memory of those who loved us, and comfort ourselves with the thought that they were unchanged to the last. The regret we feel at such afflictions has something in it that softens our hearts, and renders us better. We feel more kindly disposed to our fellow-creatures, because we are satisfied with ourselves – first, for being able to excite affection, and, secondly, for the gratitude with which we repay it – to the memory of those we have lost; but the regret we prove at the alienation or unkindness of those we trusted and loved, is so mingled with bitter feelings, that they sear the heart, dry up the fountain of kindness in our breasts, and disgust us with human nature, by wounding our self-love in its most vulnerable part – the showing that we have failed to excite affection where we had lavished ours. One may learn to bear this uncomplainingly, and with outward calm; but the impression is indelible, and he must be made of different materials to the generality of men, who does not become a cynic, if he become nothing worse, after once suffering such a disappointment.' . . .

'. . . There is something calm and soothing to me in the thought of death; and the only time that I feel repugnance to it is on a fine day, in solitude, in a beautiful country, when all nature seems rejoicing in light and life. The contrast then between the beautiful and animated world around me, and the dark narrow grave, gives a chill to the feelings; for, with all the boasted philosophy of man, his physical *being* influences his notions of that state where they can be felt no more. The nailed down coffin, and the dark gloomy vault, or grave, always mingle with our thoughts of death; then the decomposition of our mortal frames, the being preyed on by reptiles, add to the disgusting horror of the picture, and one has need of all the hopes of immortality to enable one to pass over this bridge between the life we know and the life we hope to find.

'Do you know (said Byron) that when I have looked on some face that I love, imagination has often figured the changes that death must one day produce on it – the worm rioting on lips now smiling, the features and hues of health changed to the livid and ghastly tints of putrefaction; and the image conjured up by my fancy, but which is as true as it is a fearful anticipation of what *must* arrive, has left an impression for hours that the actual presence of the object, in all the bloom of health, has not been able to banish: this is one of *my* pleasures of imagination.'

MIRACLES*

One evening at Pisa, in the drawing-room of the Countess G[uiccioli], where Byron was wont to spend all his evenings, a great discussion arose respecting a certain miracle which was said to have taken place at Lucca.

The miracle had been accompanied by several rather ludicrous circumstances, and of course laughter was not spared. Shelley, who never lost sight of his philosopher, treated miracles as deplorable superstitions. Lord Byron laughed at the absurdity of the history told, without any malice however. Madame G— alone did not laugh. 'Do you, then, believe in that miracle?' asked Byron. 'I do not say I exactly believe in that miracle', she replied; 'but I believe in miracles, since I believe in God and in His omnipotence; nor could I believe that God can be deprived of His liberty, when I feel that I have mine. Were I no longer to believe in miracles, it seems to me I should no longer believe in God, and that I should lose my faith.'

Lord Byron stopped joking, and said –

'Well, after all, the philosophy of common sense is the truest and the best.'

The conversation continued, in the jesting tone in which it had begun, and M M—, an *esprit fort*, went so far as to condemn the supernatural in the name of the general and permanent laws which govern nature, and to look upon miracles as the legends of a by-gone

*Teresa Guiccioli, *My Recollections of Lord Byron*, pp. 171–2.

age, and as errors which affect the ignorant. From what had gone before, he probably fancied that Byron was going to join issue with him. But there was often a wide gulf between the intimate thoughts of Byron and his expressions of them.

'We allow ourselves too often', he said, 'to give way to a jocular mood, and to laugh at everything, probably because God has granted us this faculty to compensate for the difficulty which we find in believing, in the same manner as playthings are given to children. But I really do not see why God should be obliged to preserve in the universe the same order which He once established. To whom did He promise that He would never change it, either wholly or in part? Who knows whether some day He will not give the moon an oval or a square shape instead of a round one?'

This he said smiling, but added immediately after, in a serious tone:–

'Those who believe in a God, Creator of the universe, can not refuse their belief in the possibility of miracles, for they behold in God the first of all miracles.'

CANT AND GOSSIP*

He on all occasions professes a detestation of what he calls *cant*; says it will banish from England all that is pure and good; and that while people are looking after the shadow, they lose the substance of goodness; he says, that the best mode left for conquering it, is to expose it to *ridicule*, the only *weapon*, added he, that the English climate cannot rust. He appears to know every thing that is going on in England; takes a great interest in the London gossip; and while professing to read no new publications, betrays, in various ways, a perfect knowledge of every new work. . . .

Byron is very fond of gossiping, and of hearing what is going on in the London fashionable world: his friends keep him *au courant*, and any little scandal amuses him very much. I observed this to him one day, and added, that I thought his mind had been too great to descend to such trifles! he laughed, and said with mock gravity, 'Don't you know that the trunk of an elephant, which can lift the most ponderous weights, disdains not to take up the most minute? This is the case with my *great* mind, (laughing anew,) and you must allow the simile is worthy the subject. Jesting apart, I do like a little scandal – I believe all English people do. . . .'

Lady Blessington's Conversations of Lord Byron, pp. 13, 28.

HIS LAMENESS*

His reverend friend, Mr Becher, finding him one day unusually de-
jected, endeavoured to cheer and rouse him, by representing, in their
brightest colours, all the various advantages with which Providence
had endowed him – and, among the greatest, that of 'a mind which
placed him above the rest of mankind'. – 'Ah, my dear friend,' said
Byron, mournfully – 'if *this* (laying his hand on his forehead) places me
above the rest of Mankind, *that* (pointing to his foot) places me far, far
below them.'

LORD AND LADY HOLLAND†

He talked of Lord [Holland]; praised his urbanity, his talents, and
acquirements; but, above all, his sweetness of temper and good-nature.
'Indeed I do love Lord [Holland],' said Byron, 'though the pity I feel
for his domestic thraldom has something in it akin to contempt. Poor
dear man! he is sadly bullied by *Milady*; and, what is worst of all, half
her tyranny is used on the plea of kindness and taking care of his
health. Hang such kindness! say I. She is certainly the most imperious,
dictatorial person I know – is always *en reine*; which, by the by, in her
peculiar position, shows tact, for she suspects that were she to quit the
throne she might be driven to the antechamber; however, with all her
faults, she is not vindictive – as a proof, she never extended her favour
to me until after the little episode respecting her in *English Bards*; nay
more, I suspect I owe her friendship to it. Rogers persuaded me to
suppress the passage in the other editions. After all, Lady [Holland]
has one merit, and a great one in my eyes, which is, that in this age of
cant and humbug, and in a country – I mean our own dear England –
where the cant of Virtue is the order of the day, she has contrived,
without any great resemblance of it, merely by force of – shall I call it
impudence or courage? – not only to get herself into society, but
absolutely to give the law to her own circle. She passes, also, for being
clever; this, perhaps owing to my dullness, I never discovered, except
that she has a way, *en reine*, of asking questions that show some reading.
The first dispute I ever had with Lady Byron was caused by my urging
her to visit Lady [Holland]; and, what is odd enough,' laughing with
bitterness, 'our first and last difference was caused by two very worth-
less women.'

*Thomas Moore, *The Life of Lord Byron*, p. 45.
†*Lady Blessington's Conversations of Lord Byron*, pp. 11–13.

Observing that we appeared surprised at the extraordinary frankness, to call it by no harsher name, with which he talked of his *ci-devant* friends, he added: – 'Don't think the worse of me for what I have said: the truth is, I have witnessed such gross selfishness and want of feeling in Lady [Holland], that I cannot resist speaking my sentiments of her.' – I observed: 'But are you not afraid she will hear what you say of her?' He answered: – 'Were she to hear it, she would act the *aimable*, as she always does to those who attack her; while to those who are attentive and court her, she is insolent beyond bearing.'

RAVENNA*

Except Greece, I was never so attached to any place in my life as to Ravenna, and but for the failure of the Constitutionalists and this fracas, should probably never have left it. The peasantry are the best people in the world, and the beauty of their women is extraordinary. Those at Tivoli and Frascati, who are so much vaunted, are mere Sabines, coarse creatures, compared to the Romagnese. You may talk of your English women, and it is true that out of one hundred Italians and English you will find thirty of the latter handsome; but then there will be one Italian on the other side of the scale, who will more than balance the deficit in numbers – one who, like the Florence Venus, has no rival, and can have none in the North. I have learnt more from the peasantry of the countries I have travelled in than from any other source, especially from the women: they are more intelligent, as well as communicative, than the men. I found also at Ravenna much education and liberality of thinking among the higher classes. The climate is delightful. I was unbroken in upon by society. Ravenna lies out of the way of travellers. I was never tired of my rides in the pine-forest: it breathes of the *Decameron*; it is poetical ground. Francesca lived, and Dante was exiled and died at Ravenna. There is something inspiring in such an air.

AIR TRAVEL†

'Who would not wish to have been born two or three centuries later?' said he, putting into my hand an Italian letter. 'Here is a *savant* of Bologna, who pretends to have discovered the manner of directing balloons by means of a rudder, and tells me that he is ready to explain the nature of his invention to our Government. I suppose we shall soon

---

Medwin's Conversations of Lord Byron, pp. 24–5.
†*Medwin's Conversations of Lord Byron*, pp. 187–8.

travel by air-vessels; make air instead of sea-voyages; and at length find our way to the moon, in spite of the want of atmosphere. . . .

'There is not so much folly as you may suppose, and a vast deal of poetry, in the idea', [said] Lord Byron. 'Where shall we set bounds to the power of steam? Who shall say, "Thus far shalt thou go, and no farther?" We are at present in the infancy of science. Do you imagine that, in former stages of this planet, wiser creatures than ourselves did not exist? All our boasted inventions are but the shadows of what has been – the dim images of the past – the dream of other states of existence. Might not the fable of Prometheus, and his stealing the fire, and of Briareus and his earth-born brothers, be but traditions of steam and its machinery? Who knows whether, when a comet shall approach this globe to destroy it, as it often has been and will be destroyed, men will not tear rocks from their foundations by means of steam, and hurl mountains, as the giants are said to have done, against the flaming mass? – and then we shall have traditions of Titans again, and of wars with Heaven.'

A STORM AT SEA*

[16 July 1823.] I was half dead with sickness the whole night. When able to rise, [Byron] said to me, 'You have lost one of the most magnificent sights I ever beheld. For a short time we were in serious danger; but the captain and his crew did wonders. I was the whole time on deck. The sight is not new to me, but I have always looked upon a storm as one of the sublimest spectacles in nature.' He appeared thoughtful, and remarked, that he considered a bad beginning a favourable omen.

With Byron to Greece I*

J. H. BROWNE

I had resided about a year at Pisa, when I was seized with a sudden ardour and enthusiasm in favour of the cause of Greece, then exciting,

*Count Pietro Gamba, *A Narrative of Lord Byron's Last Journey to Greece* (1825) p. 11.
*'Voyage from Leghorn to Cephalonia with Lord Byron, and a Narrative of a Visit, in 1823, to the Seat of War in Greece', *Blackwood's Magazine*, XXXV (Jan 1834) 56–65.

throughout Europe, the strongest sympathy. Intending to embark for the Ionian Islands, on my way to the Morea, I requested a friend at Leghorn to look out for a vessel bound to Zante, or Cephalonia. He informed me that there was not likely to be any opportunity for some time; but he strongly recommended me to apply for a passage to Lord Byron, who had just chartered an English brig for that destination. As his Lordship and I had some mutual friends, I ventured, but with some reluctance, to write to him on the subject; he returned a very polite answer, stating, that he should feel much pleasure in acceding to my request, and that I might either join his party at Genoa, or he would direct the vessel to touch off Leghorn and take me on board. As I was desirous of purchasing some sea-stock, and had other business at Leghorn, I preferred the latter plan, as I told his Lordship in a letter of thanks for his kindness; the vessel accordingly, at the appointed time, made her appearance, when I immediately joined her in the Roads, and had the honour of becoming personally known to him. My first personal introduction to Lord Byron thus took place at Leghorn, on board of the Hercules, which vessel he had caused to be chartered at Genoa, for the purpose of conveying himself and suite to the Ionian Islands, or perhaps direct to Greece.

He had kindly promised to touch off the port and take me on board, it being understood between us, that if he did not intend to communicate with Leghorn, certain signals should be displayed, when I was to lose no time in joining him.

I was accompanied to the ship, riding at anchor in the Roads, by Messrs Jackson and Lloyd, who departed immediately after seeing me safe on board, as I was apprehensive that Lord Byron might have conceived that they had come for the purpose of catching a glimpse of him. He put to me some interrogatory relative to them, regretting that I had hurried them off. On my informing him that the former gentleman was son to the Rev. Dr Jackson – who, so unfortunately for his family, rashly engaged in the Irish Rebellion, and would have suffered the death of a traitor; only escaping so disgraceful an end, by having anticipated the sentence of the law, in terminating his existence by poison, conveyed to him, it was alleged, by his lady, a very high-spirited woman, who afterwards, with her family, retired to France, where Bonaparte conferred a small pension on her – Lord Byron appeared quite conversant with the particulars of this unhappy affair, and said he should have felt a great interest in conversing with young Jackson.

His Lordship's mode of address was peculiarly fascinating and insinuating – *au premier abord*[1] it was next to impossible for a stranger to refrain from liking him.

The contour of his countenance was noble and striking; the forehead, particularly so, was nearly white as alabaster. His delicately formed features were cast rather in an effeminate mould, but their soft expression was in some degree relieved by the moustaches of a light chestnut, and small tuft *à la houssard*, which he at that time sported. His eyes were rather prominent and full, of a dark blue, having that melting character which I have frequently observed in females, said to be a proof of extreme sensibility. The texture of his skin was so fine and transparent, that the blue veins, rising like small threads around his temples, were clearly discernible. All who ever saw Byron have borne testimony to the irresistible sweetness of his smile, which was generally, however, succeeded by a sudden pouting of the lips, such as is practised sometimes by a pretty coquette, or by a spoiled child. His hair was partially grizzled, but curled naturally. In conversation, owing to a habit he had contracted of clenching his teeth close together, it was sometimes difficult to comprehend him distinctly; towards the conclusion of a sentence, the syllables rolled in his mouth, and became a sort of indistinct murmur.

It must have been almost impossible, I apprehend, for any artist to seize fully the expression of Byron's countenance, which was varying at every moment, as different ideas suggested themselves to his powerful mind. I have never seen any likeness that conveyed to me a perfect resemblance of his Lordship, with the exception of a marble bust, which was in the drawingroom of the late Honourable Douglas Kinnaird, executed, I think, by Thorwaldsen.[2] It struck me as being very like him.

Lord Byron was habited in a round nankeen embroidered jacket, white Marseilles vest, buttoned a very little way up; he wore extremely fine linen, and his shirt-collar was thrown over in such a way as almost to uncover his neck; very long wide nankeen trousers, fastened below, short buff laced boots, and sometimes gaiters, with a chip Tuscan straw hat, completed his personal equipment. He invariably paid the most scrupulous attention to cleanliness, and had a certain fastidiousness in his dress, strongly savouring of dandyism, of which he was far from disapproving; at least he infinitely preferred it to a slovenly disregard for dress. His Lordship, who had just dined, instantly ordered some hock and claret to be brought under the awning where he was sitting, which he invited me to partake of. Whilst discussing our wine, he plied me with questions relative to the Ionian Islands, and my opinion with regard to the posture of affairs in Greece; frequently observing that he did not imagine that he could render any essential service to the cause, but that as the Committee seemed to think otherwise, he was going thither in obedience to their commands. He then, as we could not avoid discerning both Corsica and Elba from the deck, changed the conversation to the subject of the life of Napoleon, exclaiming that he had been woefully deceived in his estimate of the character of that wonderful man; repeating the pain and mortification which he endured whenever he chanced to glance his eye on either of these islands, as they recalled to his recollection the humbling conviction of the weakness of human nature. 'I at one period', he said, 'almost idolised that man, although I could not approve of many of his actions; regarding other potentates as mere pigmies when weighed in the balance against him. When his fortune deserted him, and all appeared lost, he ought at once to have rushed into the thick of the fight at Leipzig or Waterloo, and nobly perished, instead of dying by inches in confinement, and affording to the world the degrading spectacle of his petty bilious contentions with the governors to whose custody he was confided at St Helena. Even if he had maintained a dignified silence amid the persecutions to which in his latter days he complained of being subjected, I could almost have forgiven him; yet this man's fame will descend to, and be revered by posterity, when that of numbers more deserving of immortality shall have ceased to be remembered.'

Byron's suavity of manner surprised and delighted me; my own previous conceptions, supported by common rumour, having prepared me to expect to find in him a man of morose temper and gloomy misanthropy instead of which, from his fecundity in anecdote, he was a most delightful associate. I had recently lost for ever one who was deservedly dear to me, and in consequence was clad in deep mourning. I apologised to Lord Byron for the unavoidable depression of my spirits; he instantly seemed to sympathise unaffectedly with my grief. I shall ever entertain a grateful recollection of the amiable and soothing attentions which he then paid me, using gentle efforts to draw me into conversation, and endeavouring at the same time to inspire me with self-possession, on perceiving that I stood somewhat in awe of him. Byron had just received communications from Moore and Goëthe; he read to me the letter of the former, who, he said, was the most humorous and witty of all his correspondents. He appeared to estimate, at its just value, the flattering and distinguished homage rendered to his inimitable poetic talent by the veteran German Bard, who, with the most profuse and enthusiastic eulogiums, panegyrised the wonderful productions of his genius.

Lord Byron expressed the extreme regret which he experienced at not being able to return the compliment by a perusal of Goëthe's works in their native garb, instead of through the cold medium of a translation; but nothing, he said, would induce him to learn the language of the Barbarians, by which epithet he constantly designated the Austrians.

On my arrival on board, the majority of Lord Byron's suite were on shore, but the wind coming fair, they returned towards the afternoon, when the anchor was weighed, and we made sail, every one assisting at the capstan and ropes, no one being more active than Byron himself. I had been but a short time on board until I perceived that the others, instead of addressing him with a prolonged emphasis on the first syllable of his name, pronounced it short, as if it had been 'Byrne', that of Byron seeming distasteful to him, so I adopted the same.

His suite consisted of Count Pietro Gamba, brother to his *chère amie*; Mr Edward Trelawny; a young man who had been engaged as his medical attendant, named Bruno,[3] who was a native of Alessandria Della Paglia; a Constantinopolitan Greek, calling himself Prince Schilizzi,[4] and a Greek Captain, Vitali.[5] He had, besides, five domestics, and the same number of horses, together with a Newfoundland and a bull dog; so that our small vessel, which did not much exceed a hundred tons burden, was sufficiently crowded. On the passage to Cephalonia, Byron chiefly read the writings of Dean Swift, taking occasional notes, with the view possibly of gleaning from that humorous writer something towards a future Canto of *Don Juan*. He also made it a constant rule to peruse every day one or more of the Essays of Montaigne. This practice, he said, he had pursued for a long time; adding his decided conviction, that more useful general knowledge and varied information were to be derived by an intimate acquaintance with the writings of that diverting author, than by a long and continuous course of study. This was relieved sometimes by dipping into Voltaire's *Essai sur les Mœurs*, and his *Dictionnaire Philosophique* – De Grimm's *Correspondence*, and *Les Maximes de la Rochefoucault*, were also frequently referred to by his Lordship; all, I should say, as connected with the composition of *Don Juan*, in which he was then deeply engaged.

A heavy tome on the War of Independence in South America, written by a *soi-disant* Colonel, named Hippisley,[6] I think, who had taken service with Bolivar, as an officer of cavalry, but quickly retired in disgust, on not finding port wine and beef-steaks to be always procurable in the other hemisphere (at least good fare seemed to him an indispensable requisite in campaigning), was invariably asked for by Byron at dinner, and at length, Fletcher, his valet, brought it regularly with the table-cloth. Its soporific qualities, he amusingly remarked, were truly astonishing, surpassing those of any ordinary narcotic; the perusal of a few pages sufficed to lull him asleep, and obtained him a comfortable siesta, even when ill disposed, or in bad humour with himself.

Dinner was the only regular meal which he partook of in the twenty-four hours. He usually eat it by himself on deck. His diet was very singular, and, in my opinion, almost nothing could have been devised more prejudicial to health in the intense heat of summer, under a blazing Italian sun. It consisted of a considerable quantity of decayed Cheshire cheese, with pickled cucumbers or red cabbage, which he quaffed down by drinking at the same time either a bottle of cider or Burton ale, of which articles he had procured a supply at Genoa. He sometimes drank an infusion of strong tea, but ate nothing with it but a

small piece of biscuit; and occasionally his fare at dinner was varied by
a little fish, if we succeeded in taking any. When he returned on deck
after the siesta, he joined us in drinking wines or other liquors,
displaying sometimes the most overflowing spirits; but in the midst of
the greatest hilarity and enjoyment, I have observed this jovial mood to
be suddenly checked. A cloud would instantaneously come over him, as
if arising from some painful and appalling recollection; the tears would
bedew his eyes, when he would arise and quit the company, averting
his face, in order to conceal his emotion. This strange conduct was
probably the effect of reaction from over-excitement, in a mind so
exquisitely susceptible; at least I have heard it thus accounted for.

Byron cherished the strongest superstition relative to commencing
any enterprise, or attempting any thing on a Friday, deeming it most
unlucky. He also seemed to repose credit in the absurd belief, so
popular among the Greeks and Turks, about the accidental spilling of
oil or wine, or the oversetting of salt, considering the first and last as
indicative of approaching misfortune, the other as possessed of a more
cheerful and favourable augury. When irritated or incensed, he did not
fail to make a profuse use of the common Italian oaths, *Faccia di
Maladetto*, *Corpo di Bacco*, *Sangue di Dio*, etc., combined sometimes with
the usual Greek malediction of 'Ανάθεμά σου, following each other in
rapid succession. He also imitated the inhabitants of the Levant, by
spitting on the deck or ground with great violence, whilst giving way to
the impetuosity of his temper. I considered Byron to be strongly
imbued with a certain religious feeling, although chary of acknowledg-
ing it. No one, he said, could be so senseless a brute as to deny the
existence of a First Cause, and an omnipotent and incomprehensible
Being, whose omnipresence all around us sufficiently evinced. He
frequently expressed considerable anxiety about attaching himself to
some particular creed, as any fixed belief would, he thought, be
preferable to the continued state of uncertainty in which he had
hitherto existed. He declared his ready openness to conviction, if the
truth could only be rendered evident to his understanding. His glowing
and fervent imagination, I feel inclined to believe, would sooner or later
have impelled him to attach himself to some particular, and, very
possibly, extreme sect.

For the religious tenets or prejudices of others, he invariably testified
the most profound respect – professing to entertain much regard for
those who were truly and conscientiously devout, believing such
individuals to enjoy great worldly felicity. On the contrary, no man
more than Byron ridiculed and detested the cant and hypocrisy which
are so much in vogue in our times. He spoke frequently of the inane
pursuits of mankind, and our limited intelligence, dwelling at some
length on a remark once made to him by the late Sir Humphry Davy,[7]
with respect to the nothingness of all human intellect, when it engages

in the ever endless task of endeavouring to explore or solve the hidden and impenetrable mysteries of nature.

To be in company with Lord Byron, and in almost constant inter-course with him for a considerable period, more especially on ship-board, where, it is affirmed, you will in a few days acquire more knowledge of an individual than from years of previous acquaintance, was, through the extreme communicativeness of his disposition, equiv-alent to an introduction to the whole course of his life. Although occasionally affecting mystery, he yet could conceal nothing. This sometimes produced rather painful confidences, relative to his own family matters, and amatory intrigues, which, if they ever actually took place, he would have shown more good sense not to reveal; but I have my doubts about some of them, more especially in respect to one lady of very high rank, whose family I had the honour to be acquainted with, and whose fair fame I had never before heard assailed by the vile breath of slander. I will, however, do Lord Byron the justice to say, that in regard to this particular case, he dealt more in innuendo than any allegation of facts.

I thence concluded that much of this *façon de parler*[8] consisted in a desire on his part, or rather weakness, if I may be permitted to term it so, to be considered amongst others as a *roué*, and man of gallantry; although I should be very far from disputing his general success in such matters; no one, from the insinuating powers of conversation, which he possessed in no small degree, and polished manner, combined with a strikingly handsome physiognomy, independently of his splendid men-tal qualifications, being more calculated to prove irresistibly attractive to the female heart. However blamable and unpleasant such revel-ations may appear to be, yet you might almost call them involuntary. Lord Byron could keep nothing secret, and occasionally astonished me by lavishing the grossest abuse on those whom I had always been led to consider as his intimate friends, and those to whom he owed the greatest obligations, which at other times he perhaps readily admitted: this fit, however, was transient as a summer shower, arising from impetuosity of temper, or some momentary personal pique; and I am persuaded, had he heard others assail them, he would have been the foremost in throwing down the gauntlet in their defence. Lord Byron entertained, or appeared to have imbibed, the most violent prejudice against the late Lady Noel.[9] He showed himself always affectionately anxious about the health and welfare of his daughter Ada. Alluding to her probable large fortune, he expressed a wish that it had been in his power to inhibit her from marrying a native of Great Britain – deeming his countrymen to have a greater propensity to fortune-hunting than the individuals of other nations – which might, by an ill-assorted union, tend to her future unhappiness and discomfort.

Lord Byron adverted, on many occasions, sometimes in a state of the most bitter excitement, to the unfortunate infirmity of his foot, and the extreme pain and misery it had been productive of to him. He once uttered a very savage observation on his lameness, declaring, that years before he would have caused the recreant limb to be amputated, had he not dreaded thereby to spoil an exercise in which he more especially excelled and delighted.

His Lordship had the strongest aversion to walking, and always performed even the most trivial distance on horseback; from a wish, I apprehend, to conceal as much as possible the slight halt in his gait. The habit of not using pedestrian exercise, without doubt, would contribute in no small degree to increase that tendency to obesity to which he was by constitution inclined; and to counteract which, he adopted the pernicious system of continually drugging himself. This early impaired his digestive organs, although they could not fail to have been also injured by his mode of living and singular diet.

In the use of the pistol, Lord Byron was exceedingly dexterous, and prided himself much on this trivial accomplishment, which, by constant practice, may easily be attained by any person possessed of a calculating eye and steady nerves. In this, as every thing else, he wished to carry off the palm; and if he made a shot which he thought could not be surpassed, he declined to share farther in the pastime of that day; and if a bad one, he did not attempt to improve it, but instantly gave up the contest. His nerves were a good deal shattered; and from his firing so well even with that disadvantage, it was evident that, when younger, his aim must have been most unerring.

Trelawny was also an excellent shot; and his Lordship and he occasionally used to kill the ducks for the cabin dinner in this way – a wicker basket was suspended from the main-yard of the mast, containing a poor duck, with his head protruding through it. I have known both of them, from the poop, to kill the bird by hitting its head at the first fire. Lord Byron possessed several cases of excellent pistols; among others, a brace which had been the private property of his old friend, Joe Manton;[10] and I was told he never grudged any expense in procuring those of superior workmanship. He frequently conversed about his former feats of skill at that celebrated maker's pistol gallery in London. He also boasted of having, about the time of his marriage, much to the amazement and discomfiture of Lady Noel, split a walking-stick in the garden at Seaham House, at the distance of twenty paces.

His lordship was within an ace of losing his life during one of these firing-matches on board. Schilizzi, who was unacquainted with the guard on English hair triggers, inadvertently discharged a pistol, the ball from which whizzed close past Lord Byron's temple. He betrayed no tremor, but taking the pistol out of Schilizzi's hand, pointed out to him the mechanism of the lock, and at the same time desired Gamba to take care, that in future he should not be permitted to use any other pistols than those of Italian workmanship. . . .

Lord Byron frequently boxed with Trelawny as an amusement, and practised fencing with Count Gamba; he was not particularly dexterous at the foils, but excelled in the other, but he could not keep up the exercise long, which had become too violent for him.

Lord Byron and Trelawny also often bathed from the ship's side in calm weather; neither of them betrayed any apprehension from sharks, which, however, are by no means of rare occurrence in the Mediterranean . . . .

On our nearing the Island of Ionza, in which Neapolitan prisoners of state are usually confined, which was then crowded with those unhappy persons who had engaged in the unsuccessful attempt at revolution in 1821, Lord Byron gave vent to his ire, uttering the most tremendous invectives against Austria, and the tyranny exercised by that nation over the minor powers of Italy; and recounted to me the history of the once expected rising of the Papal dominions, which should have taken effect when he resided at Ravenna, and in which he might have been called upon to act a prominent part; this insurrection was checked by the rapid march on Naples of the Imperialists, under Baron Frimont. It was not to be regretted that his Lordship had not found an opportunity of assisting in any revolt in Italy, which could only have ended in defeat and disgrace. . . .

Lord Byron sat up nearly all night watching Stromboli: it was, however, overcast, and emitted no flame. This was considered singular, as the volcano is supposed to be in constant activity, and always ejecting matter. He narrated to me the extraordinary story of the affidavit made by the crew of a British ship, who deposed that they had witnessed the apparition of a man, well known to them, borne through the air by two other figures, and cast into the crater of Stromboli. This raised a long discussion, with many arguments, in regard to superstition in general, and tales of spectres, to a belief in which Lord Byron either was, or affected to be thought prone.

We found the mighty Charybdis, so much dreaded by the ancients, dwindled to an inconsiderable whirling eddy, caused by the conflicting currents. The furious bellowing of the surge, which continually lashes the precipitous and cavernous promontory of Scylla, is, however, heard to a great distance.

Charybdis is reported to be still formidable in stormy weather. The strait, most probably, is now wider than it was in olden times; but I imagine that poetic licence in former days greatly exaggerated its terrors. Lord Byron much regretted its state of almost tranquil repose, and sighed, but, in vain, for a stiff breeze.

Both from attentive observation, and many circumstances which subsequently occurred, I was inclined to consider Lord Byron as a man of extreme sensibility, but decidedly of first impulses; ready at once to assist distress with purse and person; but, if the feeling were permitted to subside, and not instantaneously acted upon, it evaporated. I cannot account for this, except in supposing that his first – I do not say always better feelings, because in the objects which kindled his sympathy he was sometimes too indiscriminate – became withered things, and were deadened by suspicion of the world, or fear of ridicule; but, at all events, his second determination in such cases rarely coincided with the seeming original dictates of his heart and expressed intentions. I assert this with no view to detract from Lord Byron's charity, or to depreciate his philanthropy; but those around him were occasionally compromised by it, and placed in unpleasant predicaments – as, when a case of wretchedness was depicted to him, without stopping to institute any enquiry, he would entreat, nay, insist, that specific promises of relief should be made, which not being afterwards fulfilled, I have known one or two instances where friends of his, rather than occasion any misapprehension to his prejudice, have themselves disbursed the money. It had the effect of rendering them more wary and cautious, and caused sometimes a doubt with regard to Lord Byron's sincerity. This failing, with respect to those who did not perfectly understand his ways, was an unfortunate one, as it became the cause of much misrepresentation.

The extreme apparent candour of his disposition engendered a propensity for divulging every thing. No one who knew him well would have liked to confide any matter of a secret nature to his discretion, or even speak disparagingly about, or turn any one into ridicule in his presence, as he was sure to disclose it, and very likely to the party so assailed. In regard to this inherent infirmity, I do not wish to cast any imputation on Lord Byron, although occasionally it might have been productive of serious mischief, as I sincerely and honestly believe that he could not control this defect, or error in judgement, call it which you please; besides, in some cases, I think that he adopted this course advisedly, as a sort of test to elicit the truth, by listening to both sides. . . .

I once used the liberty of asking Lord Byron why he appeared never to have thought of writing an Epic, or some grand and continuous work. He replied, that it was very difficult to find an appropriate subject, and that, admitting he possessed the capacity to do so, he would not engage in such a composition. He remarked, that even Milton was little read at the present day, and how very few in number were those who were familiar with the writings of that sublime author; adding, 'I shall adapt my own poesy, please God! to the fashion of the time, and, in as far as I possess the power, to the taste of my readers of the present generation; if it survives me, *tanto meglio*,[11] if not, I shall have ceased to care about it.' I permitted myself to mention how generally Tasso and Ariosto were known to all Italians of any education; he answered, 'Ah! but Italy is not like England, the two countries cannot stand in comparison; besides, I consider that almost

every Italian inherits from nature, more or less, some poetical feeling.'
It is strange how little value he appeared to put on that fame which was
already acquired by his immortal literary performances; he seemed to
anticipate more lasting renown from some insignificant achievement
in Greece, which could only derive any importance from his being an
actor in it, than from any brilliant emanation of his genius.

His vivid and ardent imagination was wont to convert those every
day occurrences that related to himself into extraordinary events,
which were to exercise an influence on his future destinies; distorted
conceptions arose to his morbid fancy, from which he extracted gloomy
and desponding inferences, which no ordinary man would ever have
contemplated in idea; when in a fitful mood, as he was a most ingenious
self-tormentor, they furnished him with materials to vomit forth bitter
imprecations against his own supposed unhappy fate, and the villainy
of mankind. This miserable feeling appeared to be with him quite a
second nature, and, I venture to say, no greater calamity could have
befallen him than suddenly to find himself without a grievance, real or
ideal, of which he could complain.

Lord Byron set great store by his independence in mind and action,
but he was, however, if I may use such a term, the slave of that liberty
on which he piqued himself so highly, as in support of it he was almost
continually doing or saying something, that, on calm reflection, was the
cause of sincere regret, and bitterly lamented, on discovering that he
had been in error. He was also easily influenced and led by those who
had the tact to use their sway mildly, and allow him to suppose that he
governed them, whilst the reverse was the fact; but had any one
suggested this to him, or even hinted it, he would have been frantic at
the idea, and perhaps never after endured the presence of the party
supposed to exercise the obnoxious dominion. He sometimes on the
passage expressed his intention, should his services prove of no avail to
Greece, of endeavouring to obtain by purchase, or otherwise, some
small island in the South Sea, to which, after visiting England, he
might retire for the remainder of his life, and very seriously asked
Trelawny if he would accompany him, to which the latter, without
hesitation, replied in the affirmative.

He frequently reverted to the extreme dissolute conduct and inconti-
nence which reigned among the higher circles in his younger days,
observing, that married ladies of that class of society in England were
much more depraved than those of the Continent, but that the strict
outward regard paid to the observances of morality in the former, led
the fair sinners to be more dexterous and cunning in concealing their
delinquencies.

He professed to entertain a very indifferent opinion in respect to
habitual virtue and constancy in the fair sex; this unfair and severe
judgement may probably be ascribed to the tone of society in which his

Lordship had so unfortunately in his younger days, and afterwards at Venice, indulged; and to having early abandoned himself to the mastery of his passions, without any one to act as his Mentor and protector.

The Greek Schilizzi, by way of flattery, used frequently to insinuate that his countrymen might possibly choose Lord Byron for their King, as a considerable party were in favour of a Monarchical Government; this idea did not displease his Lordship, who said he would perhaps not decline the offer, if made, adding, 'but we shall retain our own monies; and then if our appetite disagrees with the kingly authority, we shall, like Sancho, have the alternative of abdicating'.

He often contended in favour of the Oriental custom of secluding females, and teaching them only a few pleasing accomplishments, affirming the learned education lavished so frequently in England on the sex, only served to turn their heads with conceit, and look with contempt on domestic duties; that the Greeks were sensible people in not allowing their daughters to be instructed in writing, as it taught them to scribble billets-doux and practise deception. Had he to choose a second wife, he would select one born in the East, young and beautiful, whom he alone had been permitted to visit, and whom he had taught to love him exclusively, but of her he would be jealous as a tiger.

Lord Byron could scarcely be serious in such a strange idea, and perhaps was but mystifying some of our party. He used to indulge in many mirthful sallies about his increasing love of money; when he possessed little, he said that he was extremely profuse, but now that his fortune had been so much augmented, he felt an irresistible inclination to hoard, and contemplated with delight any accumulation. From this propensity he augured that a prediction once made in respect to him would be forthwith fulfilled, viz that he would die a miser and a Methodist, which he said he intended should also be the *dénouement* of *Don Juan.*

With occasional liberality, Lord Byron certainly united a considerable degree of unnecessary parsimony, and those who had known him much longer than myself, stated that this habit was to be dated from the period of the increase to his fortune, arising from the large property which he had become entitled to at the demise of Lady Noel, his wife's mother.

Lord Byron sometimes spoke in terms of unqualified praise of the extremely careful and penurious character of old Lega, his *Maestro di Casa.* This man, he said, guarded his treasure like the Dragon watching the golden fruit in the garden of the Hesperides, and viewed his monies with the same self-satisfaction as if they were his own property, grumbling and murmuring at making the most trivial disbursement on Lord Byron's own order, and sleeping on the boxes of specie, yet was strictly honest.

NOTES

James Hamilton Browne was a Scot who sympathised with the cause of Greek independence. He had been secretary to General Maitland in Corfu and had assisted with the negotiation of a British loan to the Greeks. He joined Byron's expedition, meeting him in Leghorn in late July 1823. It was Browne who persuaded Byron to go to Cephalonia rather than to Zante. In addition to the article from which this extract is taken, Browne published 'Narrative of a Visit to the Seat of War in Greece', *Blackwood's Magazine*, XXXVI (Sep 1834) 392–407.

1. At the first encounter (French).

2. On Thorwaldsen's bust, see p. 24. The Hon. Douglas Kinnaird (1788–1830), son of the seventh Baron Kinnaird, was educated at Trinity College, Cambridge, and became Byron's banker, business adviser and friend. Byron wrote many letters to him from abroad, and Kinnaird was the first man in England to be notified of his death, the news reaching him on 14 May 1824.

3. Francesco Bruno, who joined the expedition as Byron's medical adviser, was young and inexperienced (Trelawny called him 'an unfledged medical student') and spoke no English.

4. Constantine Schilizzi (also spelt Skilitzy), who seems to have been a Count rather than a Prince, was related to Prince Mavrocordatos (see p. 154).

5. Captain George Vitali, like Schilizzi, had asked Byron to grant him passage to his homeland.

6. The reference is perhaps to G. Hippisley's *Narrative of the Expedition to the River Orinoco* (1819).

7. Sir Humphry Davy (1778–1829), chemist and inventor of the miner's safety lamp. He was a friend of Sir Walter Scott.

8. Manner of speaking (French).

9. Byron's mother-in-law (formerly Lady Milbanke).

10. Manton kept a shooting-gallery in Davies Street, London, which Byron had at one time frequented. See also p. 41.

11. So much the better (Italian).

With Byron to Greece II*

E. J. TRELAWNY

The poet had an antipathy to everything scientific; maps and charts offended him; he would not look through a spy-glass, and only knew the cardinal points of the compass; buildings the most ancient or modern he was as indifferent to as he was to painting, sculpture, and music. But

*Records of Shelley, Byron, and the Author, II, 91, 95–7.

all natural objects and changes in the elements he was generally the
first to point out and the last to lose sight of. We lay-to all night off
Stromboli; Byron sat up watching it. As he went down to his cabin at
daylight, he said –

'If I live another year, you will see this scene in a fifth canto of *Childe
Harold*.'. . .

It was now 30 July, twelve days since our departure from Genoa, our
ship would do anything but go a-head, she was built on the lines of a
baby's cradle, and the least touch of Neptune's foot set her rocking. I
was glad of this, for it kept all the land-lubbers in their cribs. Byron was
not at all affected by the motion, he improved amazingly in health and
spirits, and said, 'On shore when I awake in the morning, I am always
inclined to hang myself, as the day advances, I get better, and at
midnight I am all cock-a-whoop. I am better now than I have been for
years.' You never know a man's temper until you have been imprisoned in a ship with him, or a woman's until you have married her. Few
friendships can stand the ordeal by water; when a yacht from England
with a pair of these thus tried friends touches – say at Malta or
Gibraltar – you may be sure that she will depart with one only. I never
was on shipboard with a better companion than Byron, he was generally cheerful, gave no trouble, assumed no authority, uttered no complaints, and did not interfere with the working of the ship; when
appealed to he always answered, 'do as you like'. Every day at noon, he
and I jumped overboard in defiance of sharks or weather; it was the
only exercise he had, for he could not walk the deck. His favourite toys –
pistols – were not forgotten; empty bottles and live poultry served as
targets; a fowl, duck or goose, was put into a basket, the head and neck
only visible, hoisted to the main yard-arm: and we rarely had two shots
at the same bird. No boy cornet enjoyed a practical joke more than
Byron. On great occasions when our Captain wished to be grand, he
wore a bright scarlet waistcoat; as he was very corpulent, Byron wished
to see if this vest would not button round us both. The Captain was
taking his siesta one day, when Byron persuaded the boy to bring up
the waistcoat. In the meantime, as it was nearly calm and very hot, I
opened the coops of the geese and ducks, who instinctively took to the
water. Neptune, the Newfoundland dog, jumped after them, and
Moretto the bull-dog followed.

'Now,' said Byron, standing on the gangway, with one arm in the red
waistcoat, 'put your arm in, Tre, we will jump overboard, and take the
shine out of it.'

So we did.

The Captain hearing the row on deck, came up, and when he saw the
gorgeous garment he was so proud of defiled by sea-water, he roared
out, 'My Lord, you should know better than to make a mutiny on

board ship' (the crew were laughing at the fun). 'I won't heave to, or lower a boat, I hope you will both be drowned.'

'Then you will lose your *frite*' (for so the Captain always pronounced the word freight), shouted Byron.

As I saw the dogs worrying the ducks and geese, I returned on board with the waistcoat, pacified the skipper, lowered a boat, and with the aid of a boy, sculled after the birds and beasts; the Newfoundlander brought them to us unharmed, but Moretto the bull-dog did not mouth them so tenderly. After the glare and oppressive heat of the day, the evenings and nights were delightful: balmy air, no dew, and light enough to distinguish everything near.

NOTE

On Trelawny, see p. 27.

In Greece*

JULIUS MILLINGEN

Being, like many others, bearers of a letter of recommendation from the London Greek Committee to Lord Byron – who, as we were informed, was on the eve of his departure for Greece – we hastened [in November 1823] to Argostoli, whence we forwarded it to Metaxata,[1] a village at a few miles' distance, in which, since his arrival in Cephalonia, he had taken up his abode.

The next day, Count Gamba, a young nobleman of Ravenna, who acted as secretary to Lord Byron, came to inform us, that his lordship had come down from the country, and desired to see us. We proceeded accordingly to the Lazaretto,[2] where he received us with the greatest affability, exhibiting the most gentlemanly and elegant manners, bordering perhaps a little on affectation, but not to be surpassed by the

---

Memoirs of the Affairs of Greece with Various Anecdotes of Lord Byron and an Account of his Last Illness and Death (London: Murray, 1831) pp. 1–16, 116–20.

most finished courtier. After commending our zeal in favour of the Greek cause, and expressing his readiness to assist us to the utmost of his power, he added, that we would not, he trusted, as many had done, ascribe his prolonged stay in Cephalonia to any diminution of Philhellenism; he had remained here because, notwithstanding the repeated assurances he had received, and the promise he had made of advancing a loan of twenty thousand dollars, the long-expected division of the Greek fleet, which was to raise the blockade of Missolonghi, had not yet made its appearance. He also waited for the arrival of the deputies, which he had engaged the Greek government to appoint, in order to negotiate a national loan in England, wishing to have private conferences with them on this most important measure. To hasten their departure, and obtain at the same time a correct report on the state of things in the Morea, he had sent to that country Mr Hamilton Browne,[3] a gentleman highly qualified for the task. He flattered himself, he could not have acted more in conformity with the best interests of Greece than he had hitherto done; and it was his intention, he said, to depart for that country the moment the objects, he had mentioned, should be completely fulfilled.

He assured the German gentlemen, that he would give them letters of recommendation to the Greek government; though he felt it a duty to confess to them plainly his apprehensions, that the Greeks were not in a sufficient state of mental improvement to appreciate either their merits as military men, or the value of their services. In spite of what they had been given to understand in Europe, he feared that their acquirements would prove as unavailing to Greece, for the present, as a bridle would be to one possessing neither saddle nor horse. They would find the country agitated by civil broils and the thousand evils of anarchy, and the mind of every one absorbed by the petty passions, arising from the most absolute egotism. He dwelt in most feeling terms on the disappointment, met with by almost every Philhellene; described the miserably forlorn condition in which they returned from a land, in the defence of which they had often exposed their lives, endured the severest privations, and lost the greater part of their companions in arms. 'If, gentlemen,' continued he, 'you allow yourselves to be influenced by the same illusory ideas, which have led so many others to take a step, of which they repented as soon as reality taught them on how false a basis they had grounded their hopes, you cannot but expect to share the same fate. Yet, if you deem yourselves capable of serving Greece in spite of the Greeks, you might do well to venture on the career, which you propose to run. On the other hand, should you feel the love you bear towards so unfeeling a mistress, not to be proof against the thousand crosses, which inevitably await it, let prudence caution you in time to renounce so misplaced an attachment.'

Thoroughly imbued as we were with enthusiastic ideas in favour of the Greeks, that were then prevalent in England, we could not but feel the most grievous disappointment, on hearing observations so completely at variance with our fondest expectations and the statements, on which we had been taught to rely; and what rendered them the more impressive was the quarter from which they proceeded; Lord Byron being considered by us as a chivalrous friend of the cause.

I had afterwards repeated opportunities of observing, that, on every occasion before strangers, he sought to prove, that in the part he had undertaken, his conduct was influenced rather by prudence and judgement than by any romantic disposition; while before those, whom he treated with familiarity, he delighted in indulging the natural bent of his mind for adventurous and extraordinary undertakings. Addressing himself to me in particular, he wished me to remain in Cephalonia till he himself should embark for Greece. My professional services, he said, would always be valued in a country where there was a great dearth of medical men; and where the name of *doctore* was the best, or rather the only, introduction for a Frank; and he promised to employ me in the corps of troops, he proposed taking into his service on his arrival in that country.

In consequence of his invitation I soon after went to Metaxata, where I remained several days. On my arrival, I found him on the balcony of the house, wrapt in his Stewart tartan cloak, with a cap on his head, which he affected to wear as the Scotch bonnet, attentively contemplating the extensive and variegated view before him, terminated by the blue mountains of Ætolia, Acarnania, and Achaia. The valley below the village is highly luxuriant, and even at this advanced epoch of the year was covered with verdure, and embellished by the evergreen olive, orange and lemon trees, and cypresses towering above the never-fading laurel and myrtle. Like an oasis in the sandy desert, its aspect produced the most pleasing impression on the eye, weary of the barren and cheerless rocks of Cephalonia.

Being on the point of taking his usual ride, he invited me to accompany him. Greece and the London Committee formed, till our return, the principal topics of conversation. After I had, to the best of my power, satisfied his curiosity by answering the questions he put to me, he said, that notwithstanding the talents of most of its members, he could not help apprehending, that the well-meaning endeavours of the Committee would be attended with very limited success; because their impatience of being useful to the Greeks induced them to act before a competent knowledge had been acquired of their moral disposition and real wants. If they allowed themselves to be guided by Bellier's report, they could not avoid falling into the most egregious errors. Had they taken a correct view of the state of things, they would not have sent, as they had lately done, cavalry and infantry officers to Greece, much less have determined on establishing a laboratory. By acting thus, they not only wasted the funds, entrusted to their care by the public, and drew blame and ridicule on their proceedings, but materially injured the cause, they sought to serve, and occasioned the misfortune of those deluded young men, who placed confidence in their fair but unwarranted assurances. The most essential service, the London Committee could confer upon Greece, would be to exert their influence in facilitating the negotiation of the intended loan; for on the well-directed employment of this aid entirely depended the prosperity of the country both at home and abroad. The sums raised by private subscription could, comparatively speaking, be of trifling avail, and, at any rate, would be much more beneficial if spent upon the spot by prudent agents, instead of being devoted in England to the relief of wants that, for the most part, are imaginary, or the least urgent.

Having, in the course of conversation, often expressed my surprise at the prodigious difference between his notions with regard to the Greek character and those prevalent in England, he said, 'This should not surprise you, for I know this nation by long and attentive experience, while in Europe they judge it by inspiration. The Greeks are perhaps the most depraved and degraded people under the sun; uniting to their original vices both those of their oppressors, and those inherent in slaves. Breaking asunder the frail shackles, which checked their immorality, the late revolution has given the amplest scope to the exhibition of their real character; and it stands to reason, that it must have placed in a more glaring light the melancholy picture of their utter worthlessness. Even under the wisest government, the regeneration of a nation can only be the difficult work of time; and certainly none can be less easily improvable than this.'

As I expressed my astonishment how, having so unfavourable an opinion of the Greeks, he should have determined on leaving the comforts of peaceable life to devote his time, talents, and fortune, nay, if necessary, his very existence, for their sake, he replied, after a long pause, 'Heartily weary of the monotonous life I had led in Italy for several years; sickened with pleasure; more tired of scribbling than the public, perhaps, is of reading my lucubrations; I felt the urgent necessity of giving a completely new direction to the course of my ideas; and the active, dangerous, yet glorious scenes of the military career struck my fancy, and became congenial to my taste. I came to Genoa; but far from meditating to join the Greeks, I was on the eve of sailing for Spain, when, informed of the overthrow of the Liberals, and the desperate state of things in that country, I perceived it was too late to join Sir R[obert] Wilson; – and then it was, in the unmanageable delirium of my military fever, that I altered my intention, and resolved on steering for Greece. After all, should this new mode of existence fail to afford me the satisfaction I anticipate, it will at least present me with the means of making a dashing exit from the scene of this world, where the part I was acting had grown excessively dull.'

On dinner being served up, although several dishes of meat were upon the table, Lord Byron did not partake of any, his custom being to eat meat only once a month. Soup, a few vegetables, a considerable portion of English cheese, with some fried crusts of bread, and fruit, constituted his daily fare. He eat with great rapidity, and drank freely. There happened to be on the table a roasted capon, the good looks of which so powerfully tempted him, that, after wistfully eyeing it, he was on the point of taking a leg; but suddenly recollecting the rule, he had imposed on himself, he left it in the dish, desiring his servant to let the capon be kept till the next day, when his month would be out.

Lord Byron pretended, that the reason of his abstaining from meat, and of his taking nourishment only once in the course of twenty-four hours, was his having experienced, that his mental powers became thereby more alive and powerful; for nothing blunted or rendered them more torpid than substantial food or frequent eating. Though it is an incontrovertible fact, as indeed every one must, more or less, have experienced, that the stomach and digestive organs materially operate on the functions of the mind, this was not the cause of Lord Byron's abstemiousness: the real motive being the fear of becoming corpulent, which haunted him continually, and induced him to adopt measures very injurious to his health. I frequently heard him say, 'I especially dread, in this world, two things, to which I have reason to believe I am equally predisposed – growing fat and growing mad; and it would be difficult for me to decide, were I forced to make a choice, which of these conditions I would choose in preference.' To avoid corpulence, not satisfied with eating so sparingly, and renouncing the use of every kind of food, that he deemed nourishing, he had recourse almost daily to strong drastic pills, of which extract of colocynth, gamboge, scammony, etc. were the chief ingredients; and if he observed the slightest increase in the size of his wrists or waist, which he measured with scrupulous exactness every morning, he immediately sought to reduce it by taking a large dose of Epsom salts, besides the usual pills. No *petit-maître*[4] could pay more sedulous attention than he did to external appearance, or consult with more complacency the looking-glass. Even when *en négligé*, he studied the nature of the postures he assumed as attentively as if he had been sitting for his picture; and so much value did he attach to the whiteness of his hands, that in order not to suffer 'the winds of heaven to visit them too roughly', he constantly, and even within doors, wore gloves. The lameness, which he had from his birth, was a source of actual misery to him; and it was curious to notice with how much coquetry he endeavoured, by a thousand petty tricks, to conceal from strangers this unfortunate malconformation. If any one fixed a look of curiosity on his foot, he considered it as paramount to a personal insult, and he could not easily forgive it. Sooner than confess, that nature had been guilty of this original defect, he preferred attributing his lameness to the improper treatment of a sprained ankle while he was yet a child; and he even vented himself bitterly against his mother for having neglected to place him in time under the care of a competent surgeon.

Besides the medicines, I have mentioned, he had daily recourse to soda powders or calcined magnesia, in order to neutralise the troublesome acidities, which the immoderate use of Rhenish wines and ardent spirits continually generated in his debilitated stomach. Nothing could be more strange, and at the same time more injurious to health, than the regimen which he had been induced to adopt, and to which, during several years, he unalterably adhered. He rose at half-past ten o'clock, when, by way of breakfast, he took a large basinful of a strong infusion of green tea, without either sugar or milk; a drink, that could not but prove exceedingly prejudicial to a constitution so essentially nervous. At half-past eleven he would set out on a two hours' ride; and on his return his singular and only meal was served up. Having dined, he immediately withdrew to his study, where he remained till dark; when, more willingly than at any other time, he would indulge in conversation: and afterwards he would play at draughts for a while, or take up some volume on light subjects – such as novels, memoirs, or travels. He had unfortunately contracted the habit of drinking immoderately every evening; and almost at every page he would take a glass of wine, and often of undiluted Hollands, till he felt himself under the full influence of liquor. He would then pace up and down the room till three or four o'clock in the morning; and these hours, he often confessed, were the most propitious to the inspirations of his muse.

This mode of life could not but prove ruinous to his constitution, which, however robust it might originally have been, must necessarily sink under shocks so powerful and so often repeated. The disagreeable symptoms of dyspepsia obliged him to have recourse to the daily use of pharmacy, which, instead of annoying him, seemed to be a business of pleasure, persuaded as he was, that there was no other way of obviating the misfortune of corpulency: but after the evanescent stimulation of alcohol had subsided, hypochondriasis, the inseparable companion of intemperance, plunged him in a condition often bordering on despair.

From the moment Lord Byron embarked in the Greek cause, his mind seemed so completely absorbed by the subject, that it rendered him deaf to the calls of the muse; at least he repeatedly assured us, that, since his departure from Genoa, he had not written a single line: and though it appeared from his conversation, that he was arranging in his head the materials of a future canto of *Don Juan*, he did not feel his poetical vein sufficiently strong to induce him to venture on the undertaking. It was an invariable habit with him to write by fits and starts, when the impetuosity of his Pegasus could no longer be restrained; and he often observed, that the productions of his pen, to which he was most partial, were those which he had composed with the greatest rapidity. If he ever wrote any thing worth perusing, he had done it, he said, spontaneously and at once; and the value of his poems might, according to him, be rated by the facility he had experienced in composing them, his worst productions (his dramatic pieces) being those that had given him most trouble. *The Bride of Abydos* was composed in less than a week; *The Corsair* in the same space of time; and 'The Lamentation of Tasso', which he wrote at the request of Teresa [Guiccioli] of Ravenna, was the business only of two nights.

During his stay at Metaxata, the portion of his time, which was not employed in correspondence with the different chiefs in Greece, and his friends in England, was devoted to reading. Novels, from his earliest youth, were the works in which he delighted most, and they formed almost his sole occupation. So prodigious was the number which he had perused, and so strong was the impression they had left on his memory, that he frequently defied us to mention one, however indifferent, that he had not read, and of which he could not give some account. Sir Walter Scott's were his favourites: and so great was the pleasure he derived from them, so often had they banished from his mind the sad train of thoughts attendant on despondency, that he professed himself bound to their author by ties of the liveliest gratitude; and though habitually frugal of praise, he constantly spoke of this distinguished writer in terms of the most lavish admiration. The conversation happening once to fall on modern poets, on being asked his opinion of Sir Walter, he observed: 'I have received so many benefits from him as a novelist, that I cannot find it in my heart to criticise him as a poet.' Passing in review the rest of the poets, he gave to each, without exception, a few lashes of that playful but often caustic satire which invariably enlivened his conversation, and rendered it so piquant. Southey and Wordsworth served him as targets against which to vent his bitterest sarcasms. We were not a little surprised to find that he did not spare even *****. It was some time before he would let out what had indisposed him so much against a man, whom he had publicly called his friend; but he spoke at last of a letter, in which this friend had taken the liberty of censuring him rather freely on the immorality of certain passages of *Don Juan*; a liberty which was deemed highly misplaced, and by a person so excessively touchy as Lord Byron, and whose vanity, vulnerable on all sides, never overlooked the slightest offence, was not to be forgiven. Small reliance, it would appear, is to be placed on the friendship of poets for each other: like coquettes, they look with an evil eye at any one of their craft, who has pretensions to beauty; and the slightest incident of displeasure is sufficient to cause them to throw off the mask that concealed their enmity.

Among Lord Byron's books there were very few poetical works; and, what may appear strange, he did not possess a copy of his own. Next to the British poets, those which he read in preference were the Italian – Ariosto and Dante more especially. With respect to the ancient classics, he was too indifferent a scholar to be able to peruse the originals with any degree of pleasure. He was as partial to the French prose-writers as he was averse to their poets. He entertained a singular prejudice against every thing that bore the name of this nation; and it may be cited as a proof of the sway, which preconceived opinions exercised over his mind, that not only he would never visit any part of France, but purposely avoided even entering its confines; and absolute necess-ity alone could induce him to express himself in the French tongue. Italian was the language he used in conversing with foreigners, and he spoke and wrote it with peculiar purity and elegance. It has been supposed by many, that Lord Byron was familiarly acquainted with German literature; and critics in Europe have often laid imitation and even plagiarism to his charge; yet he certainly understood scarcely one word of that language; and the only knowledge, he possessed of the productions of the most celebrated German authors, was derived from the very limited translations of their works, that have appeared in England.

Historical works, next to novels, were those which he took most pleasure in reading; and indeed his acquaintance with both ancient and modern history might, without exaggeration, be called prodigious. He had devoted peculiar attention to that of the East, a region very imperfectly known; where his imagination always delighted to rove, and from which he drew his finest and most original poetical thoughts. We had often occasion to be astonished at the accuracy, with which he related the minutest details of the most uninteresting facts. So highly was he gifted with memory, that every word he heard that struck, or every passage he read that pleased him, left an indelible impression. Not only could he repeat the finest passages of our classics, but also the most ludicrous of *Bombastes Furioso*; and we found it difficult, after repeated trials, to cite a line from any poet, he had attentively perused, without his being able to add the lines that followed.

While a member of the Drury Lane Committee for the examination of the theatrical productions presented by different authors, it was his amusement to read the greater portion; and, to our no small entertain-ment, he often regaled us with extracts from the most nonsensical. His wonderful mnemonic faculties, the rich and variegated store with which he had furnished his mind, his lively, brilliant, and ever-busy imagination, his deep acquaintance with the world, owing to his sagacious penetration, and the advantageous positions in which, through his birth and other circumstances, he had been placed, con-joined to the highly mercurial powers of his wit, rendered his conversa-tion peculiarly interesting; enhanced, too, as it was by the charm of his fascinating manners. Far from being the surly, taciturn misanthrope, generally imagined, I always found him dwelling on the lightest and merriest subjects, carefully shunning discussions, and whatever might give rise to unpleasing reflections. Almost every word with him was a jest; and he possessed the talent of passing from subject to subject with a lightness, an ease, and a grace, that could with difficulty be matched. Communicative to a degree, that raised our surprise, and might, not unfrequently, be termed indiscretion, he related anecdotes of himself, his friends, and even of the females, to whom he had been bound by the tenderest ties, which he might as well have kept secret. Many, perhaps, will regard this circumstance as incredible; but the apparent contradictions, existing in his character, are not the less true because they appear singular. Those only, who lived for some time with him, could believe that a man's temper, Proteus like, was capable of assuming so many shapes. It may literally be said, that at different hours of the day he metamorphosed himself into four or more individuals, each possessed of the most opposite qualities; for, in every change, his natural impetuosity made him fly into the furthermost extremes. In the course of the day he might become the most morose, and the most gay; the most melancholy, and the most frolicsome; the most generous, and the most penurious; the most benevolent, and the most misanthropic; the most rational, and the most childish; the most sublime and elevated in thought, and the most frivolous or trivial; the most gentle being in existence, and the most irascible. His works bear the stamp of his character, and *Childe Harold* is no less a faithful picture of him at one part of the day, than *Don Juan* is at another. . . .

Sometimes, when his vein of humour flowed more copiously than usual, he would play tricks on individuals. Fletcher's boundless credulity afforded him an ever ready fund of amusement, and he one evening planned a farce, which was as well executed and as laughable as any ever exhibited on the stage. Having observed how nervous Parry[5] had been, a few days before, during an earthquake, he felt desirous of renewing the ludicrous sight which the fat horror-struck figure of the major had exhibited on that occasion. He placed therefore fifty of his Suliots in the room above that where Parry slept, and towards midnight ordered them to shake the house, so as to imitate that phenomenon; he himself at the same time banged the doors, and rushed down stairs, delighted to see the almost distracted engineer imploring, tremblingly, the mercy of heaven. Parry was altogether a 'curious fish', an excellent mimic; and possessed a fund of quaint expressions, that made up for his deficiency of real wit. He could tell, in his coarse language, a good story, could perform the clown's or Falstaff's part very naturally, rant Richard the Third's or Hamlet's soliloquies in a mock-tragic manner, unrivalled by any of the players of Bartholomew fair, and could always engender laughter enough to beguile the length of our rainy evenings. His description of the visit he paid to Bentham;[6] their walk; Bentham's pursuit by a lady, named City-Barge, was highly humorous, and pleased Lord Byron so much, that he purposed putting it in verse, like that of Gilpin's trip to Edmonton.[7]

It was soon perceived, that the brandy-bottle was Parry's Castalian spring, and that, unless he drank deep, his stories became dull. Lord Byron, in consequence, took constant care to keep him in good spirits; but unfortunately, partly from inclination, and partly to keep him company, he drank himself to the same excess. One evening, by way of driving away the vexation he had experienced during the day, from an altercation with some one, whose name I do not now remember, Parry prescribed some punch of his own composition, so agreeable to Lord Byron's palate, that he drank immoderate quantities of it. To remove the burning sensation his lordship, soon after, began to experience, he ordered a bottle of cider; and having drank a glass of it, he said it was 'excessively cold and pleasant'. Scarcely had he said these words when he fell upon the floor, agitated by violent spasmodic movements of all his limbs. He foamed at the mouth, gnashed his teeth, and rolled his eyes like one in an epilepsy. After remaining about two minutes in this state his senses returned, and the first words he uttered were: 'Is not this Sunday?' On being answered in the affirmative, he said; 'I should have thought it most strange if it were not.'

Dr Bruno,[8] his private physician, proposed opening a vein; but finding it impossible to obtain his consent, he applied leeches to the temples, which bled so copiously as almost to bring on syncope. Alarmed to see the difficulty Dr Bruno experienced in endeavouring to stop the haemorrhage, Lord Byron sent for me, and I succeeded in stopping the bleeding by the application of lunar caustic. The acute pain, produced by this slight operation, rendered him more than ever impatient, and made him say, 'In this world there is nothing but pain.'

The nervous system of Lord Byron, which by nature was highly irritable, and which had become more so by the immoderate use of green tea, the abuse of medicines, and habitual intemperance, could not sustain so violent a shock without some serious attendant consequences. Like a cord at its full stretch, it required but the slightest force to break it. From this moment a change took place in his mental and bodily functions. That wonderful elasticity of disposition, that continued flow of wit, and that facility of jest, by which his conversation had been so highly distinguished, returned only at distant intervals; for he fell into a state of melancholy, from which none of our reasonings could relieved him. He felt assured that his constitution had been irretrievably ruined by intemperance; that he was a worn-out man; and that his muscular power was gone. Flashes before the eyes, palpitations and anxieties, hourly afflicted him; and at times such a sense of faintness would overpower him, that, fearing to be attacked by similar convulsions, he would send in great haste for medical assistance. His nervous system was in fact in a continued state of erethism, which could only be augmented by the low debilitating diet, enjoined him by his physician. One day while I sat by him rather longer than usual, endeavouring to prove that by a total reform in his mode of living, and by following a tonic plan, he might recover his former vigour, I quoted, in support of my argument, the celebrated example of Cornaro the Venetian, who at a more advanced age, and with a constitution still more broken, not only recovered his strength by adopting a proper regimen, but continued beyond the hundredth year in the full possession of all his mental and bodily faculties. 'Do you suppose', inquired his lordship with impatience, 'that I wish for life? I have grown heartily sick of it, and shall welcome the hour I depart from it. Why should I regret it? can it afford me any pleasure? have I not enjoyed it to a surfeit? Few men can live faster than I did. I am, literally speaking, a young old man. Hardly arrived at manhood, I had attained the zenith of fame. Pleasure I have known under every form it can present itself to mortals. I have travelled, satisfied my curiosity, lost every illusion; I have exhausted all the nectar contained in the cup of life; it is time to throw the dregs away. But the apprehension of two things now haunt [*sic*] my mind. I picture myself slowly expiring on a bed of torture, or terminating my days like Swift – a grinning idiot! Would to Heaven the day were arrived in which, rushing sword in hand, on a body of Turks, and fighting like one weary of existence, I shall meet immediate, painless death – the object of my wishes!'

NOTES

Dr Julius Millingen (1800–78) attended Byron during his final days. He had been sent to Greece at the age of twenty-three as Surgeon-in-Chief to the Army of Western Greece, and was with Byron in Cephalonia (Nov – Dec 1823) and in Missolonghi. In 1832, the year after publication of his *Memoirs*, he became court physician to the Sultan's harem in Constantinople – a change of sides that led many to question the veracity of his account of the Greek campaign.

1. Metaxata is in the south-west of the island of Cephalonia, and Argostoli a few miles to the north of Metaxata.
2. Ship used to accommodate travellers in quarantine before they were allowed to enter a port.
3. See p. 137.
4. Fop (French).
5. Major William Parry was sent out to Greece by the Greek Committee in London, and arrived in Missolonghi on 7 February 1824. He lived in the same house as Byron, became a congenial drinking-companion, and saw him constantly during the last ten weeks of his life. According to Trelawny, Parry had 'a fund of pot-house stories'. Byron described him as 'a fine rough subject' and 'a sort of hardworking Hercules'. His *The Last Days of Lord Byron* (1825) contains a harrowing account of Byron's final sufferings. (It has been suggested that his book was 'ghosted' by Thomas Hodgskin.) See also p. 155.
6. Jeremy Bentham (1748–1832), English philosopher and jurist.
7. John Gilpin in Cowper's poem 'The Diverting History of John Gilpin'.
8. See p. 137.

Last Days I*

COUNT GAMBA

About seven o'clock in the evening [of 15 Feb 1824] he was taken with a sudden seizure . . . . After that he lived with the strictest abstinence: vegetables and a little fish were his only food. But he took too much medicine, as indeed he was accustomed at all times to do. He persuaded himself that diet and exercise were the best preventives against a relapse. He took, therefore, long rides every day that the weather permitted him, nor did he think that enough, for every evening, and sometimes twice a day, he played at single-stick or at the sword exercise. The continued demands of the Greeks for money were become insupportable to him. Attempts were made to keep them at a distance, but who can defend himself against the importunities of these people? When the turbulent conduct and the unreasonable pretensions of the Suliotes (a warlike tribe of Albania) had induced him to force himself from all connection with them and to abandon his favourite enterprise against Lepanto, he employed himself in the organisation of a Greek brigade to be officered by Franks, paid and commanded by himself. I was his second in command. We were on the point of having everything ready, and he counted upon leaving the marshes of Missolonghi as soon as possible.

18 March. A messenger arrived from Colonel Stanhope[1] from Athens, inviting my Lord and Mavrocordatos[2] to a Congress to be held at Salona. He hoped that journey would do good to his health and to his spirits, as had been the case last year in Ithaca. In two or three days everything was ready for his departure, but the weather was against us, the roads were impracticable. For fifteen days it was impossible to attempt the passage across the mountains. In the meantime my Lord, by persevering in the same mode of living, had become very thin; but he was glad of it, being much afraid at all times of the contrary habit of body. His temper was more irritable; he was frequently angry about trifles, more so indeed than about matters of importance, but his anger was only momentary. Frequently he complained of not feeling well, of vertigos in the head, of a disposition to faint, and occasionally he told

*'Count Pietro Gamba's Account of Lord Byron's Last Illness', in Hobhouse, *Recollections of a Long Life*, III, 365–73.

me that he experienced a sort of alarm without any apparent cause.

He wrote little or nothing, except now and then a private letter; all his letters on public business or from the various Greek leaders who annoyed him from all quarters he handed over to me.

9 April. In the morning of that fatal day he received letters from the Ionian Islands and from England full of the most gratifying intelligence, particularly one of yours containing an account of the health of his daughter Ada, together with her profile cut in black. He came out of his bedchamber early, with the portrait in his hand. He talked about it a good deal, and he remarked to me that his daughter (just as was the case with him when a child) preferred tales and stories in prose to poetry; and he then observed that it was very singular that his sister should have had a severe illness at the very time of his fit.

As he had not ridden for three or four days, he was determined, although it threatened to rain, to go out on horseback. Three or four miles from town we were caught in a heavy rain. Missolonghi lies in a low flat, on one side covered by a wide ditch, on the other washed by the sea-marshes. Our house was on the marshes. The entrance into the town and the streets are so muddy that both going and returning he always preferred being ferried in a little boat to and from the place of his ride.

When he came back to the town wall, he was very wet and in a perspiration. I wanted to go home on horseback, instead of sitting still in a boat whilst in that state, but he would not, and he replied, 'I should make a fine soldier if I did not know how to stand such a trifle as this.' Two hours after coming home, he found himself shivering all over. He had a little fever and rheumatic pains. About eight o'clock I came into his room. He was lying on a sofa, restless and melancholy. He said to me, 'I am in great pain; I should not care for dying, but I cannot bear these pains.' The doctors proposed bleeding. He refused, saying, 'Is there no remedy but bleeding?' I am afraid that one of the physicians complied too much with his prejudice against bleeding, and told him there was no necessity for it. But at that time there was not the slightest suspicion of danger, nor was there any danger then.

10 April. He was always shivering; he did not go out of doors, but he got up at his usual hour. He transacted some business.

11 April. At ten o'clock in the forenoon he would go out on horseback, an hour earlier than usual for fear that it might rain later in the day. He rode a long time in the olive-woods a mile from the town. He talked a good deal, and seemed in better heatlh and spirits.

In the evening the police acquainted my Lord that a Turkish spy had taken refuge in his house. He was a relation of the master of the house. Byron himself gave orders for his arrest. The discovery of these disgraceful and vile plots had little effect upon him, if I may judge by what he said and did.

12 April. My Lord kept his bed with a rheumatic fever. He thought that his saddle had been wet when he rode the day before, but it was more probably the effect of the wetting he had on the previous day.

13 April. He got out of bed, but did not go out of his house. His fever was allayed, but his pains still continued. He was out of spirits and irritable.

14 April. He rose at twelve o'clock. He appeared calmer; the fever was diminished, but he was weak and had pains in the head. He wished to ride, but the weather was threatening, and his doctors advised him not to go out.

It was thought that his complaint was got under, and that in a few days he would be quite recovered. There was no suspicion of danger. He was pleased at having a fever, for he thought it might counteract the tendency to epilepsy. He received many letters, and he told me to answer many of them.

15 April. The fever continued, but his rheumatic pains and his headaches were gone. He seemed easier; he wished to ride, but the weather prevented him.

He received many letters, amongst them one from a Turkish Governor to whom he had sent some prisoners that he had set at liberty. The Turk thanked him, and asked him to liberate others. This letter pleased him much.

16 April. I was confined to my bed all day by a strained leg. I could not see him, but they brought me word that he felt better, that his disorder was taking the regular course, and that there was no alarm. He himself wrote a letter to the Turk, and sent it to me to get it translated into Greek.

17 April. I contrived to walk to his room. His look alarmed me much. He was too calm. He talked to me in the kindest way, but in a sepulchral tone. I could not bear it. A flood of tears burst from me, and I was obliged to retire.

This was the first day in which dreadful doubts were awakened. He suffered himself to be bled for the first time. During the night he could get no sleep; he perspired violently on his neck and head. It was feared that the inflammation would reach his brain.

It was only then that it was proposed to send for Dr Thomas,[3] but he could not come in time. Fletcher says that he had proposed it to him two or three days before, and that he refused. But I am not aware that any one suspected his danger until 17 April – more than that, it was thought the day before he was better.

He had not been able to sleep for some nights, and then it was that he said to Dr Millingen, 'I know that without sleep one must either die or go mad. I would sooner die a thousand times.'

He said the same thing to Fletcher afterwards. In the night between the 17th and 18th he had some moments of delirium, in which he talked about going to battle, but neither in that night nor in the whole of the next morning was he ever aware of his danger.

18 April. On the morning of the 18th it was feared there was an inflammation of the brain. The doctors proposed another bleeding, but he refused.

At twelve o'clock I was standing near his bed. He asked me if there were any letters come for him. There was one from a Greek Bishop; but fearing to agitate him, I said there were none. 'I know', he said, 'there is one to Mavrocordatos and Luriottis.'[4] 'It is true, my Lord.' 'That is what I want to see.' In five minutes I returned with the letter. He opened it himself (it was partly in French, partly in modern Greek). He translated the French into English without hesitation. He tried to translate the Greek; fearing that it might fatigue him I offered to get it translated. He would not let me, but at last he made it out himself. He made several remarks upon it, and said, 'As soon as Napier[5] comes we'll do so and so.' A clear proof that at twelve o'clock on the 18th he had no notion of his danger. This being Easter Sunday, there was a grand ceremony. It is usual in Greece, after twelve o'clock, to discharge cannon and muskets on this occasion. It was thought best to march the Brigade outside the walls, and by a few distance discharges of artillery to attract the crowd so as to prevent a noise near the house. In the meantime the Governor ordered the town guard to patrol the streets to inform the citizens of the situation of their illustrious benefactor, and to exhort them to maintain tranquillity and silence near his dwelling.

Whilst we were without the city the malady increased, and he was made aware of his danger. How unfortunate that we were not at home! He tried to make himself understood by Fletcher, as he himself will have told you.

From a circumstance collected from his servant Tita,[6] I think that he was convinced of his imminent danger after the consultation held by his physicians, about four o'clock in the afternoon. There were near his bed, Tita, Fletcher, and Dr Millingen. The latter could not restrain his tears, nor could the other two. They wished to retire in order to hide them, on which he said, almost with a smile, 'Oh, what a fine scene!' And then he exclaimed, 'Call Parry; I have something of importance to tell him.' Doubtless this was some testamentary direction.

Parry was out with me. When we came he could scarcely recognise any one. He wished to sleep. He continued asleep for half an hour. About half-past five he awoke. I had not the heart to see him. I sent Parry. My Lord knew him. He tried to express his wishes, but could not.[7] About six o'clock he fell into a sleep. Alas! it was his last sleep. He breathed, however, until six in the evening of the next day, but without speaking a word or being sensible.

I collected all the words he uttered in those few hours in which he was certain of his danger. He said, 'Poor Greece, poor people (*città*), my

poor family. Why was I not aware of this in time? but now it is too late.'
Speaking of Greece, he said, 'I have given her my time, my money, and
my health; what could I do more? Now I give her my life.' He
frequently repeated that he was content to die, and regretted only that
he was aware of it too late.

He mentioned the names of many people, and several sums of
money, but it was not possible to distinguish clearly what he meant.

He named his dear daughter, his sister, his wife, Hobhouse, and
Kinnaird.[8] 'Why did I not go to England before I came here? I leave
those that I love behind me; in other respects I am willing to die.'

After six o'clock on the evening of the 18th it is certain that he
suffered no pain whatever. He died in a strange land, and amongst
strangers, but more loved, more wept, he could not have been.

NOTES

Count Pietro Gamba, younger brother of Teresa Guiccioli and an enthusiastic
patriot and revolutionary, met Byron in Ravenna in July 1820 and later sailed
from Italy with Byron's party to join the struggle for Greek independence. He
enjoyed a close and affectionate relationship with Byron, and followed his body
to England. Gamba's account of the poet's last days was originally published
as *A Narrative of Lord Byron's Last Journey to Greece* (1825) and was dedicated to
Hobhouse, who praised its authenticity. Gamba died of typhoid in Greece in 1827.

1. Leicester Stanhope (1784–1862), son of the Earl of Harrington, was
appointed an agent of the Greek Committee in London on 21 September 1823
and arrived in Cephalonia on 22 November, setting off for Missolonghi early in
December. From 5 January 1824, when Byron arrived in Missolonghi, until
21 February, when Stanhope left for Athens, the two men saw a good deal of
each other; since Stanhope's presence could be taken as constituting a challenge to Byron's authority, relations between them were somewhat strained.
Stanhope later published *Greece in 1823 and 1824, to which is added Reminiscences of
Lord Byron* (1825).

2. Prince Alexander Mavrocordatos (1791–1865), Greek patriot and
leader to whom Byron gave his support. Byron wrote to Murray (25 Feb 1824)
that 'Prince Mavrocordato is an excellent person, and does all in his power'.
He later became Prime Minister of Greece.

3. Dr Thomas practised on the island of Zante, about fifty miles south-west
of Missolonghi.

4. Andreas Luriottis had visited London in January 1823 as a representa-
tive of the Greek government to enlist British aid, and then travelled with
Blaquière to Genoa and Greece.

5. Colonel Charles Napier, commander of the British garrison on the island
of Cephalonia, and 'the only English Resident markedly favourable to the
Greek cause' (Marchand).

6. Tita was the nickname of Giovanni Battista, who had been Byron's
gondolier in Venice and accompanied him to Ravenna and Pisa, subsequently
forming part of his entourage when he sailed from Genoa in July 1823.

7. On Parry, see p. 149. His own account of Byron's last moments of consciousness is as follows (*The Last Days of Lord Byron*, p. 128):

> Byron knew me, though scarcely. He had then less of alienation about him than I had seen for some time before, there was the calmness of resignation, but there was also the stupor of death. He tried to utter his wishes, but he was incapable; he said something about rewarding his Italian servant, and uttered several incoherent words. There was either no meaning in what he said, or it was such a meaning, as we should not expect at that moment.

8. Douglas Kinnaird (1788–1830), friend of Byron and Hobhouse.

Last Days II*

WILLIAM FLETCHER

My master continued his usual custom of riding daily, when the weather would permit, until 9 April; but on that ill-fated day he got very wet, and on his return home his Lordship changed the whole of his dress, but he had been too long in his wet clothes, and the cold of which he had complained, more or less, ever since we left Cephalonia, made this attack be more severely felt. Though rather feverish during the night, he slept pretty well, but complained in the morning of a pain in his bones, and a head-ache; this did not, however, prevent him from taking a ride in the afternoon, which, I grieve to say, was his last. On his return, my master said, that the saddle was not perfectly dry, from being so wet the day before, and observed, that he thought it had made him worse. His Lordship was again visited by the same slow fever, and I was sorry to perceive, on the next morning, that his illness appeared to be increasing. He was very low, and complained of not having had any sleep during the night. His appetite was also quite gone. I prepared a little arrow root, of which he took three or four spoonsfull, saying it was very good, but could take no more. It was not till the third day, the 12th, that I began to be alarmed for my master. In all his former colds he slept well, and was never affected by this slow fever. I therefore went to Dr Bruno and Mr Millingen, the two medical attendants, and inquired minutely into every circumstance connected with my master's present illness; both replied, that there was no danger, and I might make myself perfectly easy on the subject, for all would be well in a few days; this was on the 13th. On the following day I found my master in such a state, that I could not feel happy without entreating that he

*Quoted by Edward Blaquière, 'The Last Days of Lord Byron', in *Narrative of a Second Visit to Greece* (London: Whittaker, 1825) pp. 16–21.

would send to Zante for Dr Thomas. After expressing my fears lest his Lordship should get worse, he desired me to consult the doctors; on doing so they assured me it was unnecessary to call in any additional medical advice. Here I should remark, that his Lordship repeatedly said, in the course of the day, he was afraid the doctors did not understand his disease; to which I answered, 'then, my Lord, have other advice by all means'. 'They tell me', said his Lordship, 'that it is only a common cold, which you know I have had a thousand times.' 'I am sure, my Lord,' said I, 'that you never had one of so serious a nature.' 'I think I never had', was his Lordship's answer. I repeated my supplication that Dr Thomas should be sent for on the 15th, and was again assured that my master would be better in two or three days. After these confident assurances, I did not renew my entreaties until it was too late.

The whole nourishment taken by my master, for the last eight days, consisted of a small quantity of broth, at two or three different times, and two spoonsfull of arrow-root on the 18th, the day before his death.

The first time I heard of there being any intention of bleeding his Lordship, was on the 15th, when it was proposed by Dr Bruno, but objected to at first by my master, who asked Mr Millingen if there was any very great reason for taking blood; the latter replied that it might be of service, but added, that it could be deferred till the next day; and accordingly his Lordship was bled in the right arm on the evening of the 16th. I observed at the time, that his arm had a most inflamed appearance. Dr Bruno now began to say, he had frequently urged my master to be bled, but that he always refused. A long dispute now arose about the time that had been lost, and necessity of sending for medical assistance to Zante; upon which I was informed that it would be of no use, as my master would be better, or no more, before the arrival of Dr Thomas.

His Lordship continued to get worse, but Dr Bruno said, he thought letting blood again would save his life, and I lost no time in telling my master how necessary it was to comply with the doctor's wishes; to this he replied, by saying, he feared they were not aware of his disorder; and then, stretching out his arm, said, 'here, take my arm, and do whatever you like'.

His Lordship continued to get weaker, and on the 17th he was bled twice in the morning, and at two o'clock in the afternoon. The bleeding at both times was followed by fainting fits, and he would have fallen down more than once, had I not caught him in my arms. In order to prevent such an accident, I took care not to let him stir without being supported. On this day my master said to me twice, 'I cannot sleep, and you well know I have not been able to sleep for more than a week': he added, 'I am not afraid of dying; I am more fit to die than many think.' I do not, however, believe that his Lordship had any apprehension of his fate till the day after, the 18th, when he said, 'I fear you and Tita (the courier) will be ill by sitting up constantly, night and day.' I answered, 'we shall never leave your Lordship till you are better'. On the 18th he addressed me frequently, and seemed to be rather dissat-isfied with his medical treatment. I then said, 'Pray, my Lord, allow me to send for Dr Thomas'; to which he answered, 'do so, but be quick; I am only sorry I did not let you send for him before, as I am sure they have mistaken my disease'. I did not lose a moment in obeying my master's orders, or informing Dr Bruno and Mr Millingen of it. They said it was very right, as they now began to be afraid themselves. On returning to my master's room, his first words were, 'Have you sent?' 'I have, my Lord', was my answer; upon which he said, 'You have done right, for I should like to know what is the matter with me.' Although his Lordship did not appear to think his dissolution was so near, I could perceive he was getting weaker every hour. His Lordship con-tinued the conversation by saying, 'I now begin to think I am seriously ill; and in case I should be taken away suddenly from you, I wish to give you several directions, which I hope you will be particular in seeing executed.' I answered I would, in case such an event came to pass, but expressed a hope that he would live many years, to execute them much better himself than I could. To this my master replied, 'No, it is now nearly over'; and then added, 'I must tell you all without losing a moment.' I then said, 'Shall I go, my Lord, and fetch pen, ink, and paper?' 'Oh! my God, no; you will lose too much time, and I have it not to spare, for my time is now short': and immediately after, 'Now pay attention.' His Lordship commenced by saying, 'You will be provided for.' I begged him, however, to proceed with things of more consequence. He then continued – 'Oh, my poor dear child! my dear Ada! my God, could I but have seen her! Give her my blessing, and my dear sister Augusta and her children; and you will go to Lady Byron, and say – Tell her every thing – you are friends with her.' His Lordship appeared to be greatly affected at this moment. Here my master's voice failed him, so that I could only catch a word at intervals, but he continued muttering something very seriously for some time. I then told his Lordship, in a state of the greatest perplexity, that I had not understood a word of what he said; to which he replied – 'Oh! my God! then all is lost! for it is now too late. Can it be possible you have not understood me?' 'No, my Lord', said I; 'but I pray you to try and inform me once more.' 'How can I?' rejoined my master; 'it is now too late, and all is over.' I said, 'Not our will, but God's be done.' He answered, 'Yes! not mine be done; but I will try.' His Lordship did indeed make several efforts to speak, but could only repeat two or three words at a time, such as, 'My wife! – my child! – my sister! you know all, you must say all, you know my wishes!' The rest was quite unintelligible.

A consultation was now held (about noon), when it was determined to administer some Peruvian bark and wine. My master had now been nine days without any sustenance whatever, except what I have already mentioned. With the exception of a few words, which can only interest those to whom they were addressed, it was impossible to understand any thing his Lordship said, after taking the bark. He expressed a wish to sleep. I at one time asked whether I should call Mr Parry; to which he replied – 'Yes, you may call him.' The last words I heard my master utter were at six o'clock on the evening of the 18th, when he said, 'I must sleep now';[1] upon which he laid down, never to rise again; for he did not move hand or foot during the following twenty-four hours. His Lordship appeared, however, to be in a state of suffocation at intervals, and had a frequent rattling in the throat. On these occasions I called Tita to assist me in raising his head, and I thought he seemed to get quite stiff. The rattling and choking in the throat took place every half hour, and we continued to raise his head whenever the fit came on, till six o,clock in the evening of the 19th, when I saw my master open his eyes, and then shut them, but without showing any symptom of pain, or moving hand or foot. 'Oh! my God!' I exclaimed, 'I fear his Lordship is gone.' The doctors then felt his pulse, and said, 'You are too right – he is gone!'

NOTES

William Fletcher was Byron's valet for some twenty years, first in England, then during his periods of travel and residence abroad, and finally accompanying him to Greece. When Trelawny arrived at Missolonghi a few days after Byron's death (see p. 167), he found Fletcher alone in the house with the corpse. Blaquière later quotes (pp. 29–30) Fletcher's observations on 'the habitual benevolence of his master':

I could, if you require it, fill fifty pages with traits of his Lordship's generosity, which have occurred during the time I have served with him, but will now only trouble you with a few. So long back as December 1807, a poor man came to Newstead Abbey, where we then resided, and asked alms of a youth, son to one of the farmers. Perceiving that he sent the beggar away without giving him even a morsel of bread, my master called to the lad, who was his favourite servant, and said, 'I insist on your going after that poor man, and serving him the whole of this day with every thing he wants, and in case you act in such a way again, I will make you provide a good dinner for him: and recollect if you ever insult or ill use any other person in distress, you shall be made to wait behind their chair, till they have dined, this will teach you how to behave yourself in future.'

Indeed there is no part of Europe in which we lived that I have not witnessed numerous proofs of his Lordship's kindness of heart. While we were one day walking in the woods near Ravenna, my master saw an old woman decrepit with age, gathering sticks, he inquired into her circumstances, and immediately granted her a pension for her future maintenance. It was customary to dress a dinner daily for his Lordship while at the above place, as the servants were all on board wages, and my master scarcely every dined at home, I had orders to find out twelve of the most helpless poor of the city, to whom the victuals were always given.

One of the dogs happening to get into a mill dam, a man, who saw that he was likely to be carried into the wheel, leaned over the brink so far, that he fell in, and was unfortunately drowned. My master seemed to suffer very much from this accident, and not only defrayed the expenses of the funeral, but settled fifteen shillings a week on his children, till they should grow up, and be otherwise provided for. These are, indeed, only a few instances of his Lordship's goodness; but should you require any more, I could furnish you with a thousand.

Blaquière's claim that Fletcher's testimony is 'transcribed nearly in his own words' should perhaps be treated with scepticism (see note 1 below).

In June 1818 Byron had written to Hobhouse a letter giving a mock account of his own death as Fletcher might have communicated it:

Sir, – With great grief I inform you of the death of my late dear Master, my Lord, who died this morning at ten of the Clock of a rapid decline and slow fever, caused by anxiety, sea-bathing, women, and riding in the Sun against my advice. . . . His nine whores are already provided for, and the other servants; but what is to become of me?

1. This account of Byron's last words may be compared with that given by Fletcher in a letter to Augusta Leigh dated 20 April 1824, the day after Byron's death (in Ernest J. Lovell Jr, *His Very Self and Voice*, pp. 648–9):

'Once more I understood so far as now you will Be sure to attend to all these orders.' I said, 'shall I write them Down', My Ld said, 'no theire his not time' and was Gone again at Quite a Delereious State for a few minutes when he again Commenced again saying, 'now pay great attention to all i say'. My Lord now again got me by the hand saying, 'be sure mind all I say', and at this moment his voice began to falter and I was not able to Distinguish one word from a nother. My Lord continued talking to me for more then a Quarter of an Houre – I may say nearley half an Houre when My Lord said Quite Plain, 'now I have told you all which I hope you will attend to'. i answered, 'My Lord I am very sorry but I have not understood one word which I hope you will now tell me over again.' My Lord in Great agitation said then, 'if you have not understood me it his now too Late', and in a faltering Low voice Repeated, 'I am truley sorry you have not understood me but I will try to make you understand me again but I know well it his too Late now', and in a minutes time all was over for my Lord was Delerious and continued so excepting now and Then a single word.

Last Days III*

JULIUS MILLINGEN

At no time of his life did Lord Byron find himself in circumstances, more calculated to render him unhappy. The cup of health had dropped from his lips, and constant anxiety and suffering operated powerfully on his mind, already a prey to melancholy apprehensions, and disappointment, increased by disgust. Continually haunted by a dread of epilepsy or palsy – complaints most humiliating to human pride – he fell into the lowest state of hypochondriasis, and vented his sorrows in language which, though sometimes sublime, was at others as peevish and capricious, as that of an unruly and quarrelsome child. When he returned to himself, however, he would request us 'not to take the indisposed and sickly fit for the sound man'.

Riding was the only occupation that procured him any relief; and even this was but momentary. On 9 April, prolonging his ride further than usual, he was on his return caught in a shower, and remaining exposed to it for more than an hour, he complained in the evening of shooting pains in his hips and loins; but he found himself, the next morning, sufficiently well to ride out for a short time. On his return, however, he scolded his groom severely, for having placed on the horse the same wet saddle he had used on the preceding day.

Mr Finlay[1] (then a staunch Odyssean[2]), had been deputed to engage Lord Byron to assist at the congress at Salona. This gentleman and myself called upon him in the evening; when we found him lying on a sofa, complaining of a slight fever and of pains in the articulation. He was at first more gay than usual; but, on a sudden, he became pensive, and after remaining some few minutes in silence, he said that during the whole day he had reflected a great deal on a prediction, which had been made to him, when a boy, by a famed fortune-teller in Scotland. His mother, who firmly believed in cheiromancy and astrology, had sent for this person, and desired him to inform her what would be the future destiny of her son. Having examined attentively the palm of his hand, the man looked at him for a while steadfastly, and then with a solemn voice, exclaimed; 'Beware of your thirty-seventh year, my young lord; beware.'

*Memoirs of the Affairs of Greece, pp. 128–34, 140–4.

He had entered on his thirty-seventh year on 22 January: and it was
evident from the emotion with which he related this circumstance, that
the caution of the palmist had produced a deep impression on his mind,
which in many respects was so superstitious, that we thought proper to
accuse him of superstition: – 'To say the truth,' answered his lordship,
'I find it equally difficult to know what to believe in this world, and
what not to believe. There are as many plausible reasons for inducing
me to die a bigot, as there have been to make me hitherto live a
freethinker. You will, I know, ridicule my belief in lucky and unlucky
days; but no consideration can now induce me to undertake any thing
either on a Friday or a Sunday. I am positive it would terminate
unfortunately. Every one of my misfortunes, and, God knows, I have
had my share, have happened to me on one of those days. You will
ridicule, also, a belief in incorporeal beings. Without instancing to you
the men of profound genius, who have acknowledged their existence, I
could give you the details of my friend Shelley's conversations with his
familiar. Did he not apprise me, that he had been informed by that
familiar, that he would end his life by drowning; and did I not, a short
time after, perform, on the sea beach, his funeral rites?'

Considering myself, on this occasion, not a medical man, but a
visitor; and being questioned neither by his physician nor himself, I did
not even feel Lord Byron's pulse. I was informed, next morning, that
during the night he had taken diaphoretic infusions, and that he felt
himself better. The next day Dr Bruno[3] administered a purgative, and
kept up its effects by a solution of cream of tartar, which the Italians
call 'Imperial lemonade'. In the evening the fever augmented, and
as on the 14th, although the pains in the articulations had diminished,
the feverish symptoms were equally strong, Dr Bruno strongly
recommended him to be blooded; but as the patient entertained a
deep-rooted prejudice against bleeding, his physician could obtain no
influence whatever over him, and his lordship obstinately persevered
in refusing to submit to the operation.

On the 15th, towards noon, Fletcher called upon me, and informed
me, that his master desired to see me, in order to consult with Dr Bruno
on the state of his health. Dr Bruno informed me that his patient
laboured under a rheumatic fever, that, as at first, the symptoms had
been of a mild character, he had trusted chiefly to sudorifics; but
during the last two days, the fever had so much increased, that he had
repeatedly proposed bleeding, but that he could not overcome his
lordship's antipathy to that mode of treatment. Convinced, by an
examination of the patient, that bleeding was absolutely necessary, I
endeavoured, as mildly and as gently as possible, to persuade him; but,
in spite of all my caution, his temper was so morbidly irritable, that he
refused in a manner excessively peevish. He observed that, of all his
prejudices, the strongest was against phlebotomy. His mother had on

her death-bed obtained from him a promise never to consent to being bled; and that whatever we might say, his aversion was stronger than any reason we could give. 'Besides,' said his lordship, 'does not Dr Reid observe, in his *Essays*,[4] that less slaughter has been effected by the warrior's lance than by the physician's lancet? It is, in fact, a minute instrument of mighty mischief.' On my observing, that this remark related to the treatment of nervous disorders, not of inflammatory ones, he angrily replied: 'Who is nervous, if I am not? Do not these words, besides, apply to my case? Drawing blood from a nervous patient is like loosening the chords of a musical instrument, the tones of which are already defective for want of sufficient tension. Before I became ill, you know yourself how weak and irritable I had become. Bleeding, by increasing this state, will inevitably kill me. Do with me whatever else you please, but bleed me you shall not. I have had several inflammatory fevers during my life, and at an age when I was much more robust and plethoric than I am now; yet I got through them without bleeding. This time, also, I will take my chance.'

After much reasoning and entreaty, however, I at length succeeded in obtaining a promise, that, should his fever increase at night, he would allow Bruno to bleed him. Happy to inform the doctor of this partial victory, I left the room, and with a view of lowering the impetus of the circulating system, and determining to the skin, I recommended the administration of an ounce of a solution of half a grain of tartarised antimony and two drachms of nitre in twelve ounces of water.

Early the next morning I called on the patient, who told me, that having passed a better night than he had expected, he had not requested Dr Bruno to bleed him. Chagrined at this, I laid aside all consideration for his feelings, and solemnly assured him how deeply I lamented to see him trifle with his life in this manner. I told him, that his pertinacious refusal to be bled had caused a precious opportunity to be lost; that a few hours of hope yet remained; but that unless he would submit immediately to be bled, neither Dr Bruno nor myself could answer for the consequences. He might not care for life, it was true; but who could assure him, unless he changed his resolution, the disease might not operate such disorganisation in his cerebral and nervous system as entirely to deprive him of his reason. I had now touched the sensible chord; for, partly annoyed by our unceasing importunities, and partly convinced, casting at us both the fiercest glance of vexation, he threw out his arm, and said, in the most angry tone: 'Come; you are, I see, a d——d set of butchers. Take away as much blood as you will; but have done with it.'

We seized the moment, and drew about twenty ounces. On coagulating, the blood presented a strong buffy coat. Yet the relief, obtained, did not correspond to the hopes we had anticipated; and during the night the fever became stronger than it had been hitherto. The restlessness and agitation increased, and the patient spoke several times in an incoherent manner. The next morning (17th) the bleeding was repeated; for although the rheumatic symptoms had completely disappeared, the cerebral ones were hourly increasing, and this continuing all day, we opened the vein, for the third time, in the afternoon. Cold applications were from the beginning constantly kept on the head; blisters were also proposed. When on the point of applying them, Lord Byron asked me whether it would answer the same purpose to apply both on the same leg. Guessing the motive that led him to ask this question, I told him I would place them above the knees, on the inside of the thighs. 'Do so,' said he, 'for as long as I live, I will not allow any one to see my lame foot.'

In spite of our endeavours, the danger hourly increased; the different signs of strong nervous affection succeeded each other with surprising rapidity; twitchings and involuntary motions of the tendons began to manifest themselves during the night; and, more frequently than before, the patient muttered to himself and talked incoherently.

In the morning (18th) a consultation was proposed, to which Dr Lucca Vaga and Dr Freiber, my assistant, were invited. Our opinions were divided. Bruno and Lucca proposed having recourse to antispasmodics and other remedies, employed in the last stage of typhus. Freiber and I maintained that such remedies could only hasten the fatal termination; that nothing could be more empirical than flying from one extreme to the other; that if, as we all thought, the complaint was owing to the metastasis of rheumatic inflammation, the existing symptoms only depended on the rapid and extensive progress, it had made in an organ, previously so weakened and irritable. Antiphlogistic means could never prove hurtful in this case; they would become useless only if disorganisation were already operated; but then, when all hopes were fled, what means would not prove superfluous?

We recommended the application of numerous leeches to the temples, behind the ears, and along the course of the jugular vein a large blister between the shoulders, and sinapisms to the feet. These we considered to be the only means likely to succeed. Dr Bruno, however, being the patient's physician, had, of course, the casting vote, and he prepared, in consequence, the antispasmodic potion, which he and Dr Lucca had agreed upon. It was a strong infusion of valerian with ether, etc. After its administration, the convulsive movements and the delirium increased; yet, notwithstanding my earnest representations, a second dose was administered half an hour after: when, after articulating confusedly a few broken phrases, our patient sunk into a comatose sleep, which the next day terminated in death. . . .

[During Byron's last days] Two thoughts constantly occupied his mind. Ada[5] and Greece were the names, he hourly repeated. The

broken complaints he uttered, lamenting to die a stranger to the sole
daughter of his affection, not only far from her embrace, but perhaps
the object of the hatred, which he thought had been carefully instilled
into her from her tenderest infancy, showed how exquisitely his paren-
tal feelings were excited by these sad considerations. The glory of dying
in Greece, and for Greece, was the only theme he could fly to for relief,
and which would dry up the tears, he abundantly shed, when pro-
nouncing Ada's name. In the agony of death – that dreadful hour
when, leaving the confines of life, the soul is launched into eternity –
his parting look, his last adieu, was to Greece and Ada. I was present
when, after taking the first antispasmodic mixture, he spoke to Fletcher
for the last time, recommending him to call on his sister, on Lady
Byron and his daughter, and deliver to each the messages, which he
had repeated to him before. His feelings, and the clouds of death, which
were fast obscuring his intellect, did not allow him to continue: 'You
know what you must say to Ada; – I have already told it to you; you
know it, do you not?' On hearing Fletcher's affirmative, he replied
'that's right.'

On the 18th he addressed me, saying: 'Your efforts to preserve my
life will be vain. Die I must: I feel it. Its loss I do not lament; for to
terminate my wearisome existence I came to Greece. – My wealth, my
abilities, I devoted to her cause. – Well: there is my life to her. One
request let me make to you. Let not my body be hacked, or be sent to
England. Here let my bones moulder. – Lay me in the first corner
without pomp or nonsense.'

After his death I informed Count Gamba of Lord Byron's dying
request; and at the same time urged the imperious obligation, he was
under, of executing it with religious punctuality. The count replied,
that a great man belonged to his country; and that it would be a
sacrilege to leave his remains in a place, where they might, one day,
become the sport of insulting barbarians. He desired us to embalm the
body carefully; his last duty to his friend would be performed when he
had deposited his body in the same vault, that contained his illustrious
ancestors.

It is with infinite regret I must state, that, although I seldom left
Lord Byron's pillow during the latter part of his illness, I did not hear
him make any, even the smallest, mention of religion. At one moment I
heard him say: 'Shall I sue for mercy?' After a long pause he added:
'Come, come, no weakness! let's be a man to the last.'

Before concluding this melancholy portion of what I have known of
this celebrated man, during the last six months of his life, I beg that
inexactitude may not be laid to my charge, if I have passed over in
silence many of the particulars, which belonged to the character of this
strange compound of opposite passions. I have cursorily mentioned the
excellent qualities of his heart; but I am incapable of enumerating the

faults of one, from whom I received so many marks of kindness, merely
to gratify the curiosity of the idle or the malice of his enemies. To all
future inquirers, I prefer saying with the poet;

> No further seek his merits to disclose,
> Or draw his frailties from their dread abode.
> There they alike in trembling hope repose,
> The bosom of his Father and his God.[6]

Before we proceeded to embalm the body, we could not refrain from
pausing, in silent contemplation, on the lifeless clay of one, who, but a
few days before, was the hope of a whole nation and the admiration of
the civilised world. After consecrating a few moments to the feelings,
such a spectacle naturally inspired, we could not but admire the perfect
symmetry of his body. Nothing could surpass the beauty of the forehead; its height was extraordinary, and the protuberances, under
which the nobler intellectual faculties are supposed to reside, were
strongly pronounced. His hair, which curled naturally, was quite grey;
the mustachios light coloured. His physiognomy had suffered little
alteration; and still preserved the sarcastic haughty expression, which
habitually characterised it. The chest was broad, high vaulted, the
waist very small, the pelvis rather narrow; the muscular system well
pronounced; especially that of the superior extremities; the skin delicate and white; and the habit of the body plump. The adipose tissue
was every where predominant, a proof of his natural predisposition to
embonpoint; which his severe abstemiousness could hardly counteract.
The only blemish of his body, which might otherwise have vied with
that of Apollo himself, was the congenital malconformation of his left
foot and leg. The foot was deformed, and turned inwards; and the leg
was smaller and shorter than the sound one. Although Lord Byron
preferred attributing his lameness to the unskilful treatment of a
sprained ankle, there can be little or no doubt, that he was born
club-footed.

The following are the principal phenomena, which the autopsy
presented. The cranium resembled completely that of a man much
advanced in age; its sutures were obliterated; its two tables were united
into one; no traces of the diploe remained, and the texture of it was as
hard as ivory. The adhesion of the dura mater to the interior of the
skull-cap was extraordinarily strong. Its vessels were large, highly
injected, and it had acquired at least twice its usual thickness. Each of
its surfaces was covered with strong organised bands, uniting them
powerfully to the adjacent parts. Its prolongation, the falciform process, was perhaps even more inflamed, and adhered firmly to the
hemispheres; and the tentorium cerebelli, though in a less degree, was
also strongly injected. The pia mater presented the appearance of the

conjunctiva on an inflamed eye. The whole system of sanguiferous vessels, of the cerebrum and cerebellum, was gorged with blood, and their substance was surprisingly hard. The ventricles contained several ounces of serous fluid.

The lungs were perfectly healthy and crepitant; and what is seldom observed in natives of cold climates, had not contracted the slightest adhesion to the pleura. The appearance, presented by the heart, was singular. Its parietes were as collapsed, and of a consistence, as flabby as those of persons, who have died of old age. Its muscular fibres were pale, and hardly pronounced; and the ventricles had no thickness whatever.

The liver was beginning to undergo the alterations, observed in persons, who have indulged in the abuse of alcoholic liquors. Its bulk was smaller, its texture harder, its colour much lighter than in its healthy condition. The stomach and intestines presented no remarkable phenomena.[7]

NOTES

On Millingen, see p. 149.

1. George Finlay met Byron in Cephalonia in October 1823 and later saw him frequently in Missolonghi. At the time he was twenty-four years old and, fresh from his university studies in Scotland and Germany, had gone out to take part in the Greek struggle. Later he became a distinguished historian and published a history of Greece. He settled in that country and died in Athens in 1875. In his *History of Greece*, VI (1877) 324, he wrote of Byron,

> The genius of Lord Byron would in all probability never have unfolded either political or military talent. He was not disposed to assume an active part in public affairs. . . . Both his character and his conduct presented unceasing contradictions. It seemed as if two different souls occupied his body alternately. One was feminine, and full of sympathy; the other masculine, and characterised by clear judgement, and by a rare power of presenting for consideration those facts only which were required for forming a decision. When one arrived the other departed.

2. Supporter of Odysseus, Greek leader and rival of Mavrocordatos.

3. See p. 137.

4. Dr John Reid (1776–1822) published *Essays on Insanity* (1816) and *Essays on Hypochondriasis and other Nervous Infections* (1821).

5. See p. 30.

6. The concluding stanza of Gray's 'Elegy Written in a Country Churchyard'.

7. In her diary entry for 8 November 1820, quoted in Lorraine Robertson, 'The Journal and Notebooks of Claire Clairmont: Unpublished Passages',

Keats–Shelley Memorial Bulletin, IV (1952) 38, Claire Clairmont (see p. 54), whose love for Byron had by this time changed to detestation, gave her own imaginative account of an autopsy performed on him:

> He dead extended on his bed, covered all but his heart, which many wigged doctors are cutting open to find out (as one may be saying) what was the extraordinary disease of which this great man died – His heart laid bare, they find an immense capital I grown on its surface – and which had begun to pierce the breast – They are all astonishment. One says 'A new disease.' Another 'I never had a case of this kind before.' A third 'What medicines would have been proper' the fourth holding up his finger 'A desert island.'

At the actual autopsy, his lungs were removed and the urn containing them was placed in Missolonghi church, from where they subsequently disappeared. When the body, preserved in spirits, was shipped back to England, the rest of the internal organs were contained in four separate jars.

'More Beautiful in Death than in Life'*

E. J. TRELAWNY

It was 24 or 25 April when I arrived; Byron had died on the 19th. I waded through the streets, between wind and water, to the house he had lived in; it was detached, and on the margin of the shallow slimy sea-waters. For three months this house had been besieged, day and night, like a bank that has a run upon it. Now that death had closed the door, it was as silent as a cemetery. No one was within the house but Fletcher, of which I was glad. As if he knew my wishes, he led me up a narrow stair into a small room, with nothing in it but a coffin standing on trestles. No word was spoken by either of us; he withdrew the black pall and the white shroud, and there lay the embalmed body of the Pilgrim – more beautiful in death than in life. The contraction of the muscles and skin had effaced every line that time or passion had ever traced on it; few marble busts could have matched its stainless white, the harmony of its proportions, and perfect finish; yet he had been dissatisfied with that body, and longed to cast its slough. How often I

Records of Shelley, Byron, and the Author, II, 129–31.

had heard him curse it! He was jealous of the genius of Shakespeare –
that might well be – but where had he seen the face or form worthy to
excite his envy? I asked Fletcher to bring me a glass of water. On his
leaving the room, to confirm or remove my doubts as to the exact cause
of his lameness, I uncovered the Pilgrim's feet, and was answered – it
was caused by the contraction of the back sinews, which the doctors
call 'Tendon Achilles', that prevented his heels resting on the ground,
and compelled him to walk on the fore part of his feet; except this
defect, his feet were perfect.[1] This was a curse, chaining a proud and
soaring spirit like his to the dull earth. In the drama of *The Deformed
Transformed*,[2] I knew that he had expressed all he could express of what
a man of highly-wrought mind might feel when brooding over a
deformity of body; but when he said,

> I have done the best which spirit may to make
> Its way with all deformity's dull deadly
> Discouraging weight upon me

I thought it exaggerated as applied to himself; now I saw it was not so.
His deformity was always uppermost in his thoughts, and influenced
every act of his life, spurred him on to poetry, as that was one of the few
paths to fame open to him – and as if to be revenged on Nature for
sending him into the world 'scarce half made up', he scoffed at her
works and traditions with the pride of Lucifer; this morbid feeling
ultimately goaded him on to his last Quixotic crusade in Greece.

NOTES

On Trelawny, see p. 27. Trelawny arrived too late to be present at Byron's
deathbed, but this did not deter him from giving in a letter (*Letters*, pp. 74–5) a
detailed account of that occasion. As he explains (*Records*, II, 125),

> We had been two days winding through the mountain passes . . . when a
> messenger from Missolonghi on his way to Salona, conveying the startling
> news of Byron's death, crossed our path, as we were fording the river
> Evvenus. Thus, by a stroke of fate, my hopes of being of use in Greece were
> extinguished . . . .

The egotism of the last sentence quoted is surpassed by that found in a letter of
August 1824 to Mary Shelley in which he writes, 'I wish he had lived a little
longer, that he might have witnessed how I would have soared above him here,
how I would have triumphed over his mean spirit' (*Letters*, pp. 85–6).

    1. This represents a very striking modification of the version given twenty
years earlier in Trelawny's *Recollections* (see p. 27 above), where the passage
'was answered . . . feet were perfect' runs as follows: 'was answered – the great

mystery was solved. Both his feet were clubbed, and his legs withered to the knee – the form and features of an Apollo, with the feet and legs of a sylvan satyr.'

2. Unfinished drama by Byron, written in 1822.

Preparations for the Last Journey*

EDWARD BLAQUIÈRE

Whilst Missolonghi was deploring a loss which all those who were within its walls felt could never be repaired, the necessary preparations were made to embalm the body, and an account of the process has appeared in the *Greek Telegraph*. The most remarkable facts stated in this report relates to the quantity of brains, which are described as being at least one fourth greater than those of ordinary persons; they were saturated with blood. The heart was also very large, but its fibres were extremely relaxed, so that it must have performed its functions very feebly. The liver is represented as small. In other respects, the body was found to be perfectly sound and healthy. Dr Bruno, who drew up the report, concludes by stating, that had his illustrious patient consented to be bled when first attacked, there is no doubt but he would be still alive; arguing, however, from the exhausted state in which he found the vessels of the heart, smallness of the liver, and the peculiar structure of the cranium, added to a want of more precaution with regard to his health, not to mention his excessive literary occupation, the doctor adds, that his Lordship could only have survived a few years.

There being no possibility of procuring sheet lead at Missolonghi, the body was placed in a strong tin case, and elevated on a bier covered with black cloth. The arms of the Byron family were represented at one end of the coffin, while the sword and cap which his Lordship had intended to wear at the siege of Lepanto, were placed on the top.

The necessary arrangements being made for conveying the body to the principal church in the town, this ceremony was omitted in consequence of a suggestion that the rugged state of the pavement might lead

Narrative of a Second Visit to Greece, pp. 23–5.

to some accident happening to the coffin; it was therefore determined that instead of the corpse every object would be answered by merely conducting the heart in procession. A separate case having been made for this, it was accordingly substituted for the body. The procession took place on the 24th, and was attended by the clergy, civil and military authorities, as well as the whole population. On reaching the church, the case was placed on an elevated pedestal prepared for the occasion, upon which a solemn service was pronounced by the Bishop of Arta Porfirius; this was followed by the chaunting of a requiem. The mournful ceremony concluded with a funeral oration from the pen of my friend Spiridion Tricoupi. This composition, so creditable to the talent of the writer, contains a very eloquent and affecting tribute to the memory of his Lordship.

It being necessary to wait for the vessels sent over by Mr Barff,[1] the body was not embarked until the 30th, when another procession took place. The coffin was carried down to the sea side, on the shoulders of four military Chiefs, and attended in the same order as before; minute guns continued to be discharged till the moment of embarkation; these were followed by a salute of thirty-seven cannon.

The vessel which bore the body, appeared off this Island about two o'clock, on the 4th instant, and was recognised at a considerable distance, owing to her colours being lowered. She entered the Mole towards sunset. The corpse was accompanied by the whole of his Lordship's attendants, who conveyed it to the Lazaretto, on the following morning.

NOTES

Edward Blaquière had been sent to Greece by the Greek Committee, which had been established to help the cause of Greek independence and had held its first meeting in London on 28 February 1823. He had stopped off in Genoa on 5 April and met Byron there. On 7 April Byron wrote to Hobhouse, 'I saw Captain Blaquière, and the Greek Companion of his mission [i.e. Luriottis: see p. 154], on Saturday. Of course I entered very sincerely into the object of their journey . . . .'

1. A merchant on the island of Zante, Samuel Barff (1793–1880) handled Byron's business affairs.

'A Great Sensation'*

MARY SHELLEY

[To Edward J. Trelawny, 28 July 1824.] You will not wonder that the late loss of L[ord] B[yron] makes me cling with greater zeal [to] those dear friends who remain to me – He could be hardly called a friend – but connected with him in a thousand ways, admiring his talents and with all his faults feeling affection for him, it went to my heart when the other day [12 July] the hearse that contained his lifeless form, a form of beauty which in life I often delighted to behold, passed my window going up Highgate Hill on his last journey to the *last* seat of his ancestors. Your account of his last moments was infinitely interesting to me. Going about a fortnight ago to the house where his remains lay, I found there Fletcher and Lega. Lega looking a most preposterous rogue – Fletcher I expect to call on me when he returns from Nottingham – From a few words he imprudently let fall, it w[oul]d seem that his Lord spoke of C[laire] in his last moments, and of his wish to do something for her at a time when his mind, vaccillating between consciousness and delirium, would not permit him to do any thing. Did F[letcher] mention this to you. It seems that this doughty Leporello[1] speaks of his lord to strangers with the highest respect – more than he did a year ago – the best, the most generous, the most wronged of peers – the notion of his leading an irregular life quite a false one. Lady B[yron] sent for F[letcher] he found her in a fit of passionate grief, but perfectly implacable, and as much resolved never to have united herself again to him as she was when she first signed their separation . . .

His death as you may guess made a great sensation here [i.e. in London], which was not diminished by the destruction of his memoirs, which he wrote and gave to Moore, and which were burned by Mrs Leigh and Hobhouse. There was not much in them I know, for I read them some years ago at Venice, but the world fancied that it was to have a confession of the hidden feelings of one, concerning whom they were always passionately curious. Moore was by no means pleased he

---

The Letters of Mary W. Shelley, I, 298.

is now writing a life of him himself, but it is conjectured that notwithstanding he had the MS. so long in his possession, that he never found time to read it.

NOTES

On Mary Shelley, see p. 57. On hearing of Byron's death, she had written in her journal for 15 May 1824 (*Mary Shelley's Journal*, pp. 193–4),

This then was the coming event that cast its shadow on my last night's miserable thoughts. Byron had become one of the people of the grave – that miserable conclave to which the beings I best loved belong. I knew him in the bright days of youth, when neither care nor fear had visited me – before death had made me feel my mortality, and the earth was the scene of my hopes. Can I forget our evening visits to Diodati? our excursions on the lake, when he sang the Tyrolese Hymn, and his voice was harmonised with winds and waves. Can I forget his attentions and consolations to me during my deepest misery? Never.

Beauty sat on his countenance and power beamed from his eye. His faults being, for the most part, weaknesses, induced one readily to pardon them.

1. Manservant to Don Giovanni (Don Juan) in Mozart's opera.

Byron's Funeral Procession*

THOMAS MOORE

1–9 July [1824]. Began to think whether it would be *necessary* for me to go up to Lord Byron's funeral. Wrote to Hobhouse, who told me his own wish had been to have him buried in Westminster Abbey; but that Mrs Leigh had decided for Newstead, and that therefore the only mark of respect would be sending carriages.[1]

9th. Saw in the papers that the friends of Lord B would accompany the funeral out of London, and determined to go up; wrote to Rogers to-day, to know what his intentions are; cannot, however, wait his answer, which would not arrive till Sunday (the day after to-morrow), and the funeral is to be on Monday. Resolved to start to-morrow morning.

10th. Mrs B went with me in the gig to Buckhill, where I took the coach and arrived in town five minutes after six; no rooms at 15 in Duke Street; was obliged to go to a glazier's opposite.

11th. Called on Rogers after breakfast; said he had written in answer to my letter, that I need not disturb myself to come up, as there was no occasion. Hobhouse had asked him to go in one of the mourning coaches, but he did not intend it; seemed inclined, however, to change his mind: and at last I persuaded him to accompany me to the funeral.

12th. Was with Rogers at half-past eight. Set off for George Street, Westminster, at half-past nine. When I approached the house, and saw the crowd assembled, felt a nervous trembling come over me, which lasted till the whole ceremony was over; thought I should be ill. Never was at a funeral before, but poor Curran's.[2] The riotous curiosity of the mob, the bustle of the undertakers, etc., and all the other vulgar accompaniments of the ceremony, mixing with my recollections of him as was gone, produced a combination of disgust and sadness that was deeply painful to me. Hobhouse, in the active part he had to sustain, showed a manly, unaffected feeling. Our coachful consisted of Rogers, Campbell, Colonel Stanhope, Orlando[3] (the Greek deputy), and myself. Saw a lady crying in a barouche as we turned out of George Street, and said to myself, 'Bless her heart, whoever she is!' There were, however, few respectable persons among the crowd; and the whole

The Journal of Thomas Moore, pp. 103–5.

ceremony was anything but what it ought to have been. Left the hearse as soon as it was off the stones,[4] and returned home to get rid of my black clothes, and try to forget, as much as possible, the wretched feelings I had experienced in them. Stanhope said in the coach, in speaking of the strange mixture of avarice and profusion which Byron exhibited, that he had heard himself say, 'He was sure he should die a miser and a bigot.' Hobhouse, to-day, mentioned as remarkable, the change in Byron's character when he went to Greece. Finding that there was ardour enough among them, but that steadiness was what they wanted, he instantly took a quiet and passive tone, listening to the different representations made to him, and letting his judgement be properly informed, before he either urged or took any decided course of action. Walked with R into the park, and met a soldier's funeral, which, in the full state my heart was in, affected me strongly . . . .

　　14th. Breakfasted with Rogers to meet Leicester Stanhope. Much talk about Lord Byron, of whom Stanhope saw a good deal at Missolonghi. Byron entirely guided in his views by Mavrocordatos; 'a mere puppet in his hands'; Mavrocordatos always teasing him for money, till Byron hated the very sight of him. The story of Byron's giving four thousand pounds to raise the siege of Missolonghi not true. A little money goes an immense way in Greece. A hundred pounds might sometimes be the means of keeping a fleet or army together. Mavrocordatos appointed B to command the army of western Greece. Stanhope thought this appointment of a stranger injurious to the dignity of the Greek nation, and told B so, which annoyed him. S expressed the same to some members of the Greek government, who said it was done by Mavrocordatos, without consulting them. In the passage from Cephalonia, the ship, aboard which were Count Gamba, Byron's servants, packages, etc. etc., was taken and carried into a Turkish port; but, by some management, got off again. Byron himself, next morning, at break of day, got close in with a Turkish frigate, which, however, took his small vessel for a fire-ship and sheered off. B gave but little money. After his severe attack, when he was lying nervous and reduced in bed, insurrection took place among the Suliots, who would frequently rush into his bedroom to make their remonstrances. Byron would not have them shut out, but always listened to them with much good nature; very gallant this. Asked Stanhope as to his courage, which I have sometimes heard the depreciating gossips of society throw a doubt upon; and not long ago, indeed, was told of Lord Bathurst's saying, when somebody expressed an apprehension for Lord Byron's safety in Greece, 'Oh, never fear, he will not expose himself to much danger.' Stanhope said, on the contrary, he was always for rushing into danger; would propose one day to go in a fire-ship; another time, to storm Lepanto; would however, laugh at all this himself afterwards, and say he wished that —— (some one, I don't know whom, that was expected to take a command) would come and supersede him. Stanhope had several stormy conversations with him on business. In one of them Byron threatened to write a pasquinade against him; and Stanhope begged him to do so, and he would give him a hundred pounds for the copyright. Said it was an extraordinary scene when the leeches had bit the temporal artery in his first attack; and two physicians squabbling over him, and he, weak as he was, joking at their expense. Captain Parry was his favourite *butt* at Missolonghi.

NOTES

On Moore, see p. 58. On 9 and 10 July, Byron's remains lay in state in the front parlour of Sir Edward Knatchbull's house in Great George Street; admission was by ticket, and 'several of the nobility and gentry called in the course of the day' (*The Times*, 10 July). The body was not visible. At 9 a.m. on the 12th the funeral cortège left the house and proceeded north. Overnight stops were made at Welwyn, Higham Ferrers and Oakham, the body arrived in Nottingham on the 15th, and burial in the family vault at Hucknall Torkard church took place on the 16th.

1. According to Hobhouse's diary, 'about 47 carriages', many of them empty, followed the body through the London streets (for those not attending in person, to send an empty carriage was considered a mark of respect). *The Times* (13 July) listed four mourning coaches and nearly forty carriages, referring also to 'many others'. Chapter 39 of George Borrow's *Lavengro* (1851) contains an episode apparently based on his observation of the procession: in Borrow's version, 'three or four mourning coaches' were followed by 'a very long train of splendid carriages, all of which, without one exception, were empty'.

2. John Philpot Curran (1750–1817), Irish judge.

3. Jean Orlando, a friend of Mavrocordatos. With Luriottis, and acting on behalf of the Greek government, he had asked Byron for a loan of 30,000 dollars 'for the payment of the Greek fleet'. Byron had agreed to give two-thirds of the sum asked for.

4. Off the paved streets; beyond the city limits.

Last Recollections (1824)*

J. C. HOBHOUSE

The *Times* of yesterday announced his death in a manner which is, I think, a fair sample of the general opinion on this event. The writer is,

*Recollections of a Long Life, III, 41–2, 49, 56, 64–70, 134.

however, mistaken in saying that others may have *been more tenderly beloved* than *Lord Byron*, for no man ever lived who had such devoted friends. His power of attaching those about him to his person was such as no one I ever knew possessed. No human being could approach him without being sensible of this magical influence. There was something commanding, but not overawing in his manner. He was neither grave nor gay out of place, and he seemed always made for that company in which he happened to find himself. There was a mildness and yet a decision in his mode of conversing, and even in his address, which are seldom united in the same person. He appeared exceedingly free, open, and unreserved with everybody, yet he contrived at all times to retain just as much self-restraint as to preserve the respect of even his most intimate friends, so much so that those who lived most with him were seldom, if ever, witnesses to any weakness of character or conduct that could sink him in their esteem.

He was full of sensibility, but he did not suffer his feelings to betray him into absurdities. There never was a person who by his air, deportment, and appearance, altogether more decidedly persuaded you at once that he was well born and well bred. He was, as Kinnaird[1] said of him, 'a gallant gentleman'. . . .

19 June. Went to Mr Hanson's[2] in Chancery Lane, and thence with him to Doctors' Commons, where we deposited Lord Byron's will of 1815 for safe custody. We were accompanied by Mr Glenarie, partner of Mr Farquhar of the Commons. By a curious coincidence, Hanson told me that the room in which we delivered in the will was the very one to which he accompanied Lord Byron when my friend applied for his marriage licence. Lord Byron, at that time, said very gravely to the Doctor of the Commons: 'Pray, sir, what is the proportion of those who come here first to make marriages, and then afterwards to unmake them?' . . .

1 July. I heard that the *Florida*, with the remains of Byron, had arrived in the Downs, and I went, the same evening, to Rochester. The next morning I went to Standgate Creek, and, taking a boat, went on board the vessel. There I found Colonel Leicester Stanhope, Dr Bruno, Fletcher, Byron's valet, with three others of his servants. Three dogs that had belonged to my friend were playing about the deck. I could hardly bring myself to look at them. The vessel had got under weigh, and we beat up the river to Gravesend. I cannot describe what I felt during the five or six hours of our passage. I was the last person who shook hands with Byron when he left England in 1816. I recollected his waving his cap to me as the packet bounded off on a curling wave from the pier-head at Dover, and here I was now coming back to England with his corpse. . . .

2 July. The *Florida* anchored at Gravesend, and I returned to

London. . . . .On the following Monday I went to Doctors' Commons and proved Byron's will. Mr Hanson did likewise. Thence I went to London Bridge, got into a boat, and went to London Docks Buoy, where the *Florida* was anchored. I found Mr Woodeson, the under-taker, on board, employed in emptying the spirit from the large barrel containing the box that held the corpse. This box was removed and placed on deck by the side of a leaden coffin. I stayed whilst the iron hoops were knocked off the box, but I could not bear to see the remainder of the operation, and went into the cabin. Whilst there I looked over the sealed packet of papers belonging to Byron, which he had deposited at Cephalonia, and which had not been opened since he left them there. Captain Hodgson of the *Florida*, the captain's father, and Fletcher were with me: we examined every paper, and did not find any will. Those present signed a document to that effect.

5 July. Mr Woodeson came into the cabin and told me the body was placed in the coffin, and asked me if I wished to see it. I believe I should have dropped down dead if I had ventured to look at it. He told me, as did the physician, Bruno, that it had almost all the freshness and firmness of life. I remained on board, and continued leaning on the coffin, which I had now covered with a lid and the ship flag. I felt an inclination to take a last look of my friend, just as one wishes to jump down a precipice, but I could not, and I walked away, and then I came back again and rested on the coffin. Lord Byron's large Newfoundland dog was lying at my feet. I wished I was as unconscious of my loss as he was.

At intervals Fletcher talked to me of his master. He told me that he had said he loved me better than any man on earth, and yet had never passed twenty-four hours without quarrelling with me.

After the removal of the corpse into the coffin, and the arrival of the order from the Custom-house, I accompanied the undertaker in the barge with the coffin. There were many boats round the ship at the time, and the shore was crowded with spectators. We passed quietly up the river, and landed at Palace Yard stairs. Thence the coffin and the small chest containing the heart were carried to the house in George Street, and deposited in the room prepared for their reception. The room was decently hung with black, but there was no other decoration than an escutcheon of the Byron arms, roughly daubed on a deal board. . . .

I ascertained from Mrs [Augusta] Leigh[3] that it was wished that the interment should take place at the family vault at Hucknall in Notting-hamshire.

The utmost eagerness was shown, both publicly and privately, to get a sight of anything connected with Byron. Lafayette[4] was at that time on his way to America, and a young Frenchman came over from the General at Havre, and wrote me a note requesting a sight of the deceased poet. The coffin had been closed, and his wishes could not be complied with. A young man came on board the *Florida*, and in very moving terms besought me to allow him to take one look at him. I was sorry to be obliged to refuse, as I did not know the young man, and there were many round the vessel who would have made the same request. He was bitterly disappointed; and when I gave him a piece of the cotton in which the corpse had been wrapped, he took it with much devotion and placed it in his pocket-book. Mr Phillips,[5] the Academician, applied for permission to take a likeness, but I heard from Mrs Leigh that the features of her brother had been so disfigured by the means used to preserve his remains that she scarcely recognised them.

6 July. Went down to George Street with Kinnaird. Hanson had just been looking at Lord Byron. He told me he should not have known him, except he had looked at his ear and his foot. I followed Kinnaird into the room, and, drawn by an irresistible inclination, though I expected to be overcome by it, approached the coffin. I drew nearer by degrees, till I caught a view of the face. It did not bear the slightest resemblance to my dear friend. So complete was the change it did not seem to be Byron. I was not moved so much scarcely as at the sight of his handwriting or anything that I knew to be his. I did not remark what Hanson told me he had observed in his life-time, that his left eye was much larger than his right.

7 July. I wrote a note to Mrs Leigh, telling her that I should return the £1,000 left to me by Lord Byron to one of her family.

11 July. Lord Byron's coffin, etc., *lay in state*, as it is called, yesterday and the day before. Immense crowds applied for admittance.

12 July. I attended the removal of my dear Byron's remains, as mourner and executor. . . . On the whole, as much honour was done to the deceased as circumstances would admit of. He was buried like a nobleman, since we could not bury him as a poet. . . .

16 July. Went with Lord Rancliffe to Nottingham. The town was crowded in every street leading to the inn in which the coffin lay, and much feeling and sympathy were exhibited by all classes. Hodgson, translator of Juvenal, afterwards Provost of Eton, whom Byron had much befriended, and Colonel Wildman, owner of Newstead, attended as mourners. The Mayor and Corporation of Nottingham joined the funeral procession. It extended about a quarter of a mile, and, moving very slowly, was five hours on the road to Hucknall. The view of it as it wound through the villages of Papplewick and Lindley excited sensations in me which will never be forgotten. As we passed under the hill of Annesley, 'crowned with the peculiar diadem of trees' immortalised by Byron, I called to mind a thousand particulars of my first visit to Newstead. It was dining at Annesley Park that I saw the first interview of Byron, after a long interval, with his early love, Mary Anne Chaworth.[6]

The churchyard and the little church of Hucknall were so crowded that it was with difficulty we could follow the coffin up the aisle. The contrast between the gorgeous decorations of the coffin and the urn and the humble village church was very striking. I was told afterwards that the place was crowded until a late hour in the evening, and that the vault was not closed until the next morning.

NOTES

On Hobhouse, see p. 12. When, on 14 May 1824, Douglas Kinnaird received tidings of Byron's death, he wrote immediately to Hobhouse.

1. See p. 155.

2. John Hanson, a solicitor with offices in Chancery Lane, was Byron's attorney and business adviser and became, with Hobhouse, his executor. It was he who introduced Mary Chaworth (see note 6 below) to Byron.

3. Augusta Byron, later Mrs George Leigh (1783–1851), was Byron's half sister and the daughter of Byron's father by his first wife. In 1807 she married her cousin Colonel George Leigh. Her relationship with Byron became a matter of common gossip at the time of his separation from his wife. See Peter Gunn, *My Dearest Augusta* (New York, 1968).

4. Marquis de Lafayette (1757–1834), French aristocrat who had fought in the American revolutionary army.

5. See p. 83.

6. A distant cousin of Byron, she lived at Annesley Hall, not far from Newstead Abbey. Byron's mother wrote to John Hanson on 30 October 1803, when Byron was fifteen, that 'the Boy is distractedly in love with Miss Chaworth'. She did not return his feelings and, according to Moore, asked her maid, 'Do you think I could care any thing for that lame boy?' In 1805 she married John Musters.

Index

Addison, Joseph, 93
Albrizzi, Countess, 78
Ariosto, Ludovico, 145
Aristotle, 6
Arnold, Matthew, xiii

Baillie, Joanna, 18
Bankes, William, 36, 37
Barff, Samuel, 170
Bayle, Pierre, 93, 94
Blaquière, Edward, 155, 158–9, 160–70
Blessington, Lady, xvi, 28–30, 105–6, 107–8 110–11, 112–16, 119–21, 122–4
Boswell, James, 106–7
Bowles, W. L., 6, 107
Braham, John, 63, 70
Browne, J. H., 125–37
Brummell, George, 42, 43
Bruno, Francesco, 129, 137, 148, 155–6, 161–2
Burges, Sir James, 40
Burns, Robert, 37, 81
Burr, Aaron, 104
Butler, Henry, 5
Butler, Joseph, 4–5
Byron, Ada, 29, 30, 154, 163–4
Byron, Augusta, 154, 171, 173, 177, 179
Byron, Catherine, 1, 3, 43
Byron, Lady, 44–7, 123, 154, 171
Byron, Lord, works of:
   Bride of Abydos, The, 69, 84, 145
   Cain, 102
   Childe Harold's Pilgrimage, xi, 18, 32, 33, 34, 35, 47, 60, 84, 147
   Corsair, The, 13, 84, 145
   Deformed Transformed, The, 168
   Don Juan, 26, 56, 64, 92, 117, 129, 136, 144, 147
   English Bards and Scotch Reviewers, 8–10, 123
   Lara, 41, 84
   Marino Faliero, 53, 75
   'Weep, daughter of a royal line', 13

Campbell, Thomas, 18, 173
Charlotte, Princess, 14
Chatterton, Thomas, 112
Chaworth, Mary, 178, 179
Churchill, Charles, 46, 47
Clairmont, Claire, 51, 54, 167, 171
Clinton, George, xiv–xv
Cobbett, William, 101, 104
Coleridge, S. T., 26, 49, 107
Cowley, Abraham, 120
Cowper, William, 118, 147
Croker, J. W., 40, 43
Croxall, Samuel, 93, 94
Curran, J. P., 173

Dallas, R. C., 8–10, 31–3
Dante Alighieri, 107, 118, 145
Davies, Scrope, 7, 8, 41–2
Davy, Sir Humphrey, 130, 137
Disraeli, Benjamin, 81–2
Drummond, Home, 81
Drummond, Sir William, 30

Eldon, Lord, 9, 10
Eliot, George, xiii

Falkland, Lord, 8–10
Finlay, George, 160, 166
Fletcher, William, 12, 16, 46, 53, 91, 129, 147, 152–3, 155–8, 159, 164, 167–8, 171, 177
Frye, Northrop, xi

Galt, John, xv, 14–17, 30–1, 34–5, 79–80
Gamba, Count Pietro, 80, 84, 91, 125, 129, 132–3, 139, 150–4, 164
Gibbon, Edward, 93, 119
Godwin, William, 113
Gordon, Sir Cosmo, xii
Gray, Thomas, 165
Gronow, R. H., 40–3
Guiccioli, Teresa, 2, 53, 75–83, 84, 90–1, 121, 145

Hanson, John, 176–7, 179
Hay, John, 84–90
Hippisley, Colonel, 129, 137
Hobhouse, J. C., 11–14, 15–16, 36, 42, 43–6, 50–1, 107, 154, 159, 173, 175–9
Hodgson, James T., 7, 178
Hogg, James, 56
Holland, Lord and Lady, 81, 123
Holmes, James, 77, 83
Hoppner, Richard, 54
Hunt, Leigh, xiii, 20–2, 36, 55, 90–4, 97, 106–7, 111, 113

Jackson, John, 20, 22
Johnson, Samuel, 106–7, 118

Kean, Edmund, 13–14
Kilgour, Alexander, 2
Kinnaird, Douglas, 154–5, 176, 178

Lafayette, Marquis de, 177, 179
Lamb, Lady Caroline, 19, 20, 32–3
Landor, W. S., 64, 110–11
Leigh, Mrs, see Augusta Byron
Luriottis, Andreas, 153, 154, 175

Manton, Joe, 41
Matthews, Charles, 37
Matthews, Charles Skinner, 41
Mavrocordatos, Alexander, 150, 154, 174
Medwin, Thomas, 23–4, 74–5, 107, 108–9, 110–12, 116–19
Milbanke, Annabella, see Lady Byron
Milbanke, Lady, 44–6, 131, 132
Milbanke, Sir Ralph, 44–6

Mill, J. S., xiii
Millingen, Julius, 139–49, 152–3, 155, 160–6
Milton, John, 93, 102, 107, 117
Montaigne, Michel de, 129
Moore, Thomas, xiii, xvi, 4–5, 13, 18, 21, 35, 37, 57–62, 66, 77–8, 81, 111, 173–5
Murray, John, 13, 14, 25–6, 27, 36, 38, 64, 100

Napier, Charles, 153, 154
Napoleon Bonaparte, xi, 127–8
Noel, Lady, see Lady Milbanke
Noel, Thomas, 44, 47

Orlando, Jean, 173, 175

Parry, William, 147–9
Peacock, T. L., 56
Phillips, Thomas, 77, 83, 178
Polidori, J. W., 47–9
Pope, Alexander, xiv, 105–6
Prince Regent, 14, 63, 65
Prothero, R. E., 3–4

Radcliffe, Ann, 91
Rancliffe, Lord, 178
Reid, John, 162, 166
Roberts, Daniel, 89–90
Rogers, Samuel, xiii, 18–20, 45, 48–9, 65, 123, 173
Rose, William, 36
Rossini, Giacomo, 92
Rousseau, Jean-Jacques, 36

Sandys, George, 93–4
Sanders, George, 77, 83
Schilizzi, Constantine, 129, 132, 136, 137
Scott, Sir Walter, 18, 35–9, 40, 81, 108–10
Shakespeare, William, 63, 93, 105–6, 107, 168
Shelley, Mary, 27, 49, 55–7, 66–7, 82, 113, 168, 171–2
Shelley, P. B., 25–7, 36, 49, 51–3, 56, 63–4, 66–7, 84, 94–8, 107, 111–12, 119, 121

Simmons, J. W., xiv
Smith, Eliza, 81
Southey, Robert, 110, 118
Spenser, Edmund, 93
Staël, Madame de, 107–8
Stanhope, Leicester, 150, 154, 173–4
Stendhal, 82
Stowe, Harriet Beecher, xii
Swift, Jonathan, 26, 149

Taaffe, John, 84–90, 118
Tasso, Torquato, 117
Tennyson, Lord, xii
Thomas, Dr, 152, 154, 156–7
Ticknor, George, 42–3
Tita, 99, 153, 154
Todd, John, 89–90

Trelawny, Edward, xiii, 24–7, 56, 62–70, 84, 94–8, 129, 132–3, 137–9, 167–8

Vaccá, Dr, 88–90
Virgil, 102
Vitali, George, 129, 137
Voltaire, 107, 118, 129

Watkins, John, xii
Webster, J. W., 41
Wesley, John, 118
Westall, Richard, 77, 83
Wildman, Colonel, 81, 178
Williams, Edward, 56, 84–90, 94–8
Williams, Jane, 84–90
Wollstonecraft, Mary, 113
Wordsworth, William, 21, 110